Cyberville

Cyberville

CLICKS, CULTURE, AND

THE CREATION OF AN

ONLINE TOWN

Stacy Horn

WARNER BOOKS

A Time Warner Company

Grateful acknowledgment is made to reprint from *New and Selected Poems* by Robert Penn Warren. Copyright © 1985 by Robert Penn Warren. Reprinted by permission of Random House, Inc.

Warner Books, Inc., 1271 Avenue of the Americas, New York, NY 10020
Visit our Web site at http://warnerbooks.com

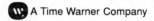 A Time Warner Company

Printed in the United States of America
First Printing: January 1998
10 9 8 7 6 5 4 3 2 1

Library of Congress Cataloging-in-Publication Data
Horn, Stacy.
        Cyberville : clicks, culture, and the creation of an online town /
Stacy Horn.
            p.   cm.
        Includes index.
        ISBN 0-446-51909-X
        1. Echo (Online service)--Social aspects. 2. Electronic
discussion groups--Social aspects.   I. Title.
ZA4251.E25H67 1998
302.23--dc21   97-12323
                                                                    CIP

Book design by H. Roberts

In loving memory of H. L. "Jim" Grace

ACKNOWLEDGMENTS

I want to thank the people at Warner Books: Karen Kelly for calling me out of the blue and buying this book, Larry Kirshbaum for saying "Yes!" when I asked him if I could chuck the original outline, Anne Milburn for helping me through the first draft, and finally Danielle Dayen for getting it, and for her ruthless, right on the money editing. Janis Vallely, my agent, responded to countless panicked phone calls with valuable advice and encouragement, and Christine Hegarty, Steven Levy, Aly Sujo, and Marisa Bowe read early drafts and told me the things that only your good friends will tell you.

There are so many Echoids who have helped me over the years, Rob Diamond for early technical support, Sanyaku Amare for hosting Echo in the beginning, everyone at The Meta Systems Design Group, and Cliff Figalo at The Well. Then there are the people who helped so much Echo wouldn't exist if it weren't for them: Jim

Baumbach, Kevin Krooss, Bob Knuts, Mark Abene, Dan Swerdlow, the late Kathleen Creighton, Joe Battle, Andrew Brown, once again Marisa Bowe, Lianne Smith, Eric Hochman, Liz Margoshes, Betsy Richter, Rosemary Bray, David Ross, all hosts past and present, there's simply too many to list them here but God I wish I could, they shaped the place bigtime. Scott Connor was here so much every step of the way for the first few years his stamp is all over the place. Sue Grady, Josh Chu, Abby Bowen—my first employees—Echo would have been dead for sure if it weren't for them, and Hadley Taylor, Andrea Pillsbury, Jessica Millstone, Molly Ker, Quinn Moo, John Adams, Mary Ellen Kennel, Steve Rivo, as current and former employees of Echo their hearts and minds are also all through this community, and I can't forget my original core group and, of course, all Echoids, past and present.

I'd like to thank Red Burns for her endless love, help and support and for believing in me even when she wasn't entirely immediately convinced of my ideas, Pat O'Hara for introducing me to virtual communities in the first place, Josianne Caggiano for helping me get to where I could even attempt to make my dreams come true, my mother and step-father, Jeanne and the late Jim Grace and my brother Douglas, for supporting me every way they could, and finally Joe Rosen and again Christine Hegarty, my closest friends. If I've accomplished anything at all it was winning the love of the two best people I have ever known.

"The time had come, in the history of mankind,
to obtain freedom by giving up faces."

From *Carnival*, by Isak Dinesen.

"Now there are some things we all know,
but we don't take'm out and look at'm very often."

From *Our Town*, by Thornton Wilder.

". . . This is the way we were: in our growing up and
in our marrying and in our living and in our dying."

From *Our Town*, by Thornton Wilder.

CONTENTS

ECHO POLL

Source: From an online survey of 242 members of Echo, May 1995.

Margin of Error: I'm told this has no scientific validity whatsoever.

Remembering how you spent your day yesterday, would you have been better off just going to the movies instead?

44% said yes.

7% actually did go to the movies the day before.

AND NOW?

Face-2-Face And Now? Mystery Button

And now? It's a question my computer asks me every time I turn it on. Whenever I want to do something, I have to type it in at the And now? prompt. AND NOW? And now what would you like to do Stacy? Of all the things to do in the world, just what would you like to do next? Hmm? Make up your mind. Come on. The words glow with choice. Direction. Anything you want.

> And now?
> And now?
> And now?

My response? Fuck you.

It's my favorite reply. Fuck you. You got that? What a relief. My friend Marisa says it's my Catholic upbringing. I'm rejecting my inner Mother Superior. That's it. I spent the first thirty years of my life wondering what to do next and that's enough time to spend with any one question. My twenties were particularly terrifying because all of a sudden it really, really mattered. Time was running out. I had to figure it out. And now? Have a career. Get a husband. Yeah, yeah, shoot me, I was raised that way. No, shoot my family. And now? I was trying to figure this out at five.

By the time I hit thirty I was thoroughly depressed and in a job I hated. That's when I came up with the endlessly useful response of: Fuck you. (Variations: Fuck it. Fuck this.) I give up. Uncle. I can't figure it all out. I didn't know what the hell to do with myself. Fuck you was freedom. Enough already. I'll just do whatever comes into my head next, and if nothing comes into my head? I'll go to the movies. Or dancing.

So in 1986, when I said to myself, "And now," I thought: Graduate school. What better place to sit this decision out? One of my professors lured me online my first year. I was in something called the Interactive Telecommunications Program at NYU and I was having the time of my life, finally. That place is heaven. But I wasn't too enthusiastic about cyberspace. I hate computers. She must have seen it in my face. "John Cage is online," she told me. That was all it took. I hooked my computer up to a telephone line, called up The WELL, an online service in California, and my very first month online I racked up a bill so high I couldn't immediately pay it. It wasn't the fact that I could talk to John Cage that sucked me in—I never did find him—it was all the other people. All the other people I never would have met otherwise. People I love, people I hate—when I'm online I'm drawn to people I hate as much as to people I love. A lot of people are like this, I've discovered. Because they are not really there, and you have an easy out—you can always hang up—it becomes less threatening. You stay. It's like walking right up to a traffic accident instead of slowly driving by. They are not right there in front of you. You can do it. Safely. And it isn't even considered rude.

Think about it. You're at a party or on the street and someone starts spouting some perfectly hideous idea. Or, as I like to put it, some stupid fuckhead idea. I don't know, it's hard to come up with a universally hideous idea. Something racist, something sexist. Depending on my mood, either something in me will collapse at the reminder that there are such people out in the world—aren't they all dead yet? (Never, never, if my online experiences are proof of anything.) Or I'll go through something like a mini-explosion. Either way, I never say anything coherent because I'm either collapsing or exploding. Deep down, all I really want to do is get away. *Monsters! Monsters!* When someone says something like this online, after the initial revulsion and retreat, I can step back up and take a closer look at the accident inside that person's head. Or heart. You can even see it happen. You can watch the action unfold in excruciatingly slow motion. It changes you. It makes you think. And it's irresistible. We are who we are and people are perverse. They get online, and like those drivers at a traffic accident—they can't look away.

Here's how it works. You've got a computer. You can sit down to that computer, like I'm sitting here right now, and type in anything you like. It could be perfect garbage. I've been participating in an ongoing debate with a bunch of women about blow jobs—spit or swallow? Or it could be something terribly important like death. There are people online with terminal illnesses who literally share the day to day progress of their death. Think of it like a letter to a friend or a phone call.

Next you stick a modem onto your computer, plug a phone line into that box, and your words are sent to a place where lots of people can see them. And respond. People all over the world. Or people typing a couple of hundred feet from you. By now you're either thinking: *Cool.* Or: *What a bunch of losers.* Yeah, yeah. I've seen every reaction there is, but I've also seen how very quickly people get online and decide, "I can hang out here." Where? And what are we taking with us when we go?

Everything. Even our bodies get into the act in cyberspace. Much as we might dearly love to sometimes, we can't leave ourselves behind when we get online. Even when someone is just playing around or in disguise, something true is revealed, it is never completely invented. I've never seen someone who was faking it who wasn't still disclosing something. People are incredibly tenacious when it comes to their personalities. If anything, people open up more. What is it about cyberspace? It conceals what gets in the way of revealing. No one's right there. It's like being anonymous but not quite. It's more like wearing a mask. "A mask tells us more than a face," Oscar Wilde wrote. When you get online, *you tell.* Frankly, sometimes people tell me more than I want to know.

I hate Koreans. Koreans are evil because they eat dogs. A woman expressed this online a couple of years back. She also hated Filipinos. And a whole bunch of other groups, I forget the rest. We'd been talking to this woman every day for a year; who knew? Once this came out we started talking to her even more. Why? Why? Why? We were stunned. One of her best friends online read that and said, "I guess we can't be friends anymore. I'm Filipino." Well there you go. We all waited for her awakening. Wasn't this the promise of cyberspace? No more bigots because thoughts and feelings are without race, right? Online, we make friends or enemies while temporarily blind. And she had really come to like this guy.

Normally she'd be online many times throughout the day—after this we didn't see her for twenty-four hours. We waited. We were dying for her response. Where was she? Why wasn't she logging on? Then we learned why cyberspace wasn't going to stop wars, wasn't going to bring peace and understanding throughout the world, tra-la-la-la. Cyberspace does not have the power to make us anything other than what we already are. Information doesn't necessarily lead to understanding or change. It is a revealing, not a transforming, medium. Again, we are who we are. Understanding or change happens, but it is as rare and as hard to get to online as it is anywhere else. I was almost going to call this book: *We Will Never Learn and I Have Proof.*

She came back with a long and involved explanation of how it was okay to hate a group of people and still like an individual member of that group and how it wasn't racist to condemn certain Asian groups. We knew that she was engaged to be married once and that her fiancé went to Vietnam and was killed. She admitted to us that she liked her cats better than people. They were nicer to her. The women knew that she was self-conscious about her hair; she was slightly bald. And now we came to know she had tremendous limitations. I know I'm supposed to hate her, and I do sort of, but things are different now. I can't see her simply as the evil cartoon racist. Her best friends are cats, for Christ's sake. My hate can't be as simple as hers. It's disturbing. I have to think.

And this is what got me. It wasn't just the fact that there are a lot of people online. I live in Manhattan. I'm surrounded by millions of people. It's the access to them, the line I have straight into their hearts and minds that keeps me calling back. But the key is the repeated access. To really know a person you have to talk to them again and again. Like when we were kids.

We all have friends. Talking to them is satisfying, right? I'll tell you what I missed though, I missed hanging out every day, day in and day out with the same people. Like we did when we were kids. Friendships evolved over years of talking to the same kids about everything, every last thing, the same subject over and over—it was the process of discovery that we shared—adding a new piece of information or idea to every thing we talked about. Years of seeing the same people practically every day. Not a few parties a couple of times a year. I knew these kids so well I could tell what was up with any one of them by a single gesture. A look. A look could tell me instantly and completely what was going on with them. We had history. No one hangs out like that anymore.

Virtual communities are like that. They exist in time. They give you a place to come to again and again, and when I was in my last year of graduate school I thought, that's what I'll do. I'll make a place like that. A place where we can have history again. And I started Echo. When everyone else was going on in such great, big terms—super highways and global villages of millions—I was thinking, a small town in the big city might be nice. Echo would make New York City manageable. That's how I always thought of it, as a local hangout. I didn't want Echo to lose the feel of the place I call my home. Cyberspace shatters geographic boundaries so that, in an instant, I can visit sunny places like The WELL, a service with a distinct West Coast feel, which is great. This is part of its charm. What good is it to be able to go all over the world if you don't feel like you've arrived *somewhere*? If they are all the same? Keep the cultural boundaries. On a day to day basis, I chose to hang out in New York fucking City. A darker city. When I get online it's the same. Give me a place that has character. National online services like America Online or Compuserve feel like malls.

And now we get to the heart of the matter. The WELL was wonderful, but it wasn't enough. If cyberspace didn't offer anything beyond a virtual connection I'd have hung up that phone years ago. Here were all these great people, but I wanted to see them, really see them. Just what do you look like anyway? Perhaps it shouldn't matter to me, but it does. Especially if I have a crush on them. Actually it's the most natural thing in the world and the urge is quite common. If someone you talk to online is at all interesting, you want to meet them. It isn't so much what they look like, you simply want to be with them *in the flesh*. I don't just want to talk about movies with people, I want to also go to movies with people. Besides, on The WELL, they weren't into many of the things I was into and they talked funny. Not really—but there is a virtual accent that is unmistakable. New Yorkers have a different style of communicating, regardless of where they happen to be, and they talk about different things. Even online, I wanted to be with *them*. The people on The WELL were physically, and virtually, too far away. I wanted something closer to home.

When the company I was working for packed themselves off to Virginia, *and now* became: Take your severance pay, thank you very much Mobil Oil, and start Echo. It'll be a place of heart and mind like no other. And it will be fabulously successful. Right away, too. I'll be able to sit back and write books about sex and death in my brownstone in the city or on the porch of my country home on a river upstate. No more five-story walkups for me, boy. That was the plan. Not that I cared about money, a fact that would become painfully obvious as I repeatedly slammed my head into the wall of trying to create a viable business without an adequate respect for making money. I didn't know what I was doing. I wasn't a techie, I didn't have a business background.

In fact, I am such a lame-o business person I had to run Echo out of my one-bedroom apartment on my *Day-of-the-Triffids*-like tree-lined street in the West Village for five years because in 1989 I couldn't convince anyone the Internet was going to be hot. This kills me. No one, but no one, would believe me. So Echo began on roughly $20,000—all the money I had in the world.

This is the story of one small corner in cyberspace: Echo. Just as people are people wherever you go, one virtual community is pretty much the same as another—the few differences that exist are superficial and secondary. Echo is as good an example as any of what really goes on in a small online community. This is not Bill Gates' cyberspace. When Bill and others go on and on about how you can talk to all these people, they always forget to mention how fucked up most people are. Life on Echo is like some bizarro *Our Town*. Think: Grover's Corners—the Dark Side. Don't get me wrong, I love it here. I love this place and everyone in it, even the people I don't want to know and don't particularly like. When we were growing up we didn't get to pick who lived in our neighborhood, but you got something out of having to spend time with people you dislike. It stretches those tolerance muscles. Cyberspace is just like any small town in the physical world. If you like the place, you either resolve the conflicts or learn to live with them. Online, we rediscover how societies are built and how they hold together. Every virtual community has its town cranks and drunks, psychos and saints, good girls, bad girls, good guys, bad guys—if it's out there, it's in here. I'm not looking for utopia. And like any other small community, it's intimate and supportive, mean-spirited and petty—you're not alone and you're never alone. A small town life is a public life: everyone knows everyone else's business. It may take a long time for the secrets to come out, but you can't hide forever—even online where no one can see you. Over time, personality and character is inevitably revealed, reputations are established. (Also, Echo is not anonymous. Here, everyone knows your real name.) In the end, people can't help being themselves. I once heard Maya Angelou comment on Thomas Wolfe's idea that you can't go home again. Her take was: *You can never leave.* The first thing we do when we get online is recreate the world as we have always known it.

This is the thing about cyberspace: it is full of personalities. It's a social place. We are who we are and we're not always very nice. But there's something about this place. It has that perfect blend of distance and intimacy that just makes some people feel like they have nothing to lose by telling the truth. That doesn't mean people are going to hear it however. For some people cyberspace is a world of fantasy and projection, a narcissist's paradise, they got nuts in here. The same distance that allows some to finally say what they really think, allows others to imagine whatever they like. We're not there, they can't see us, so they see devils or angels, whatever they long for, it's their mirror. Most of us are a combination of the two. Either way, we come back for all of it, heaven and hell, we want more.

MBA-types are forever asking me: What's the next big thing? And now? What a bunch of maroons. It's right there in front of them. We're soaking in it. Maybe they can't see it because it seems like such a tiny thing compared to superhighways. History likes to tell big stories. Well, people like to tell the smaller ones. Our own cuts and scrapes and blowjobs, new jobs, lost jobs, whatever, this is what we think about, gossip about, the things that happen every day, the stuff we talk about endlessly. These are the stories of our lives and this is what you need to know to know a person. You have to hang out with a person day in and day out to hear these stories. Stories like these unfold over time. Who has that kind of time?

And if you had the time, where would you go?

We get online to tell these stories. We tell them again and again, each time getting it a little more right, each time we tell we understand a little better what happened and who we are. Old stories, new stories, we act, we act out. It is the electronic theater that allows us to explore and to explain ourselves. We're stars! It's life with a Mystery Science Theater commentary running underneath. We live, fall in love, pulverize each other and die here and everyone has something to say about it. It's a place to share our drama and this, I will say over and over to anyone who will listen, is the big thing about cyberspace, the *killer app*.

And now? Just watch.

ECHO POLL

Source: From an online survey of 131 members of Echo, June 1995.

Margin of Error: I guess it depends on what you call an error.

Do you lie online?
Do others lie online?

20% said they lie online.
52% believe that other people lie online.

ECHO POLL

Source: From an online survey of 165 members of Echo, October 1995.

Margin of Error: What do 165 Echoids know anyway?

Who is your favorite person on Echo?

13% said Garbled Uplink.
24% said "myself."
02% said "Fuck off," or "Blow me."

ECHO POLL

Source: From an online survey of 217 members of Echo, May 1995.

Margin of Error: You try coming up with just one.

Note: These are the fifteen books that got the most votes.

Name your favorite book!

Pride and Prejudice
A Hundred Years of Solitude
Catcher in the Rye
Perfume
Gravity's Rainbow
White Noise
Candide
Time and Again
Green Eggs and Ham
Bastard Out of Carolina
Travels in Hyperreality
Pale Fire
Ulysses
Middlemarch
Madame Bovary

ECHO POLL

Source: From an online survey of 247 members of Echo, October 1995.

Margin of Error: I didn't ask first if they had any taste.

Note: These are the fifteen movies that got the most votes.

Name your favorite movie!

Bladerunner
Brazil
Pulp Fiction
Wings of Desire
The Producers
The Piano
The Philadelphia Story
Breakfast at Tiffany's
Harold and Maude
The Godfather
(The rest tied for tenth place.)
      The Wizard of OZ
      Buckaroo Banzai
      Casablanca
      Citizen Kane
      2001: A Space Odyssey

ECHO POLL

Source: From an online survey of 233 members of Echo, October 1995.

Margin of Error: I wonder about the Echoids sometimes.

Why do you lurk?

21% said "I have nothing to say."

16% said they were shy, or intimidated, or felt like an outsider.

12% said "To learn," or "To get the lay of the land."

7% said they were voyeurs.

3% said there was nothing worth responding to.

THE RUBBER-NECKERS

If you're not online you wonder: Who *are* these people? Like cities or towns, or anyplace else anywhere, different online places attract different people.

John F. Kennedy, Jr. stopped by Echo briefly and called himself "flash." This was the login id he chose. Everyone has one. Whenever you call Echo you have to type in this login id and a password—it becomes part of your identity online, like a nickname, it's the beginning of your online persona. Most people choose some form of their name; their first name, their last name, their initials. I use "horn." It's your first snapshot of someone and it gives you your first insight. Thatgirl. Clambake. Topper. Bikebabe. Earache. These names were chosen for a reason. Someone on Echo recently changed her login id to sterno because she thought it would make people leave her alone. Beware. Easily ignitable. Her name is Leslie Sternbergh Alexander and she draws pictures for *Mad Magazine*.

Last week they gave her an assignment to draw Madonna and she *can't wait*. On some online services, like Compuserve, people use numbers for names. I call them the prison people.

A few times a year we get guys picking login ids like, bigdick. Sure you do. Uh-huh. Right. They rarely call and actually use these id's once we give them to them and if they do they never stay. That's one of the nice things about Echo. It has always been self-selecting. The true assholes—well, we're all assholes from time to time, I'm talking your relentless, never let up for a second, how-do-they-get-through-their-lives-type assholes—they don't stick around. (Glaring exceptions to be noted later.) For the record, we let people have whatever id they want. Go ahead, call yourself bigdick. See if I care. I think people would rather know than not know that you are the kind of person who would call themselves bigdick. It says something about you. Login id requests we got today: dogstyle, mestud. Okay. I admit it. I like dogstyle for an id. Now you know just what kind of girl I am.

Why did JFK, Jr. pick flash? To be perfectly honest, I was a bit stunned to have him sitting next to me while I showed him how to get around Echo, so I didn't ask. I could barely get what I needed to say out, I'm embarrassed to say. John F. Kennedy, Jr. is like, three inches away from me, ferchristsakes. He brought his bike with him—and I live on the fifth floor of a five-story walkup—so I figured his name had something to do with his bike. Who knows. He has no scent whatsoever.

Now, while people can choose anything they like for a login id, we do not have anonymity on Echo. Your real name appears every time you log in and anyone can look up your name at any time. How can you create history with people if you don't know who they are? Besides, I'd seen what happens on anonymous systems. They feel more like computer games. Anonymity freed everyone's inner two-year-old. Oh joy. If Echo was to be more like home, rather than a computer game, it would have to be real. And, I believed, people will be more real if they know their names were going to be attached to everything they said.

There's one exception to this rule. We offer the ridiculously famous the option of using a pseudonym. They can be anonymous if they are so well known they cannot, in a real sense, be themselves. JFK, Jr. asked me if he should use his real name. Okay, I was torn, I admit it. I wanted the whole world to know he was on Echo. The online medium was only just beginning to get attention and we were still struggling. It would be good for business.

Use your real name, I said. (I have no shame.) The Echoids are not going to come after you for a virtual autograph. They are more sophisticated than that. They would not humiliate themselves that way. They'll be cool, I'm sure they'll be cool, better fucking be cool, I'm thinking.

We log in, side by side. I show him some of the political discussions on Echo and a few of the commands. The whole time he's logged in he's left entirely alone, no one says a word to the guy. Not a peep out of them. Three inches away, however, my computer is beeping like mad. There's a way of sending a message to someone that will cause that message to pop up on their screen right there and then, right in the middle of whatever they are doing. It's called a YO. By typing yo horn at the AND NOW? prompt someone can ask me immediately, *Is that really JFK, Jr.??* YOs are accompanied by three beeps. This is to make sure the sender really has your attention. Popping up, in your face, in the middle of your screen is not enough—we added three beeps. There's an urgency to YOs. Someone wants you to see what they have to say NOW NOW NOW. And as one YO after another cascades down the screen, my computer is beeping like a nest of baby birds:

> *That's not really John F. Kennedy, Jr., is it?*
> *JFK, JR! What does he look like??*
> *Tell him he should be studying!*

Echoids. That's what we call ourselves. Echoids. I picked it. I got it from Mr. Mergatroid, some cartoon from my childhood. On The WELL they call themselves Wellbeings or "pern." Different place, different style. It's not our style to call ourselves "beings." Like that godawful word that some people online use to describe the physical world: meat-space. You wanna talk about meat-space? Find another virtual community. Echo attracts the kind of people who think meat-space is a stupid trendy word.

This is what online communities offer: a connection to people. That's all any virtual community has to offer. Period, end of story. If you don't like the people on Echo, for instance, and what they have in their heads and hearts and how they express it, then there is no reason to stay. This is all we have. This strange group of people and the society we have created. It's a community of personalities. If we didn't bring our personalities, what makes us unique, then it wouldn't matter who you talked to, one person would be much the same as another. You wouldn't be drawn to anyone or anyplace in particular and you might as well join a database.

On Echo, filmmakers argue with priests, artists talk about music that changed their life with lawyers, writers, choreographers, singers, actors, students, a lot of media people (this is New York after all)—who are these people and why are they attracted to cyberspace and each other?

Garbled Uplink, a former stockbroker, currently a circus roadie, and many people's favorite Echoid, started out as the most feared. He claims to have J. Edgar Hoover's head in a bowling ball bag. His cats quote Beckett to him just before dawn, he drinks too much and in person he talks REAL LOUD. Is he sane? everyone asked me. How should I know? We met him when he came to the White Horse Tavern one night. We could see that he meant us no harm, and while he can be tiresome when he's on a tear, everyone decided they liked him. Even though we are communicating via words and we are reading, not listening, the other day he wrote: "Shut UP, all of you. I am trying to THINK."

Or take Bruce Schechter. A physicist turned writer turned Disney imagineer and now back to writer, Bruce fell in love with Carmela Federico at an Echo jam session because she sang out without fear even though she was brand-new to Echo and didn't know us very well. When I was mourning the death of my Sea Monkeys (those pets that are advertised in the back of comic books—they're brine shrimp, actually), Bruce wrote:

> "They may lead very short lives. But they are also full and intense lives. Sea Monkey's feel sorry for humans, who they view as immortals. They feel our lives are long and empty, they can't understand how we can bear the burden of eternity. Their lives are a blaze of glory.
>
> "If Shakespeare had been a Sea Monkey he would have written: 'Tomorrow and tomorrow, and then you drop dead.'"

We've got Embraceable Ewe, preop transsexual woman who wants to hang out in a women-only area on Echo. Now what? Jonathan Hayes, aka Jaze, is thrilled she's here. Stacy, Stacy! We have our first transsexual! That is so Jonathan. Every time I visit him he positively beams as he shows me his growing cyber-porn collection and tells me how late he stayed at a rave the night before. And Marisa Bowe, aka Miss Outer Boro, or MOB for short. She makes me spit out my coffee on my keyboard more than any other person on Echo. Marisa is the editor-in-chief of *WORD*, an online magazine. (She and Jaze went out for about a year.) There's Matthew Ehrlich, aka Oedipa, who recently commiserated with me about the phone company. If you run an online service you grow to hate, I mean really hate, the phone company. Matthew, who works for MTV, tells me the story of calling information:

> ". . . they can't even figure out who we are.
> 'MTV? Could you be listed under another name?'
> I suggested that we might be listed under the name Bob.
> They looked."

So if you get here and you don't care for these people, you might as well go someplace else. That's pretty much all there is. Us. And Internet access which you can get anywhere. Big deal. Echo, and places like it, are the people.

Rob Tannenbaum, freelance writer and lead singer in a band composed entirely of Echoids, says we hang out online because we all had unsatisfactory family experiences. I buy it, except doesn't that describe *everybody*? Whatever the origin of the need, there is definitely a common desire for a sustained, ongoing connection to the same group of people. A family, a gang, a group or a crowd, whatever you want to call it. I hate the word community but I'm going to use it a lot anyway. From my experiences online and off, I'd say that everybody—from executives of large corporations to out-of-work actors, from know-it-alls to know-nothings, everybody has a trace of an ache—some eternal disappointment, or longing, that is satisfied, at least for a minute each day, by a familiar group and by a place that will always be there.

And that is why the first thing I do every time I call Echo is type o. It tells me who is online at that moment. I'll repeat this off and on the entire time I'm online. I gotta know this. I don't feel like I'm someplace until I know: Who's here? Once the o command was broken briefly and it was like I had lost all my senses. I was in blackness. Soundless. I was alone in the most complete sense of the word and there was no point in being there. I was in some forgotten ghost city, left with their artifacts but not their warmth.

Here's what you get when you type o.

Login/Userid	Name	Echo Name
cityjen	Jennifer Pirtle	cityminx
jat	Jennifer Tanaka	Ebola Tank Grrrl
cabal	Alan Cabal	Garbled Uplink
twister	Stephen Berg	Berg Man of Alcatraz
mame	Amy McCutchin	McIndian Mame
cafephrk	Cathy Young	cafephreak
coollit	Lisa J. Cooley	Lazy J. Cooley
neander	Liz Margoshes	Neandergal
danis	Dani Shapiro	dani shapiro
eileen	Eileen Lottman	eileen—aka Tough Old Broad
kwk	Kevin W. Krooss	Peconic Kev
susan	Susan Campbell	SuZin
msegall	Margaret Segall	Margaret
petit	Marianne Petit	MRPetit—aka Marianne
mono	Morgan Noel	Dirtbag MoNo
patd	Patricia Decker	Ms. P.
wallich	Paul Wallich	ragged paul
peterme	Peter Merholz	Peter Driftwood
randallf	Randall Rothenberg	Randall Rothenberg
baap	Reuben Radding	Clemless

If you look, everyone has three names. That login id that I already mentioned, their real name—having everyone's real name appear made all the difference in the world in the evolution of Echo, it made us all accountable and, more importantly, it led to friendships outside Echo—and then there's what we call their Echo name. It's like a nickname or pseudonym. It can be whatever anyone likes and it can be changed with a simple command. This is the name that will appear whenever they write something online, but *their real name is still attached to that pseudonym.* Everyone knows that Clemless' real name is Reuben Radding, Neandergal is Liz

Margoshes, and so on. Important information is contained within the evolution and mutation of these Echo names.

For example, Mark Abene worked for us for a while. He's a well-known hacker, aka Phiber Optik, and on the day he went to prison for a year and a day (he pled guilty to unauthorized computer access) everyone changed their name to include part of his name. Everyone was either, Stacy Optik or Neanderoptik or Lisa J. Optik. You get the idea. If you logged on that day for the first time and typed o, you would have thought everyone on Echo was related. It was our tribute.

These names are a form of expression. Nothing online is wasted. Every tool, every stroke is put to use to explain ourselves. Because we have fewer means—you can't give someone the look, no body language here—we pounce on every command and wring out every last drop of its power to let us say it this way, no, that way. No wait, this way. It's no fun if you can't get a real sense of the people and if you can't give a real sense of yourself. We want to understand and be understood, and so Echoids turn everything into self-expression.

Playing with your Echo name adds to your story, your persona, it gives it shape. I've changed my Echo name maybe three times in five years. I think it has to do with after years of aimlessness, my identity with Echo is so important to me I want there to be no confusion: I am Stacy Horn. Others use it as an opportunity to communicate, and they do it in different ways. Miss Outer Boro lives in Brooklyn. It's part of her identity. Peter Dworkin, who started out calling himself New York Jew, constantly changes his name to play on the word Jew. Invariably I have to explain to some new user that, no, no, he's not some rabid anti-Semite, and that Peter is, in fact, a Jew from New York City—he's just rude. (You got a problem with that?) At one time or other, Peter was posting under the names below. (Posting—more online lingo. Posting refers to adding your response to a discussion. When you say something in an online topic you are posting a response, which has been shortened to simply "posting.")

> *O. Jew Simpson*
> *The Jew in the Crown*
> *Was it good for Jew¿*
> *And Now¿ j ew*

I have to explain that last one. When you call up Echo, there are different places to go, different areas, like forums, only we call them conferences. Echo is made up of these different areas, or conferences, and each of these conferences has a name that describes what people talk about when they are in there. We've got Movies & TV, Culture, Books, Angst (a big pastime on Echo), Politics and Zines, to name a few. To get from conference to conference you type j (for join) followed by the first few letters of the conference name. You don't have to type in the whole name. That's because we take pity on the poor Echoids who have to type in these commands. Big of us. So to get to Culture, at the And Now¿ prompt, you type j cul. And Now¿ j ew. Get it¿ More of Peter's names:

> *Jewboyz II Men*
> *Inka Dinka Jew*
> *Takes Jew to Tango*
> *Jewvenile Delinquent*
> *Tess of the J'ewbervilles*
> *Jew Me Up, Jew Me Down*

Terri Senft, Ph.D. candidate in performance studies, occasional phone sex worker, and darling of the philosophical set on Echo, likes to call herself Jane Doe.

Jane Doe, Postructuralist Ho
Sugar Free Jane Doe
Springtime Fresh Jane Doe
Happy Little Jane Doe
Jane Doe Hates New York
Jane Doe Loves Nantucket
Jane Doe and Her Travelling Circus
Jane Doe! The Musical

The names of NancyKay Shapiro, aka Perpetual Dawn, who accompanied me to the movie *The Rocky Horror Picture Show* when we both had the same attack of nostalgia, are all about her moods.

You Treat Your Perpetual Mean
Heard that lonesome Perpetual Dawn blues
Perpetual's Turn to Cry
Crystal Blue Perpetual
Feel Like Going Perpetual
Take Another Little Piece of My Perpetual

I like this one. A user of ours who moved here from Canada changed his name to *Goth, still Canadian!* after Quebec voted against secession. Goth, aka visigoth, aka Doug Cooper, is a novelist and one of the many voluntarily bald men on Echo. (Frequently muttered on Echo: Way too many bald guys.)

Next. Everyone gets a space where you can post a public bio. If I read something that cracks me up and I think, Who is *this* person? (or, if I'm reading something particularly lame: Who *is* this person?), I can type see followed by the person's login id or Echo name and read their bio. Some of these bios say it all. Right behind changing names, changing your bio is the favored way of saying what is up with ME, ME, ME. Some read like personal ads. Rarely a successful approach on Echo. Take this one, for instance.

6 feet, 210 pounds, college grad, black hair, brown eyes.

That's all it says. I wonder about the people who offer this kind of information by way of introducing themselves. For them, the most important thing for you to know, what they want you to know first above anything else is their height, weight, and coloring.

Not a good sign.

It can get worse.

DWM, 45, 165, 5'10" WALL STREETER, MOST WOMEN LIKE MY LOOKS. WEST SIDE, SAG HARBOR ON THE WEEKENDS. WORLD TRAVELER, SOPHISTICATED, INTELLIGENT. LIKE ATTRACTIVE LADIES, 20'S TO 40'S WITH QUICK MINTS AND A SHARP WIT, WHO HAVE DONE SOMETHING WITH THEIR LIVES.

Very scary. What's a quick mint? And what's with all the caps? It's like he's shouting at us. And sophisticated? Isn't that like saying you have a great sense of humor? These people rarely stick around. To be fair, some, when they discover that the culture of Echo favors the bizarre, drop what they're doing and reveal their true demented selves.

How did JFK, Jr. describe himself?

JOHN KENNEDY (FLASH)

I'M an Assistant D A in New YORK city and am also learning to type.

Very perfunctory but it'll do. Some people are just better at this. The ones who can write and who get that writing in the online medium is different than anyplace else, they have the most vivid personalities. Look at these bios. Look at how these people work them. Whom do you want to talk to?

FREAK SINATRA'S FORMER SIDEKICK MONO (MONO)

— Partial transcript of a tape found in deceased's apartment after fire of 2-15-95 —

"Yeah, I remember the Freak. We called him the Freak because anybody stupid enough to stay in show business like he did and keep that last name WAS freak. Anyhow, he used to play this mean trombone, and I would sit in sometimes on bass back when Kerouac still thought the Road was something you hit when they closed the bar.

"So, Freak—his real name was Bob, Bobby Sinatra the tromboning fool—one time takes this bad mushroom and the next thing we know he's preaching this Freak Love thing, where you turned your brain around and started dancing the hoochie-coochie or some such shit, and you'd be turned on to Freak's Cure for the Hate in the World. Friggin Idiot.

"Can I have another one of them smokes? Thanks. So, Freak, he starts to try and convince me to join his traveling preaching show, but I ain't having none of that. I had just gotten a steady gig on a Broadway show, and I wasn't going to waste time all over the damn boondocks with Freak Sinatra and his Freak Love Show.

"Next time I saw Freak, it was thirty-five, forty years later."

—Tape ends, fire seems to have destroyed the rest.

signed,

John Rogers, Investigating Officer.

Mono writes the best bios. MOB (Miss Outer Boro) went out with him for a while too. She always goes straight for the smart ones. (Echo is a very, very small town.)

JAGUAR (IVN)

I AM THE GLORIOUS RULER OF THE UNIVERSE, THE LUMINES-CENCE FROM WHICH ALL FORMS EMANATE, THE POSSESSOR OF SOULS, THE DESTROYER OF THE EVIL ONE AND HIS MINIONS, THE ESSENCE OF TRUTH AND ITS UPHOLDER, THE DARKNESS IN THE DARKNESS AND THE LIGHT IN THE GLORY!

Not.

I could fall for a guy like that except he's going out with Jackie Blue, who dated an ex of mine after we broke up. (Yup. VERY small town.)

JNEIL (JNEIL)

All right . . .
      . . . move it along . . .
            . . . fun's over, folks . . .
                  . . . nothing to see here . . .

GOAT NOISE (PJAMES)

"I'd like to fuck George Jetson
on a Friday afternoon
between martinis on a monorail
that's headed for the moon"
  —Wallace Stevens (channeled)

LAZY J. COOLEY (COOLLIT)

I'm doing it. I'm fucking doing it. I'm writing a play about Tonya Harding. I'm 2 paragraphs into it. It's happening.

"You know what my crime was? I prayed to God to take away her landing leg."

It's gonna be fuckin beautiful.

It takes all kinds to make up a place. People take their real-life, in-person dramas and bring them into cyberspace. If you're an asshole out there, you're going to be an asshole in here. You just can't help yourself. Alas. People participate online as they do in life, and we have a variety of styles of discourse. While these patterns appear everywhere in cyberspace, because different places attract styles, Echo may have a few less lurkers (we can't shut up) and other places may have a few more freaks (okay, maybe Echo has a lot more freaks), but people are people and these patterns are all over cyberspace.

Lurkers

They follow the action but rarely jump in. They read but do not post. They are the voyeurs of cyberspace. It's allowed. Even desirable. It's a stage and there isn't room for everyone. Someone's got to be the audience. And some people are only lurking until they get a feel for the place. Lurkers are shadows. We need them. We see their names day in and day out, and while we don't know much about them, we depend on their presence. They are a quiet but uncritical audience. 58% of the people on Echo lurk. This is a lot lower than most online services, it probably has to do with the fact that we are all mostly local.

Addicts

Then there are the people who are here over 200 hours a month. That's more time than many people spend at their jobs. What are they getting out of this that they can't hang up? What is so worth it to them? "Echo is better than TV!" I hear that a lot. (Which is why I think the publishing industry can just relax about cyberspace. It's the television industry that should be having anxiety attacks. Tiny anxiety attacks anyway.) So let's say Echo has replaced TV for some—what would have filled those other hours? What were they doing when they didn't have Echo? This question haunts me actually. What did they do before Echo? But it's a mistake to dismiss all of them. If you had someplace to go where you could make friends, lovers, business contacts, and you had access to an incredible extent of information contained within the minds of a group like Echo and other online places—how much time would you spend there?

Some are on a lot because they're working. Jane Doe is thrashing through her dissertation in a private conference called House of Thought. When told to get a life because of all the time she spent online she shot back:

> "Here is a newsflash for those of you who think I sit around doing nothing and taking prescription drugs: I am an academic. It's what I do. Writing is what I do. It constitutes: A Life.

> "Teaching, and facilitating discussions, is a large part of what helps me wake up in the morning. Your dismissal of that has more to do with *your* disrespect for people here than it does with anything innate to my personal character."

From Lana Tuna, English teacher and former actress.

"Everyday, because of Echo, I interact personally with about 3 to 10 people a day through yo's, and who *knows how* many dozens by conference participation. Almost every weekend, I do at *least* one thing with the new friends I've met in the past year (yeah, it's only been about a year!). But I like and even love as friends several of the 3,000 plus posters. They have added immeasurably to my life.

"You know, Dean [her boyfriend] and I went to the same college. Never met. Both participated in similar political groups. Never met. Met, finally, on Echo."

Because they are on *always*, talking everywhere, they tend to set the tone. If Jane Doe or Garbled Uplink is in a mood we feel it. If someone has just fallen in love it's everywhere. What the vocal users feel is inescapable. This is great when it's someone smart and funny like Marisa or Jane Doe. It's a nightmare when it's a freak.

Freaks

The online world is famous for its democracy—everyone has a voice! You gotta modem, you can talk. This is not always something to celebrate. Cyberspace sometimes attracts people everyone else has stopped listening to. I'll be talking about some of the more dramatic examples later, but before you think I am heartless, I am not talking about people who are not charming or funny. I am talking about people with more serious problems, anything from those with no social skills whatsoever to psychopaths. On a place like Echo they can put their two cents into any conversation, whether you're interested or not. They are in Heaven. We are in Hell. One person like this can strangle the place. Imagine the creepiest person you have ever known in your life. Now imagine what it would be like if that person found a way to participate in every conversation you were having everywhere all the time. These people have no idea how to communicate and they believe that, unlike anywhere else, they don't have to figure it out. They just think, Finally, a place where people have to listen to me. They have no concern for their audience—the community. You can't get away with having absolutely no social skills online. It's a social medium! You must possess some social artistry. What people sometimes do to the electronically feeble in here is not pretty. A virtual *Lord of the Flies*. Which leads me to the utopians.

Utopians

Ultimately, utopians are mean. They come here looking for a better world. We're not going to make the same mistakes here that we have made out there, we're going to be better to each other. There won't be sexism because we don't have gender. There won't be racism because we have no color. Everyone gets a wake-up call in cyberspace—maybe this time, we think—but nothing matches the bitterness of those who came expecting more. The meanest people of all are the people who thought we'd be nicer. Cyberspace is not OZ. It's Kansas. Okay, it's not Kansas either, but it's closer to Kansas than OZ. We're not better in here. And no worse. We are who we are and we always come back to ourselves. Frankly, it amazes me that anyone would think that we'd start behaving ourselves the minute we turn on a computer. Let's get Charlie Manson online and see how it transforms him.

Right now we're tracking down a member who has been reading other people's private mail. They took the most personal and private message they could find, something of a sexual and romantic nature, and posted it publicly. It was particularly mean because the person whose mail she had posted had recently broken up with another Echoid. Now that Echoid had to learn, along with everyone else, that he had found somebody new. The petty day-to-day evils that we are all capable of are played out in cyberspace. Being online does satisfy an almost universal homesickness. However, the utopians have forgotten that home wasn't always such a nice, safe place.

Hackers

They've been here since the beginning. Good guys? Bad guys? I take them on a case-by-case basis. Here's a story that'll tell you something about hackers. A few months after I started Echo I went to a panel about computer crime. On the panel were a journalist from the *New York Times*, a New York State police investigator, a lawyer, and the hacker I mentioned before, Mark Abene, aka Phiber Optik. When it was over, I went up to each of them and introduced myself. Down the line I went. "Hi. I'm Stacy Horn and I'm starting this online thing called Echo." I got to Phiber last.

"Hi. I'm Stacy Horn. What's your name?"

"Phiber."

"No. Your real name."

"What, does the name Phiber scare you or something?"

(Mark was 18 or 19 at the time and he had that teenage boy bravado.)

"No, no. Phiber's cool. Hi."

For a year I'd run into him here and there, I always said hello, he was always very friendly. Then one night I was on a radio show on WBAI called "The Personal Computer Show." Mark was on a show right after called "Off the Hook." He listened to me wail and moan and curse the computer gods about all the problems I was having with our software, then he came up to me after the show and offered to fix them. Now I know this sounds incredibly generous, and it was, but you have to understand why my first reaction was: "Uh, uh, um, uh."

Mark was a hacker. One of the most famous of all. Whenever I saw him he was talking about hacking. He'd been picked up by the police once already and that didn't stop him, he was still talking about hacking wherever he went. In order to fix my particular problems he would need the password for the login ID called root. When hackers hack, this is what they are after: the password for root. Whoever has the password for root can do anything they want on a system: read your email, destroy it, anything. This is the hacker holy grail: root access. And here's Phiber Optik, the Billy the Kid of cyberspace saying give me your root password and I'll solve all your problems.

Half of me is wondering, What do you think I am, an idiot? The other half trusted him. In the end, my instincts told me the offer was sincere and that he wouldn't do a thing to hurt us. And he didn't. He worked day and night for Echo, sometimes going for 48 hours or more straight, without sleep. This was his style. He did everything he said he would. (While playing Tchaikovsky's Nutcracker Suite so many times I don't think I can ever listen to it again.) And I fed him, listened to his girl troubles, did what I could to keep him out of jail, visited him when he went to jail, and I gave him a job when he got out. While he was inside, everyone fought to wear buttons Binki made that said: *Phree Phiber Optik*. When he left we threw him a good-bye party. When he came back we threw him an even bigger one.

In the beginning he was quick to lay the ground rules. "I don't care about all this community stuff. I'm not interested in Echo and the people, just the hardware and software. I like fixing things." Uh-huh, fine. Except if you're going to fix things you have to listen to people so they can tell you when things go wrong. We reached a compromise. Mark would oversee the technical discussions on Echo and one topic in particular, the one where people post about their problems getting on and around Echo.

He was so good at solving people's problems and downright gifted at explaining technical stuff to people who didn't care about any of it, they only wanted get online to talk about the book they just finished, that they fell in love with him. He was our hero. And he couldn't resist the adoration. We sucked him right in. Pretty soon he was going to our parties, hanging out, making friends, contacts for future jobs, he fell in love with an Echoid—he never had a chance. He even came to prefer his real name over Phiber Optik and his Echo name became: The Artist Formerly Known As Phiber. It was like growing up.

Ultimately, it didn't work out. He left in a huff one night and I said, Fine, see if I care. But we've made up, we're friends now. He's gone off to bigger and better things and I have the lovely sound engineer now unix-techno-geek-genius Hadley Taylor as my system administrator. Phiber's experience is common, though. Like you can forget that there are people here.

The Core Group

I couldn't begin Echo with just me, talking to myself. Come to this empty space I've got here and talk to me! There had to be conversations for people to join in on. So I did what I've done my whole life, I dragged my friends into it: people from ITP (the Interactive Telecommunications Program at NYU), my boyfriend, KZ, a woman about town whom I had met in a place called The Source, a couple of people from The WELL. A few are still here. The WELL people departed quickly; they already had their online home. It was an early and important lesson for me. For the most part, once people find an online home they are happy with they don't move. People who like Echo don't move to The WELL and vice versa. When the place becomes theirs, they will stay. The true founders evolved from the holdouts from this group and the earliest members. Every new virtual community needs some sort of early seed group to begin to establish a sense of place.

Our first meeting. It's in my apartment. I rent two long tables and twenty chairs, and Scott Connor, now known as Scottso, my then boyfriend, goes out for pizza. It had to be John's Pizza and John's doesn't deliver. He runs into Joe Rosen, now joro on Echo, a friend of mine and fellow ITP Adjunct Assistant Professor (Joe and I were students there together). Joe's on his way over, so he helps Scotty carry all the pizza, six pies, and five bottles of soda. I cover the tables with red tablecloths, and in front of each chair I place a pen and a notepad which I had stamped with pictures of lobsters the night before.

I called this group my core group. I was such a serious person back then. I was probably wearing a suit. I laid out my plans and hoped that no one noticed that I didn't know what I'm doing. I was fucking terrified. Later I took a public speaking course. I had to. I still have a tape of me from my early days: *dead person*. I've got a picture of the core group sitting at those tables. They all look so friendly and trusting—I gave each of them a tiny share of Echo in return for their help.

One of our first big uproars on Echo was over this core group. An early member demanded to know who they were. He thought they were being paid to talk to him, like people on those 900 numbers. Nothing they said was sincere, he thought, they're just here to keep me online, talking. Not true. And anyone who didn't want to be there was long gone. We tried to tell him, but the guy was just paranoid. There's so much room for projection when you can't see someone. Echo is a living Hell for people with a paranoid streak. So of course Echo has become a lightning rod for the paranoid. We're so paranoid we've got an acronym for it. WTAM? *Was that about me?* Whenever there's a post that's critical of someone without mentioning who that someone is, it's sure to be followed with WTAM?

One member of the core group is dead now. Kathleen Creighton. I knew her from The WELL. Eccentric to the extreme, downright scary in person, she was nonetheless one of my best sources in a crisis. She paid attention better than anyone else. She missed nothing, so she always knew exactly what to do. I loved to talk to her on the phone; we'd gab for hours and hours. She got this medium like no one else. RIP. KACK KACK KACK. Her original login id was kac, her initials, and she was livid when she learned that people pronounced that in their heads as "kack." She hated kack. She immediately changed her login id to casey and I'd call her kack to piss her off. Now I know that I'm the kind of person to annoy my friends in life *and* in death.

Her words are still here, we rarely throw anything out. When I come across them it's like seeing a ghost. She's haunting me. That's something that doesn't happen anywhere else. Unless they are famous, the words of the dead are typically stored away in closets, forgotten.

Hosts

From the opening of *War and Peace*, where Tolstoy describes Anna Pavlovna managing her soirée:

> "As the foreman of a spinning mill, when he has set the hands to work, goes round and notices here a spindle that has stopped or there one that creaks or makes more noise than it should, and hastens to check the machine or set it in proper motion, so Anna Pavlovna moved about her drawing room, approaching now a silent, now a too-noisy group, and by a word or slight rearrangement kept the conversational machine in steady, proper, and regular motion."

I'm going to go to Hell for this—I'm like the mother who admits she has a favorite kid, but I love the hosts. Every conference on Echo has one, usually two, and they oversee the place. Behind every killer party or every successful business meeting is an excellent host. On Echo they are absolutely essential. (Other online services are slowly figuring this out.) Our hosts work the room, tweaking conversations, making sure they sparkle and flare, they settle disputes, introduce new arrivals around. Or not. We've got some tough love hosts who are downright rude and they are equally popular. Garbled Uplink, the guy who drinks too much and yells a lot? When he first got here he went through Echo like a blowtorch. We made him a host. (It didn't work out.) Steve Berg (aka Berg Man of Alcatraz), whom I adore, was made the cohost of the Books Conference when he started a topic there called, *This Conference Scares the Piss Out of Me.*

From Jonathan Hayes, one of the hosts of the Movies and TV Conference:

> " . . . the great thing about this conference is that the hosts have decided to adopt a wicked laissez-faire attitude to conflict. Indeed, we prefer to camp out ringside, eating popcorn, rooting for our favourites and leaping to our feet, thumbs jabbing emphatically downward at key moments. Far from feeling demeaned by endless fighting, we actually kind of like it."

Echo is Echo because of the hosts. And they come almost entirely from the user base. From the conversations we have with each other every day, certain people emerge and rise above the others—they create connections and conversations effortlessly. When they do we grab them and make them hosts. This is one of the first things we did really right that made Echo such a singular place in cyberspace. We recognized the importance of hosts. The relationships we have are formed by what we tell. Hosts get us to tell each other *everything*. They know how to ask just the right questions, and that is what we want: the stories.

The flavor and style of Echo comes from the atmosphere that the hosts set up and nurture in their conferences. The conferences are the subcultures of Echo. Like different chat rooms on America Online (AOL), each conference has its own feel. They are not all the same. They develop their own identity, and Echoids may talk one way in one conference and assume an entirely different tone in another. What goes in one conference may not go in another. You know how you are when you're in McDonald's is different than how you are when you're eating at Bouley, or any other fancy restaurant? (Or not.) Well, you suit up into the strongest armor you can find for some of the discussions in Politics, or dust off the degrees before flashing your two cents' worth in the Whitney's Conference. You talk differently in WIT or MOE (the private conferences for women only and for men only) than you do in the Music or New York Conferences. The feel of a conference evolves between the host and the people who are active in that conference, or between the regulars and a convincing newcomer.

A host must have a commitment to the community; they have to like the place and the people. It can be a love/hate relationship, that's perfectly acceptable. Okay, preferable. The point is, they're engaged. Even more crucial, something must be in it for them. Business contacts, romance, friendship, probably other more bizarre or completely wacked-out reasons I don't want to think about, but something. They have to be dying to do it. Hosts who don't meet these requirements never work out.

The greatest host we ever had was Miss Outer Boro. I miss her hosting to this day. She's still around, she just doesn't host. She started as a user, I begged her to be a host, then she went on to be my first conference manager. She oversaw all the conferences on Echo. Queen of Queens. Host of Hosts.

My oldest friend once told me that when we were growing up she thought of me as the Queen of Androgyny. We first met in the girls' locker room after gym when we were thirteen. I was telling a story to a bunch of my friends. She said I had the assumption of power, like a man, but I was total girl—red lipstick, the shortest miniskirt I could get away with, girl voice, girl gestures—this is Miss Outer Boro or MOB. She knows she's smart, powerful and beautiful, part tart, total queen, half of Echo was dying of love for her for the longest time. She is only flirtatious from time to time now. I still rely on her opinion. I read every word she posts. Here's a favorite. A few Echoids were playing with high-school-speak and MOB was responding to her friend Mia Lipner, who was calling herself Grasshopper at the time.

"Y'know Grasshopper honey it just BREAKS my HEART, you actin' this way t'me . . . <adjusting pushup bra>

"Cause I always LIKED ya, y'know?

"I mean I always stood up forya . . . <snapping open compact, peering into mirror and applying fresh coat of Revlon Fire and Ice lipstick to pouty-but-sweet lips>

"Like f'rinstance just the other day, your boyfriend was hittin' on me like he ALWAYS does . . . and he was dissin' you an' shit and I wouldn't listen

". . . <snapping shut compact>

"and THEN he said you didn't know the FIRST THING about givin' HEAD!! Y'know, and I told him to SHUT UP that was JUST NOT TRUE . . .

" . . . 'Cause everybody ELSE I know says you're really not that bad at it . . .

" 'Specially considering the PRICE!!!

" <walks off twitching little ass under tiny miniskirt>"

I'm also very partial to Neandergal, formerly cohost of the Love Conference and now cohost of PSYCH. Neandergal's a therapist. She hates us. She loves us. I've got the same love/hate thing going, so I am comfortable with her. She met and fell in love with Echoid Jim Baumbach and they just bought a building on East Seventh Street. A favorite Neandergal post:

"When Bottomaire [Jim] and I move to our house in Alphabet City we will throw many parties: parties to celebrate winners of The Cutest Labia Contest, parties for the losers of the Brandenburg Concertos Played on Comb Marathons, parties where we stare at the sky and sob for dear life, parties where we will put on rubber loincloths and go wading in the Toys 'r Us Family Size Wading Pool (because we will have a backyard!), parties where we exclaim our love of prime grade sirloin, all kinds of parties, so it is very important that we learn who has not invited us to their parties, so we will not make any Important Mistakes in the invitation arena."

Lianne Smith, aka Topper, replaced Miss Outer Boro as conference manager. She's a singer. When she hit the stage at Mark's welcome home party we had MOE (men on Echo) meltdown. She does this thing with her foot when she sings that pins both men and women to the spot. They can't move, can't look away, stunned in place by the movements of Lianne's black leather-clad foot. She's smarter than most. And because her writing is so right to the point crystal clear she often has the final word.

And Joey X. Joey X has a independent record label called Stickboy Records (so of course we call him Stick Boy). He cohosts the Music Conference. Meen Host, we call him. He hates the Grateful Dead but most of all he hates David Crosby. Before he logged into The WELL for the first time I YOed: "Bring me the liver of the CROZ." "It's yours!" he YOed back.

Staff

Sue Grady was Echo's first employee. A former student of mine, Sue worked for me for a year as an intern before I hired her for real. Sue's a nice Irish Catholic girl. She likes to raise a few every St. Patrick's Day with a group of gorgeous, but "probably married," firemen in a bar called Rosie O'Grady's up on Seventh Avenue.

Sue and I worked side by side, working, gossiping, flirting with the customers, a weird business this. Clients, friends, it's impossible to define the relationship. Mark, who usually worked until he dropped, slept through it all over on a couch three feet away from where we sat laughing or yelling. I would have gone out of business if my customers didn't help me. Bob Knuts gave me legal advice. Longtime Echoids Jim Baumbach and Kevin Krooss, a post office employee, a happy and satisfied post office employee, still help out in a technical pinch. When we needed it, my brother Douglas, who works for Merrill Lynch, lent us a business-like air. On the one hand this was bad business, not having enough staff, but on the other hand, it made the business. It worked. We grew.

Sue Grady liked flirting with Spingo, a user who later became a host, and they would YO each other throughout the day with bad poetry. I sat inches from her so I couldn't help seeing them. I even helped her compose them from time to time. My favorite from Spingo:

> Sue Grady, Sue Grady,
> Are you upset?
> Sue Grady, Sue Grady,
> Did you step on a pet?

Sue Grady did not like my cats.

She also hated the pigeons that had built a nest underneath the air-conditioner outside my window. All day we heard them; they sound like doves. Occasionally the cats would divebomb the window thinking every time that this would be the time they would get to those birds. Sue had had enough. She and Scotty planned one day to poison those poor birds. Pigeon murderers. I found out and put a stop to their evil, pigeon-killing ways. "Well you can't turn on the air-conditioner then," Sue said.

Why not? "Oh right, one might get sucked in and, oh God, poor thing, ripped to shreds, good thinking Sue."

She looked at me. "NO. Pigeon germs. Those things are diseased. If you turn on the air-conditioner we'll all get sick!"

I figured she was making this up to get me back for foiling their plans for a pigeon holocaust, so I started a discussion on Echo to see if it was true. That's another great thing about cyberspace. Where else can you say, "Okay, let's see what several thousand people (or millions) have to say about this?" The collective wisdom of Echo sided with Sue. I had to clean out the air-conditioner and all around it before turning it on that summer. For the record, Sue loves animals. It must have been the tiny apartment, no room to move, cats crashing into glass inches from her face, birds, people everywhere. Temporary insanity. It's the only explanation.

When Mark left we hired Josh Chu (aka Slacker) and Abby Bowen, another former student of mine, and they took over the couch as their desks/office. Pity them. We really had our share of troubles in the beginning. At one point the hardware problems were so bad we would scream at the phone when it rang: "*Go away! We suck!*" When things got too much we rented movies. We had to. It's much better now. The equipment is stable and we have offices in the only part of town where I found peace when I was on the edge.

Before I went to graduate school, when I was so depressed the world vibrated like Van Gogh paintings to me, the only way I could calm down was to walk for hours and hours, and the most soothing part of town for me went from Debrosses to Reade, between Hudson Street and the Hudson River. At the time, this part of town was a deserted, empty, time-tripping forgotten patch of Manhattan, made up of mostly warehouses and gutted five- and six-story tenements with Shaftway–Shaftway–Shaftway signs running up and down the front. I longed to live in those empty buildings. I remember thinking, there's probably thousands of people in New York City at this moment who are depressed. Some are drowning their sorrows, some are sleeping, reading, or at their therapists. How many people are wandering around in these empty streets? One. Still, it made me feel better. I'd skulk about until I felt well enough to go home and sit still. Now I have an office right smack in the middle of it. Life is good. For a minute here and there.

So who are these people online? Well, not JFK, Jr. He didn't stay long. Not on Echo, at any rate. The others? It's a mixed bag. Of just people. Living breathing people. Virtual communities are alive with people. Your mother, your father, sister, brother, boss, ex-lover. Newcomers to cyberspace forget this. There are real people here, and what you say or do here has consequences in your life and in theirs.

John Perry Barlow is often quoted as saying: "The prana is missing . . . " from cyberspace. Prana is a Hindu term for "the breath of life." Say what? When we were kids, my brothers and I used to love to hunt for salamanders in the streams and rivers around our house. Saying there is no prana is like pulling up one rock, finding nothing underneath, and saying, "Well. No salamanders here," before checking a few more rocks. Barlow gets online, forgets himself in the glory of his words, and says, "Well. No prana here." You can't take one moment out of life and say life is this or life is that.

Step back. This moment is linked to that moment which is linked to the next moment and one moment you forget yourself, lost in your head, it's so easy to do but the next moment you're catching your breath, heart pounding and you're jumping in a subway to meet the people who just reminded you that you are all alive, together, the ones you've been talking to online day after day, who are composed of flesh and not flesh. Have you ever jumped in a car after hanging up the phone with someone and raced to see them because you had, had, had to tell them something? Oh, that's not cyberspace? Well, how did I get here in this room with all these people? Again, the idea that you can isolate anything, any one piece of your life, and try to define it without referring to all that is connected to it is nonsense. Not very Hindu for someone who dragged Hinduism into it. Life is a series of moments. Hell, they believe life is a series of lives.

If there is no prana in cyberspace, where does it go? I don't feel as if I'm having an out-of-body experience when I'm online. I don't know a single person who describes it that way. Here I am online, good-bye prana. I'll let you know when I get back. At what point was I separated from my prana?

One moment has little shape, you can barely smell it if you try to separate it from the rest. Some people find comfort in separating everything, in drawing lines and giving names. "Here's prana and here's prana, no prana here, though," or "Here's real life, and here's virtual life." Any one piece pulled out from the whole of anything doesn't say much. Cyberspace exists in the connections. Between people. Who have life and prana. We don't become zombies at the sound of the modem tones. Is a snapshot of someone the person? Is the photo album the family? Are the hard drives that contain the data the people? Again and again I say that what happens here happens over years. This is what is important. It is the very fact that it does continue over time that makes it valuable. It takes time, what is exchanged online: the lives that meet, cross, connect, explode, the loves, the babies where there were no babies, the friendships, jobs, companies—where is the prana, where is the prana not? I tell you cyberspace is packed with prana.

And it doesn't end when you hang up the phone.

Face-2-Face   And Now?   Mystery Button

ECHO POLL

Source: From an online survey of 208 members of Echo, October 1995.

Margin of Error: Left margin or right?

What do you like to talk about most?

16% said myself.

10% said gossip or other people.

9% said sex.

4% said culture.

3% said either books, politics, music, art, food, or feelings.

Face-2-Face   And Now?   Mystery Button

GOD, EVIL, MOM AND DAD AND FRANK SINATRA

In cyberspace we are what we talk about. The electronic dialogue is at the bottom of everything. This is how we communicate our personalities. It is what we fall in love with, what we fear, it is how we connect. I can hate you for what you say. My friends who aren't online, who think we're all a bunch of losers for being here, ask, What do you people talk about in there anyway? The same things we talk about anywhere else. These conversations are more of a reflection of the people having them than the medium or place. Place is a factor only because different "places" attract different people who want to talk about different things. So a hot topic on The WELL may be completely absent on Echo and vice versa. On Echo we talk endlessly about books, movies, the existence of God, evil, our childhoods, love, and work, other Echoids—the ones we love, but especially the ones we hate. And Frank Sinatra. (The men on Echo are obsessed with

Frank Sinatra. Then there's the secondary issue: Who is cooler—
Dean Martin or Frank Sinatra? On The WELL it's the Grateful
Dead. I gotta say, this is definitely a guy bonding thing. As far as I
can tell, the need to settle on a clear, musical/cultural front runner
has not emerged among the women.) You'll find us talking about
anything from the Talmud or performance art to *Beverly Hills 90210*
and *Melrose Place*.

A little orientation. I explained conferences. Well, each conference is filled with conversations. In Movies & TV, one of Echo's
most popular conferences, we talk about good movies, bad movies,
trash TV, cop shows, medical shows, whatever. All the topics that
have to do with film and television are there. These conversations
take place in what's called non-realtime. All it means is this: I can
start a conversation in Movies & TV called: *Bad TV.*

I could have started this topic months ago (except on Echo they
are called items, not topics, because the software was written by
people who could have called the "conferences" something more
intuitive like forums, only they didn't). When someone starts an
item they'll be asked to write a brief description of what the item
is about. Using the topic example of *Bad TV*, someone might begin
the discussion with a simple question. "Okay, what's the worst
show on television?" More complicated subjects, such as, *Sweet
Mother of Christ, Explain Duchamp for Me* (a topic started by Jane
Doe), or *Does consciousness require the experience of a unified Self?* (a
question raised by Neandergal), will require a longer explanation.
Typically, the person who started an item will be first to express
their thoughts. "I'm sorry, but I'm a TV slut. I'll watch anything
and love it."

This item, and that first response, is now up in Movies & TV
for all to see. The people who log in afterwards can read the new
item, respond with their opinions, and those opinions will be added
to the discussion. People who log in months or years from now can
read all that has been said so far and continue to add to the discus-

sion. So a non-realtime discussion simply refers to one that goes on over time, and the people participating are not necessarily logged in together at that moment.

Conferences that are always in the top ten most visited include: Books, Media, Love, and New York. The granddaddy of all: Culture. Since the beginning, Culture has consistently blown every other conference away. American culture mostly, both highbrow and lowbrow, the bizarre and the commonplace. It's popular, ultimately, because the subtext of all these conversations is ME, ME, ME. My experiences, my knowledge and ideas about anything is drawing a picture of ME. After that, YOU, YOU, YOU. On Echo we love to talk about you. In a word: gossip. Fuck anyone who is turning up their noses at this. Gossip doesn't deserve the bad rep that it has. It's what holds us together. This is true everywhere, and it is also true on Echo and anywhere in cyberspace that has people who visit regularly. It's how we keep in touch, make friends. "Did you hear that Nemo and Nancy are getting married?" Or enemies. Like I said, it's not better in here. We don't like everyone. Our gossip can be either vicious or loving.

Over time, you learn what topics people love to talk about, which ones they are sensitive about, what makes them furious or depressed, who's knowledgeable, or thinks they are knowledgeable, about what. You also quickly discover that the possession of some conversational skills are just as important online as they are anywhere else. For instance, you know how some people can go on and on about the same thing wherever they go, no matter what you're talking about? There are people who do the same thing online. They turn every item into a discussion about their pet issue. Like anywhere else, this can be a real bore. Cyberspace doesn't make such behavior suddenly fascinating. And, like anyplace else, work or school, you learn to live with these people. You tune them out mostly, or tell them to shut up sometimes when you lose it. Or, because life is complicated, sometimes you just like them anyway.

I've listed some of the items in Culture below. Each one gets a number, and the number in parenthesis is the number of responses. The title of the item is to the right of that.

Item 153 (1303)   NOIR
Item 232 (1108)   Class of '92: Amy Fisher
Item 272 (1287)   Office Family Values & Culture
Item 281 (1808)   Your School Daze—Tell Us About Them
Item 348 (125)   PRIDE
Item 349 (62)   COVETOUSNESS
Item 350 (1338)   LUST
Item 351 (89)   ENVY
Item 352 (407)   GLUTTONY
Item 353 (550)   ANGER
Item 354 (333)   SLOTH
Item 361 (854)   Suicide
Item 362 (1097)   God, do I HATE SPORTS!
Item 376 (778)   Aging
Item 426 (595)   East Meets West: Right and Left Coast Culture
Item 462 (391)   Afrocentricity
Item 466 (161)   BEAUTY and its Cultural Standards
Item 512 (406)   Who/What is on your refrigerator?
Item 516 (68)   The 40th Anniversary of the "TV Dinner"
Item 519 (314)   You asked for it . . . Murder
Item 545 (670)   Evil
Item 547 (247)   God for a Day
Item 609 (348)   ECSTASY and/or TRANSCENDENCE
Item 620 (525)   The Seventies
Item 621 (32)   Volitional Communities, or Addams Family
                  meets Levittown?
Item 630 (388)   Dean Martin: Symbol of an Epoch
Item 635 (358)   Asian-Americans: Great at Ping Pong, Good
                  at Math?

Item 645 (129)   It seems we all love drag queens.
Item 647 (180)   THE MASONS: secret world rulers or brick layers?

It's a strange mix. The hottest topic for a while was a discussion about shampoo. Shampoo! Who would want to talk about shampoo? And yet the conversation is oddly revealing. A lot of information about a person is contained within their explanation of which shampoo they use and why. It says something about them. We have conversations where people simply list what is in their pockets, their medicine cabinets, or their refrigerator. It gives a surprisingly intimate snapshot. It's personal.

Think about how you talk to your friends or family. You're not always talking about existentialism and free will, for example. You're talking about your dog's fleas, or should I call him or wait for him to call, or what did you do when your kid did this? On a day-to-day basis, we keep in touch through the mundane. Again, gossip.

A student of mine said she'd rather talk to her family than the people online. I can see it. But if her family were online she'd talk to them there and find it satisfying. It isn't "online" that she was having a problem with. She didn't know anyone there. The medium is not what is intimate or not, it's the connection you have or don't have with the people there. Over time, through these conversations, connections are made, and some are stronger than others. In life, most of the people you know are acquaintances, few are really close friends. It's the same online. The opportunity for a worthwhile conversation is more a reflection of the people having it than the place. Exception: Some online services, for whatever reasons, attract complete and utter idiots, so it's hard to separate the two. They become the stupid places.

As long as people want to talk about something, we'll keep the item around. Some items have been around as long as Echo has been around because there are some issues we will never settle. Evil for one. One of my earliest experiences of the power of words, and the power of place online, came from the ongoing discussion of evil in the Culture Conference.

With the exception of Nazis, and that was only because we didn't have any Nazis on Echo at the time, we could never come up with an example of evil that everyone could agree on. Then people did more than disagree. Someone suggested the artist Joe Coleman as an example of evil. Joe is a performance artist, painter, probably other things that I don't know about. He bit the heads off live mice in an earlier act. Surely, this person thought, no one would disagree that killing things as part of a performance was evil. He thought wrong. Plenty of people disagreed. And when they did this person immediately closed his account. Why, why? I asked him. Don't participate in this discussion anymore, and don't talk to the people who disagreed with you if it upsets you, but don't leave. I couldn't talk him out of it. He didn't want to be in the same room with people who felt like that. Same room. No one was anywhere near the guy. In fact, he didn't know where they were and they didn't know where he was. But he felt he was *that close* to evil and had to get out of here fast. I never forgot it. This place is real. As a place.

And some people want nothing to do with it. (I have been trying to get Joe Coleman online ever since. Whenever someone says they know him I plead, "Oh please get him to call Echo." No luck so far. Damn him.)

Another similar example. Mario Cuomo was going to come on Echo during his last race for Governor until one of his staff found an item titled, *Junkie Tipping: The Urban Answer to Cow Tipping*. Thanks but no thanks. He never logged in. I'm sure his staff could see the headline: Governor Supports Violence Against Addicts. I wonder if he would pull a book of his from a bookstore because some of the other books contained objectionable material?

The discussion, Junkie Tipping, came from a conference called Plain Wrapper. It was started by my good friend Joe Rosen—joro.

This is how we got to a discussion called Junkie Tipping: You can say whatever you like on Echo with two exceptions, no personal attacks and no harassment.

It didn't start out that way. When we began we didn't have rules of any kind. Fuck rules. It's the former bad girl in me, the one no one was allowed to hang out with. The one the teachers did their best to get thrown out of school. I wore too much makeup, smoked, drank Scotch in the girls' bathroom, did drugs briefly, went to classes when I felt like it, talked back. I was your typical troubled kid and everyone was sure I'd come to no good. In college, and later at work, rules were helpful, but they always seemed to help someone else, to protect *their* position, not mine. I was forever on the wrong side of those rules. Nope. No rules on Echo. It didn't last. This is how communities evolve. Rules emerge naturally. As a community grows in activity and reach we're caught by something unacceptable.

The first rule came fast. Some controversy had worked its way through Echo. It always happens like this—an argument will arise and it will run through the place like a brush fire, each conference working over some detail, depending on the nature of the conference. Right now we're all going on about the Nazi. We have a Nazi on Echo. The discussion about him in the Politics Conference is different from the one in the Culture Conference, which is different from the one in the Feedback Conference, where everyone talks about Echo, what they like, don't like, should we have Nazis on Echo, etc. You know how a subject can take over a place. I remember when I was a student in Boston how, in the summer, no matter where you went, everyone would be talking about the Red Sox. For a while on Echo we were all talking about the verdict (in the O.J. Simpson trial). A mood can also work its way through Echo. Like hope. Steve Berg, aka Herb, aka Berg Man Of Alcatraz, who had a particularly hard winter, declared last summer "The Summer That Will Not Suck." He made this pronouncement with so much heart and yearning many people came to believe him. It was *everywhere*. Something good will happen this summer. This is the Summer That Will Not Suck. We longed for it.

Arguments in cyberspace can erupt with little warning. In person, I can look at you and say: "I don't agree with a single thing you have said," and depending on how I said it, we can still go back and forth, arguing or not, no hard feelings. Because you can look me in the eye or hear the sound of my voice you can get a better idea of how I meant it. Say the same thing online, and I mean *the very same thing* and, absent of all the visual clues, people will hear that as if you said:

"I don't agree with a single thing you've said because you're a brainless idiot. How did you get here anyway? You are stupid, stupid stupid. Go away. I hate you."

It's common for people to project a lot into what you say and they often assume the worst. When text stands alone on a screen it gains a lot more power. In no time you're down to, "Oh yeah? Well you're a fuckhead," "No, you're a fuckhead." It's called flaming. It happens everywhere in cyberspace. People fight. But I'd seen it consume some of the places I visited and I didn't want Echo to be reduced to one big flamefest. To get past contributions like this, I said, That's it, I'm the fuckhead, and from now on, attack the idea, not the person. My first rule.

The management of Echo believes in freedom of expression. However, personal attacks are not acceptable behavior on Echo. Remember: Attack the idea, not the person. Repeated attacks may lead to being placed on read-only status, or, in extreme cases, the closure of your account.

I would like to take this back. I feel like everyone's mom. Now, now. Be nice. Nothing can make people be nice. People will go away rather than be nice when they don't feel like it and I agree with them. Fuck being nice. All the time that is. But it's too late. It's part of our culture. The good thing about it is it allows conversations to continue, and if you want to call someone a fuckhead, you can. You just have to find a more effective way of doing it. By taking apart what they say you can demonstrate that they are a fuckhead and in the end make a much stronger point. It takes more time. You have to think harder in order to tell someone what you really mean by fuck you.

I have been criticized for the vagueness of this policy. What is a personal attack? I have resisted getting more specific. Some believe this allows me to be selective and biased in my enforcement. That's probably true, but I keep this policy, and all Echo's policies, a little vague to give them flexibility. Life is complicated. Hell, sometimes personal attack is called for. The more rigid the definition, the more policies I would need to cover every contingency.

Read only, by the way, means just that. You can read the discussions but you can't participate in them.

We don't have censorship on Echo. Who decides what's okay and not okay on Echo? The Echoids. They develop their own standards. You'll hear me say again and again if you ever come to hear me speak: We don't need special laws—things aren't more wrong in cyberspace and the laws we already have are just fine. Community standards is one criterion for defining pornography. Well, cyberspace is the new community. A community of minds that is capable of deciding for themselves what is tolerable. Especially a small service like Echo. Complaining about what you find somewhere is like complaining about pornography on Forty-second Street. If you don't like it, don't go there.

I came up with the no-personal-attack rule, but that's because personal attacks are more of a behavioral issue online. The policy limits certain actions, not expression. It's the online equivalent of "take it outside." And that's as far as I'm going to go. It's not that I'm a free speech absolutist; I don't know if I am, it's a tricky issue as far as I'm concerned. I just gave up trying to make rules about it. After the rule about personal attacks—which has always been problematic—I couldn't come up with a single policy about speech that was fair and just.

Now, while I may have decided that there will be no censorship on Echo—you can talk about having sex with your dog for all I care, you can talk about having sex with your *dead* dog if you like—the people on Echo tend to censor themselves. It's mostly a matter of common courtesy. We're so polite. Echoids won't talk about having sex with dead dogs in a conversation about pets, for example. It's a new medium, however, and I have ideas about new speech. I want people to experiment.

And that's how Joe came up with Plain Wrapper, where the item on Junkie Tipping appeared, a place where you can say what you don't feel comfortable saying anywhere else on Echo. Anything goes. No talk of sex with dead dogs to date, but there is a particularly horrifying story about a rat the Echoids begged me to include in this book, but my answer was, "That'll be a big fat NO." The first thing you see when you go into Plain are great, big words that spell FUCK YOU.

Juvenile, I know. You give people a place where anything goes and you'll get a lot of stuff that makes you wonder, "Who are these people and why are they here?" And then you find something so brilliant it stops you dead in your tracks. It makes sense. Most experiments fail. Most of the things you try don't pan out. But sometimes you hit it. A lot of the stuff in Plain Wrapper is stupid and tasteless, even ugly, but it's worth it for those few moments of glory.

We made Plain Wrapper private. Anyone can get in, I just wanted the hosts (Joro was later joined by Scottso, and together they made it into the horror/wonder that it is) to warn people that it was offensive before letting them in. People were complaining to me regularly and I wanted to be able to say to them, Well we told you it was offensive, why'd you go in there? When Cuomo declined to visit, I thought, Should people avoid New York altogether because we have a few rough neighborhoods? Plain Wrapper is Echo's bad part of town. Again, it's a very tricky issue. One of my favorite Echoids, the author Rosemary Bray, stopped going into

Plain Wrapper because of a conversation she felt was racist. I agreed. It wasn't deliberately racist, it had to be explained how it could be seen that way, and when it was the conversation stopped. Even when anything goes, people create limits. They're basically decent. (Except when they're not.)

Plain is dead now. For years it was always one of the top three most popular conferences, but it has been replaced by a different conference that took their experiment even further: Xenophobia. More about Xenophobia, which we now call X, later. Here are some of the items from Plain Wrapper.

Item 8 (978)	This item available for private parties
Item 10 (713)	This item was raised from the dead.
Item 18 (632)	Getting to know the Borough President within
Item 25 (300)	GUESS WHICH SHELL SAMMY'S GLASS EYE IS UNDER
Item 45 (491)	Another Day in Hell
Item 65 (118)	This is the DEAD TOM CARVEL ITEM.
Item 102 (296)	Barber Comb FLUID (GERMICIDE or ORNAMENT)
Item 136 (158)	This is the LIBERACE Item
Item 186 (59)	Why is Charles Foster Kane so famous. He ain't even real!
Item 269 (260)	Please don't have sex with this item.
Item 301 (29)	FISH BED
Item 353 (133)	The Men's Room Wall
Item 354 (28)	The Ladies' Room Wall
Item 414 (186)	Tell Jim Baumbach to Stay the Hell Outta My Dreams
Item 420 (271)	Where's my new tattoo?
Item 430 (994)	Your Personal Daily Angst-o-Meter: an Experiential Workshop
Item 536 (323)	Things I'd like to smack with a baseball bat
Item 542 (287)	Jamie Lee Curtis: Hermaphrodite or what?

Item 599 (792)	That Really Really Fat Guy With The Braids Died
Item 621 (105)	Don't speak French in this item
Item 695 (59)	I'll end up a "shower toy" on Riker's Island
Item 729 (680)	SHUT THE FUCK UP !
Item 837 (54)	I Am Sick With Grief That So Many Enjoy Lima Beans
Item 855 (98)	Sundays Are The Lamest Days <tm>
Item 858 (90)	I Wanna Be An Amish Farmer!!!
Item 874 (199)	I like this item
Item 875 (74)	I like this item better
Item 900 (78)	This Is The First Item Of The Rest Of Your Life
Item 1011 (6)	Norman Rockwell Goes to Hell
Item 1053 (30)	Fuck Nancy Kerrigan

Those <tm>s you've been seeing? It stands for trademark. I'm not sure who started them, I think it was joro. Someone said they started out on the Internet. Whatever. We made the practice ours. They are now an Echo tradition. When someone says a word or a phrase that would typically be said by someone else, they give that person credit, or quickly <tm> it for themselves. For example.

Amy R: . . . GOODFELLAS didn't have an unnecessary character, line or moment; CASINO had "too many notes" <tm AMADEUS>.

ChamCham: No way! I asked for it first and I need it more! It's mine mine MINE MIIIIIIIIINE! <tm 2-year-olds>

Cham/Kitten: Clickity clackity claws <tm dogs>.

SuZin: It's a "good" tired <tm annoying people>.

Charles: If this summer (that doesn't suck <tm Herb>) does not set a record for sheer number of intolerable days, I'd like to know why.

neandergal: I hate myself because my mother blames ME for HER low self-esteem. <tm Alice Miller Perversions>

Berg Man of Alcatraz: I don't want to have a Perfect Moment <tm Spalding Grey>.

SuZin: Berg has hired me to bring him food and the *New York Post* on a daily basis at the handsome salary of four rolls of Smarties <tm> a day.

Jane Doe and her "Issues": I wanna be known as the gal who can bring home the bacon, and fry it up in a pan <tm the Enjoulie <tm> perfume commercial, circa 1981>.

Jane Doe, Postructuralist Ho: He is my Spiritual Advisor and Thighmaster <tm>.

Jane Doe and her "Issues": And please do not drift from the topic at hand, which is Paradise Lost <tm a book I never read, actually>.

Jane Doe: I am wearing a look of bewilderment on my face, because I stupidly just turned down a quickie <tm> and dinner in order to have quality time with myself.

Berg Man of Alcatraz: Oh, and I'd also like a Dixie Cup <tm> stuffed with Brown 'n' Serve <tm> sausages, to eat as I walk to work, like I used to do when I was a kid and would eat them while walking to school in the morning.

The Strange Apparatus: My liver is worn out. It revealed its age last night, when my "friend" insisted we finish an entire bottle of vodka at Sammy's Rumanian and have a fight with his wife in the melodic language of porpoise. Oy <tm>, the pain <tm Dr. Smith>.

Dr. Prof. Clem: Shoot him now! Shoot him now! <tm Daffy Duck>

The language in cyberspace is evolving. While we work very hard to express our personal identity, we also spend as much time establishing the group identity. Like certain parts of the country that have their own expressions, each online place develops their own slang, their own unique way of saying things. It's an important tool in cyberspace for recognizing and identifying with your group or online home.

The <tm>'s on Echo, for example. Others: John Gabriel brought us the expression "haina" from Pennsylvania. You stick it on the end of the sentence and it means, "You know what I'm saying?" Haina? You see it all over Echo. Oy is another popular expression. Everyone loves to say oy. (Very New York.) Someone offered someone else "fitty cent" for something, and for months the value of anything was "fitty cent." We have IWBKA (I Wanna Be Known As), as in "IWBKA Miss Fleet Week." (Every year, when the ships come in, we've got a few Echoids vying for this title.) There's the Next Big Thing. This is how we refer to a controversy as it starts to move its way through Echo. The presence of a Nazi was the Next Big Thing for a while. Another favorite Echo term: huffing. When someone leaves Echo because we're a bunch of pathetic, loser, yuppie, hippie, liberal, slacker, "you think you're so smart," scum—we say they huffed. This is different than leaving the place because they thought it was too expensive or hard to use. These are the people who leave because they hate us. They can't go quietly, they have to slam the door on the way out. For example, from an Echoid on his way out:

"As a departing, very brief Echoid, I'd like to point out that, working more or less in tandem, Tom Lipscomb and Susan Brownmiller have reduced this item to a snotty gossip conference between the two of them, from which SB has lately dropped out. I was lured into Echo by the promise that New York's best and brightest hung out on it. What I found was a level of conversation comparable to what passes across a supermarket checkout counter. I'm sorry to have spoken a discouraging word (I know it's taboo), but the whole pack of you ought to be engaged in something better than this, like reading books, for instance, or writing them. On second thought, given your Echo performance, skip the latter."

We have stylistic customs. Smiley faces are frowned on here. Smiley faces are those things that look like a smile when you look at them sideways. :-). There are countless variations. ;-). That one is supposed to be a wink. They're also called emoticons, for the love of God. Well, use them on Echo and people will assume that you are without language or conversation and suggest that you go back to America Online (a place known for its liberal use of emoticons). The same with people who use a lot of exclamation points. Make your point or not. Depend on punctuation or graphics to do it for you, and you will spend the rest of your time on Echo overcoming your reputation as an electronic rube.

Another thing that is not used very much on Echo, but it's used a great deal on America Online and Compuserve, is chat. When you're in chat you're having a conversation right then and there with the people who are logged on right then and there, with you. It's live. Realtime (unlike items). The culture of Echo does not favor chat. Because the conversation is live, you can only talk as fast as you can type. And because no one can type as fast as they talk, people shorten what they say so that the conversation doesn't move too slowly. That is why chat conversations typically look like this.

Constance: Hi!

Julian: Hi!

Charles: Hi!

Merricat: How are you?

Charles: Great! You?

Julian: Just great!

Chat is not the place for an in-depth conversation. It doesn't give you the opportunity to consider what you want to say.

People do go into chat for special occasions. Like YORB night. The YORB is an experiment in interactive television on public access being conducted by ITP and NYNEX. One evening a week you can turn on your TV and see this graphic representation of a world. People can call the show, and when they get through they show up as moving lips on the TV. Everything they say at this point is heard by anyone watching the show. One person at a time can be what is called the pilot. Using their phone, they can hit numbers to go in and out of places on the world. For instance, hit the four on your phone and the screen moves left toward a building. Hit the five and you go into that building. These buildings may have graphics inside, or music, or video. The interface was written by an ITP student named Dan O'Sullivan. YORB is the nickname for the world. No one knows where the word YORB came from—someone said it stands for Your Orb, but I think they're making that up.

A few years ago Red Burns, the Queen of New Media and the woman who runs ITP, asked me to help them create a sense of community on the YORB. I said okay, but I was overextended as usual so I said "Let's cheat." Echo already has a community, let's put Echo on the world and use them like ringers to jumpstart the community on YORB. "Let's do it," we decide. A group of ITP students made it so that when a caller went into the building on the YORB for Echo, whatever people were typing in chat on Echo at the time would appear on the TV. Everything they said scrolled across the TV live. Talking to the Echoids became so popular we later changed it to keep the chat scrolling across the top of the screen during the entire show. It developed into a bizarro *Mystery Science Theater* with Echoids and callers commenting on what they were seeing, what was going on in New York or the world that day, or whatever came into their heads. I used the time to flirt with Eric Fixler, the host of the show. He's fix on Echo.

Later we added a third element: the camera. We had a camera and microphone literally hanging out the window on Waverley Place going down four floors to the street. If a caller chose the camera, we could see and talk to whoever was walking by. The sound was in one direction only so they couldn't talk back. People are resourceful though. That winter it snowed always. We were steeped in snow and ice so treacherous we walked like the ground was the enemy. Arms extended for balance, hands out, "You won't get me," we're thinking as we frown at the street. A couple of people walking by got an idea. They used the snow to talk to us. We all watched, callers, viewers, and Echoids, as they spelled out a single word in the snow. They had to keep it short. Typing is slow. Writing in snow is interminable. One letter at a time.

The callers read each letter aloud over Manhattan Cable.

I
N
S
I
D
E

Inside. Inside. "They want to come inside!" Eric cried. I think it was something like 200,000 below that night. "Come on in." Eric is a good soul. He put them on camera so we could all say hello. Week after week we continued these strange, crude, threeway conversations, the callers, the Echoids and the people on the street—Eric and I flirting shamelessly throughout—and in time we did evolve into a small but very real community. We had our regulars. My favorite was a woman named Mary Kessler, who called herself Maz. She was smart and had a great accent.

Jake from Squirt TV was into the YORB for a while. Squirt TV was a television show that began on public access, moved to MTV, and now it's gone. The show was this kid, Jake, who was fourteen years old at the time, in his bedroom in Manhattan, hanging out, talking about whatever; he had his own obsessions. Sometimes he had a friend with him. It was a New York City wise-ass kid's version of *Wayne's World*. He was terribly sweet. And smart. When I found out he was watching, I typed:

JAKE CALL ECHO JAKE CALL ECHO JAKE CALL ECHO
JAKE CALL ECHO JAKE CALL

Until he did.

One night, out of boredom, while Eric was fixing a computer problem, we all sang the ever popular "A Hundred Bottles of Beer on the Wall." The callers sang the words while the Echoids typed them. It's hard to imagine, but it worked. I laughed until my stomach ached, but I didn't think it would be entertaining for anyone else. I was sure it belonged in the "you had to be there" category.

A month later I was asked to fill in at the last moment for a talk at the Museum of Modern Art. I was intimidated, I admit it. I had never spoken in a place like that before. Talk about the Net had begun to heat up, but had it reached MOMA? First I talked about Echo. The Echoids are an eclectic group—there are tons of artists online, conversations about art are everywhere, the Whitney Museum of American Art has a conference on Echo; it fit. Then I explained the YORB. The YORB is used, among other things, as a place to showcase artwork, so I thought they might find it interesting. Nick West, the producer, made a tape for me to show. After giving them an idea of what to expect, I start the tape. My good buddy Nick had included the "A Hundred Bottles of Beer" night. It was a very highbrow audience. What were they going to think of this? "Better than Letterman," someone said to me afterward. They loved it.

Years later, I was visiting Sharleen Smith, another ITP grad who does new media development at the SciFi Channel, when her boss came in and said, "Echo and the SciFi Channel should do something together." Sure. Love to. After he leaves we say, They'll never go for it, but wouldn't it be great if we did something like the YORB? We could have people online, live, commenting on the programming, and their comments would scroll across the bottom of the screen.

Nope. They'll never go for it, we agreed. Not a chance. They went for it, with a catch. We'll let you put something together and experiment, but we're giving you the 4:00 A.M. slot. And you get one shot. Sharleen produced and designed the whole thing, Dan O'Sullivan, our friend from the YORB days did the programming, and I supplied the people and the online connection.

Except for the one hour each day when we bring the system down for backups, people are logged on. Three o'clock in the morning, four o'clock, five o'clock, there are always people there. We call them our Insomnia Crew. For the next couple of days I kept track of who was logged in at 4:00 A.M. Then I asked the cleverest to join us: Joey X and Jack Taylor, aka The Strange Apparatus, the cohost of Culture. Jack plays the ukelele and seems to live in a perpetual tropical haze. All sunshine and Hawaiian shirts and rum. In fact, I can't see Jack without thinking of Ray Walston wearing coconut shells for breasts in the movie *South Pacific*. A favorite Strange Apparatus post of mine read:

"I lived in Adams Morgan for close to five years. I love DC, in all its steamy griminess. People are friendly, and you can live like a civilized human for reasonable prices. And let me say this for the record: New York Sucks. All the great stuff we ballyhoo, like Korean Grocers, clubs, and restaurants, are pretty meager compensation for totally compromising on one's values. Every day I contemplate new career paths which could extract me from this rat-infested, junkie-populated, soot-clouded, garbage-marinaded, necropolis of perpetual robbery. But then I think, 'what, and give up Benny's Burritos?'"

There are a lot of women on Echo dying of love for Jack, but he's in love with Jane Doe, whom I also invited to join us, along with Mrs. Hippie Queen, and Molly Ker, the woman who later replaced Sue Grady as the general manager of Echo. Molly was smart and her postings made me laugh until I cried. This was more important to me than her résumé, which, by the way, I have never seen.

The SciFi people decided our one shot would be with *The Prisoner*, a very interesting British television series from the sixties. So a couple of weeks later, at four o'clock in the morning, while *The Prisoner* aired, the Insomnia Crew logged into Echo and alternately mocked and praised the show and their comments appeared at the bottom of the screen. Some of it was very funny, not all; it was hard to be clever at four o'clock in the morning. Also, *The Prisoner* was a poor choice. We begged them to give us something truly bad to play with. Often we were reduced to comments on the set: "Either those drapes go or I do." The acting: "Oh go back to summer stock, you." The dialogue: "Panoply? Who talks like that?" The SciFi people loved it. They gave us the rest of the run of *The Prisoner* to refine it.

Sharleen got a ton of email. Anything from "You must be stopped" to "Go, go, go!" She invited a few from each camp to join us. One poor soul who called herself Roses logged in every week to defend *The Prisoner* from what she felt was our utter lack of respect. The best stuff happened during commercials. Sharleen should have just kept us on—Mrs. Hippie Queen patiently explaining to Roses that we admired the show too, "We're just teasing," the rest of us ripping into the commercials. People called in from around the country, and we became our own CNN as we gave quick news and weather updates for our hometowns. I love this about the Net. Before the Internet we relied on very few people for our news; the select few who wrote for the papers we read or appeared on the TV. Now when something happens I can also read about it online, often from people who are there, people I know and trust. When we had riots in Tompkins Square Park I read about it from the people who lived there, people who were right in the middle of it. When the bomb went off in the World Trade Center people logged in to ask each other, "What was that?" Because our words are saved, it gives history back to us and not just the people who write about it later.

Sharleen didn't censor much. She let most of what we said go straight through to the TV screen. In addition to experimenting with creating community on national television I was also further-ing a romance with an electronic—soon to be in the flesh—lover who lived in Los Angeles. While he watched I snuck in comments that only he would understand. I did my best to cleverly disguise what I was saying as cultural commentary about the show and media and the sixties, but sometimes something I said would illicit a collective "huh" from the Insomnia Crew or a call from Sharleen to ask me if I was on crack. I had said something about snow, we had this private thing about snow, and we were in the middle of the worst heat wave in years at the time. Seconds later, in response to this particular comment about snow, my screen came alive with beeps as my Los Angeles lover breathlessly YOed: *Will you marry me?* He was smitten.

Again, the SciFi Channel experiment was all very *Mystery*

Science Theater 3000-y. We borrowed from it shamelessly and the connection is important. Cyberspace is one great big *Mystery Science Theater 3000* really. The appeal is the same: We want to talk back. We have something to say about everything. On the television show, Joel and the bots do it for us—online, we get to have our say. In cyberspace we have a running commentary on ourselves and our culture and all we know and don't know, which connects us to ourselves, each other, and everything in front of us.

All the power and the allure of virtual communities is in this ongoing, evolving commentary, and the bonds and knock-down, drag-out fights that invariably arise when you give people a place to talk for as long and as often as they like. The conversations we have online are our identity. They are all we have to explain ourselves, the only way to be known. The topics we choose to discuss define the community. They set the tone; they tell what kind of place you're in. People who come looking for a hot chat session run screaming from Echo when they see the kinds of conversations we have here.

And, along with revealing who we are—pretty okay folks or complete and total idiots, or more usually, a combination of the two—the things we say as individuals establish our relationship to the other people around us.

For example, from longtime Echoid Simon Egleton:

"My father smashed my mother's brains in with a hammer when I was 14 years old. My brother and I knew something was coming. My Mother had been behaving like a scared animal for a couple of weeks. I feel guilty, because I know I should have stayed home from school the morning it happened. Mind you, he would probably have killed me too. I left for school; 15 minutes later it happened.

"He hit her 17 times with the hammer—snuck up behind

her in the bathroom. The official verdict was that she drowned in the bath (she fell into it). My mother was my only source of love and care. I used to say that after that I went off the rails at school. My friend Sandy says, nah your Dad took the track away.

"He got 2 years on a manslaughter charge. Best QC (read, lawyer) money could buy. When he came back from prison, he dated trashy, tarty women, it was strange to hear them fucking in the next room. Some of them were really into the fact that he had killed a woman.

"My father is not a clever man. His father forced him into the family business at the age of 13. He has been a drunk since the age of 13. His father was a horrible man. In his own way my father has been horrible to me.

"I still talk to him on the phone a coupla times a year. He doesn't listen to me at all, there is no sense of a two-way conversation.

"Part of me still loves him. Mind you, I got love to burn."

That story told you something about Simon. The fact that he told it at all tells you something about the place where he said it. But his words also had an effect on the community and Simon's relationships with the people in it. They brought some Echoids closer to him. They made others uncomfortable. What we say in cyberspace has a powerful effect. Whether used as an assault or a kiss, the fact that these things are said online changes little. If someone says, "I love you" or "I'm coming to kill you," over a telephone, for instance, you would still feel love or fear. The things we say to each other in cyberspace don't sit innocent and powerless on the screen—they can build friendships, inflict pain, fear, destroy lives, get you a job, or inspire a proposal of marriage. In cyberspace we build worlds with the things we say.

*   *   *

I Hate Myself. This is one of the most enduring items on Echo. Yup. That's us. The dysfunctional family Echo. Echo has a very in-your-face, New York style of communicating. On The WELL, when they need support, one of the topics they go to is *Request for Beams.* People say what is wrong in their life and ask for Wellbeings to send best wishes and hope in the form of "beams." "Sending Well beams to . . ." they'll cry. On Echo we have *I Hate Myself.* Echoids regularly post in *I Hate Myself* as a way of checking in with each other. It's how we keep tabs on what is going on with our friends. These conversations are one of the most important functions of a virtual community. On Echo we care about each other as much as the people over on The WELL do, it's just that our best wishes take a different form or style. The meaning is the same. I mean, what are the true differences between Wellbeings and Echoids? Or in how a Californian or a New Yorker cares? None. But loyalty and a sense of belonging, or commitment, to a place are expressed and strengthened with an identification with the form these conversations take.

I can't send beams to someone, it's not my style. I can commiserate with self-loathing, however. "It's a quintessential Echoidian thing," Miss Outer Boro, the quintessential Echoid, says.

I HATE
MYSELF...

606:8) Kiwi

I hate myself when my love for myself wanes.

606:9) Spingo

Which is RARE.

606:10) howl

If at fucking all.

606:29) Chameleon

I hate myself because no one missed me while I was gone for like a whole month. "Out of Echo, out of mind."
I hate myself for hating myself when I should be hating alla ya that didn't send me E-stacks of E-mail wondering "Where's the Chameleon?"

606:30) jneil

I hate myself for not filling Chameleon's mailbox while she was gone.

606:34) Chameleon   **17-JAN-92 11:56**
I hate myself for making people feel guilty for something that was my own fault.

606:36) SuZin   **17-JAN-92 22:25**
I hate myself for making Chameleon hate herself because I felt guilty.

606:45) SuZin   **18-JAN-92 12:10**
I hate myself for sleeping too late and missing all the fun stuff.

606:46) Neandergal   **18-JAN-92 12:27**
I hate myself for sleeping too late and missing nothing.

606:48) praam   **18-JAN-92 18:44**
I hate my feet.

606:50) SuZin   **18-JAN-92 21:09**
I hate myself for buying big piles of new clothes and trying to convince myself I really NEEDED them.

606:58) Jim Baumbach (another item to forget) **19-JAN-92 23:33**
If it weren't for guilt, no one would ever do anything.

606:59) Miss Outer Boro 1991   **20-JAN-92 0:04**
What about shame?
I've always found that a good motivator, along with guilt.

606:60) Jim Baumbach (another item to forget) **20-JAN-92 0:05**
I'm ashamed to admit I forgot shame.

606:61) praam   **20-JAN-92 0:10**
Still hate my feet.

606:84) Miss Outer Boro 1991   21-JAN-92 0:11

I hate myself for being chicken.
And for living in a pigsty.
A whole barnful o' self-hate.

606:86) Joey Hibachi   21-JAN-92 0:13

I hate myself for not being able to sleep, being surrounded by dirty tissues, empty beer bottles, and stinky clothes. Calgon—take me away.

606:87) Miss Outer Boro 1991   21-JAN-92 0:14

Joey—have we switched identities?

606:88) Joey Hibachi   21-JAN-92 0:17

I hate myself for switching identities with MOB without asking permission first.

606:89) Miss Outer Boro 1991   21-JAN-92 0:18

TAKE my identity—PLEASE! <tm Henny Youngman on acid>.

606:90) Joey Hibachi   21-JAN-92 0:21

I hate myself for giving Henny Youngman the last hit of acid.

606:91) praam   21-JAN-92 1:10

Speaking of empty beer bottles . . .
There's a sea 'o 'em in my sleeping/computing area . . . with many unfinished novels collecting dust . . .
Then there's the (at least 100) unmarked discs (both computer and music) strewn throughout the home . . .
Then there's the newspapers I promise that I'll someday read when I'm rotting in hell.
Then there's the . . . never mind.

606:92) SuZin   21-JAN-92 1:12

The severed head of your cousin?

606:97) Andrew Grant   21-JAN-92 1:25

I hate myself for letting my Chia Pet die.

606:121) Chameleon   21-JAN-92 10:16

I am awash in deep-seeded self-loathing that keeps threatening to explode outta me and flood the apartment with the essence of true Self Hatred, and then it will seep through the cheap construction of the building and infiltrate the lives of shiny happy people holding hands and they will turn into rusty disgusting people tearing hair, and I will have been responsible for their fall into the putrescent pit of self-loathing and ruin the agonizing solitary misery of the place. And they won't know why this has happened to them, and I won't tell them because it's all my fault and I hate myself.

606:124) Miss Outer Boro 1991   21-JAN-92 18:24

I hate myself for being Shallow and Inarticulate in my self-hatred, unlike the Great Chameleon who is showing us all How It's Done.

606:226) Neandergal   06-FEB-92 2:16

I hate myself for feeling murderous and vindictive.

606:227) Neandergal   06-FEB-92 2:16

I hate myself for loving an inappropriate person.

606:228) Neandergal   06-FEB-92 2:17

I hate myself for being a fucking addict.

606:229) Neandergal   06-FEB-92 2:17

I hate myself for hoping against hope.

606:231) Neandergal   06-FEB-92 2:18

And for living in a fantasy.

606:232) Neandergal   06-FEB-92 2:18

And for being a fucking wimp.

606:233) Neandergal   06-FEB-92 2:19

And dumb.

606:267) Joey Hibachi   20-FEB-92 20:34

If elected Pope, I'll hate myself for having to work Sundays.

606:286) Neandergal   25-FEB-92 9:14

I hate myself for being irresponsible about money and having to be arrested (I KNOW I will be) and sent to Bedford Hills Correctional Facility where Jean Harris and I will do some excellent work and publish articles together, the money from which will go to the IRS in my case and the family of Herman Tarnower in hers.

ECHO POLL

Source: From an online survey of 332 members of Echo, December 1995.

Margin of Error: Is this a trick question?

Can you tell if someone is a man or woman online?

18% said yes.

37% said no.

16% said most of the time.

26% said sometimes.

BOYZ AND GURLZ

Face-2-Face　And Now?　Mystery Button

The only gender differences online are the ones that are expressed with words. You can't see anyone. There's no scent of perfume, no sweat. Nothing soft, nothing hard. We are stripped of everything but our words. And if you take everything away from us but our words, what are the differences between men and women?

"Please let me into WIT." Someone is sending me email to get into one of our private conferences for women only. I get a few of these requests every day. They have to email me first to get in, and I don't let them in until I verify that they are female. We do this with a phone call. Someone at Echo calls every woman who asks to get into WIT, and then they do their best to determine if the person asking is a woman. This is not 100% effective, as you can imagine.

Sue is desperately trying to get my attention, *"Pick up the phone,"* she mouths to me. She's talking to someone who has asked to get into WIT. I quietly pick up my phone. Now I see the problem. This person has a low, gravely voice, there's simply no way to tell, and Sue and I are just too damn polite to say, "But you sound like a guy." We let her or him in. Such wimps.

This time it's Embraceable Ewe, a preop transsexual asking, "Please let me into WIT." Oh God, now what, I'm thinking. I'm in over my head. As I said earlier, no one else in the world can agree on this issue: Is gender a biological or social construct? Echo makes the question even more interesting. If I let her into WIT, will it feel like there is a man in the room, or a woman?

I had two experiences very early in my online life that begin to answer that question. The first was on CompuServe. This was back in 1986, when I was exploring all the online places I could for that NYU class. Someone suggested that I try CB on CompuServe. CB is a live chat area. When you go into CB you're asked to pick a name—this is the name that will appear whenever you say anything. I don't remember what I picked. Let's say Fish Head. I'm sure it was something like that. Whenever I had to come up with a name in those days I was always picking a name with fish in it. I don't know why. I don't want to know why.

It was my first time doing this so I started asking questions. "How do I see who is here," or "What do those funny characters mean?" I'm ignored. Okay, maybe I'm not asking the right way. Geeks are very fussy about how you pose questions. "Could someone please tell me what command I would use to see who is in this chat area besides me?" Nothing. Then a few very rude comments.

Okay, no one wanted to answer my technical questions. People were mostly saying hi and bye to each other as they came and went so I tried to start a conversation. I said something about movies. This time I got a whole barrage of nasty comments. I gave up. "Okay, no one wants to talk to me? Fine. I'm outta here," I typed.

Then: "Don't go Fish Head! There's a bunch of cute girls here."
Huh?

It took me a full minute to get it. A bunch of cute girls, a bunch of cute girls, no one will answer my questions, no one wants to have a conversation with me, many are insulting me, but I should stay because there are a bunch of cute girls here. Oh my God, I've got it.

"Do you think I'm a guy?"

"Well aren't you Fish Head?"

"No."

Phone numbers started flying at me. "Please call me!" "Let's chat on the phone!" I'm getting messages from guys explaining how we can go into a private channel to talk, just the two of us. "Talk to me," they're all begging, "talk to me." The best were these online roses that they started to send, one after the other. Using the characters on their keyboard they were able to create fairly decent representations of roses. And now everyone's a movie buff.

"Too late," I told them. "You had your chance to be nice!" And I logged off. I was younger and less generous then.

Now, based on whatever fish name it was that I picked and the fact that my first words were questions, they all thought: guy. This experience made it clear, you can't always tell. At first.

One other thing about this incident I have never forgotten. While I was taking that minute to figure out the mistake, a number of women were trying to convince me to stay. They adopted a slightly slavish position while coming on to me at the same time. It broke my heart. I wanted to grab their hands and say, "Get up, get up!" I found their subservience horrifying. Sexuality, it's all very complicated. I just remember thinking, How can guys like this? Since then I've caught myself doing the very same thing, I don't think I ever would have noticed this about myself had it not been for this chat.

Something to remember with respect to this experience. Every online service develops its own culture, which attracts a certain kind of person. Even within one service you will find many different subcultures. CB, or chat in general, does not attract the kind of people who might have had a more sophisticated exchange. Or rather, chat is where you go when you don't want to think anymore. Wait a minute. What am I saying? I hate thinking all the time. I am so there.

The second experience was on The WELL. I was carrying on a conversation with a number of people, and from the start, something was different. It was subtle. People were responding to me in a way that was just a little bit off. Whatever it was, it felt very, very good. I couldn't put my finger on it. It was like respect, but I'd experienced respect once or twice before, and this was a different kind of respect. Fuck it. It felt good, I just went along with it. Perhaps this is what people in California are like? I was new to The WELL and I had never been to California.

Then someone referred to something I had said and they called me "he." I was a guy again. The people on The WELL are more sophisticated than the people I found in chat that particular day on CompuServe. When I corrected them there wasn't an immediate turnaround. But it came.

Once I knew what had happened I went back through the conversation carefully. The only thing I could find to explain what I felt right from the start was I had never had to prove myself.

Whenever I go dancing, there's always a jostling of position while dancers of equal ability find each other. You have to establish that you are in each other's league. It sounds horrifying, but the dance is no fun for either person if there isn't something of a match in skill. (And of course it can get more complicated than that. Sometimes you want someone a little better, so you can stretch your skills. Sometimes you want to be the teacher, and so on.)

I go through the same thing whenever I get into a conversation with a bunch of men. There is always a short period where I have to prove that I'm a good match for this discussion. I don't have to go through this with women. It doesn't mean that I don't have to prove myself with women, it's just that certain things are a given. If it were a sword fight, it would be like someone handing me the sword without first asking me to demonstrate that I can use it. I still have to fight once I have it in my hand, I just don't have to prove that I can handle the sword. While I was a guy in this discussion, the fact that I was competent enough to join the fight was a given. All I had to do was get down to the fight at hand. No swordly third degree. I could get right to the fun stuff. That was why it felt so good.

But then I was a girl. And slowly, people started asking me to prove what I was saying. Every statement I made had to be put to the test before it was accepted. There is always a certain amount of this in any discussion, but I was definitely getting it more. There were only two other women in this conversation and they weren't saying much, so I can't really compare how the men were responding to them, or how the two women were responding to me. There also wasn't enough of a response from the women to see if there was any kind of before and after thing happening with them. At least they weren't doing that unsettling subservient/flirty thing the women on CompuServe had done.

So you can't always tell. At first. But you can often tell over time. The illusion of free and unbiased communication can only be maintained, and then only briefly, as long as people hide. It's a trick. In time, if you act like yourself, gender is revealed, because we do take our bodies with us. I don't log on and suddenly forget I'm female. Oh, I'm online! Now I can forget a lifetime of socialization. There it goes, right out the window! Right. You don't forget your body online any more than you do in the physical world. Or remember it. Sometimes you get caught up in your head, sometimes you're aroused, and when there is a conflict with respect to sexuality or gender, you remember which side you're on.

I'm not talking about the true differences between men and women, by the way. I don't know what those differences may or may not be. I'm only talking about the differences we think or have been taught to believe are there. Learned or innate, we project those differences into cyberspace. Men and women are taught to communicate differently. If you spend time with someone online, you can tell if they are a man or a woman. However, if someone is out to fool you and they are clever, they can. Or they can me anyway. But what does that prove? If someone does not act like themselves you will make mistakes about them? If someone does act like themselves and you make mistakes about their gender, *then* you have something to look at.

But Embraceable Ewe is not out to fool anyone. While she believes she is a woman, she is also very open about the fact that she has a dick. "Honey, I'm more man than you'll ever be, and more woman than you'll ever have!" That's what Embraceable Ewe answers when someone asks if she is a man or a woman. It's how a man would answer. Using the word "honey" like that is a dead giveaway, too. She sounds like a drag queen. The cultural differences come through loud and clear.

Most of the time, though, when I'm talking with her I honestly do feel as if I am talking to a woman. The fact that she occasionally sounds like a man actually makes her more real as a woman. We are all a combination of stereotypical male and female responses. If she was always, always feminine, she would be more like a cartoon.

Here's where it gets tricky. I created WIT as a space for women to talk with each other in the way that they talk when men aren't in the room. Our shared history created this need. If you didn't grow up female, where would that need come from? Can you adopt or assume a history you did not live through? There is a set of behavior easily recognizable as female, the subtleties are hard to fake, only people who grew up female can do it (for the most part).

And why would you want to fake it? Aren't you, ultimately, simply trying to be yourself? So why assume the cultural artifacts of a history you never had? I wonder what male-to-female transsexuals mean when they say that they are women. When I say I'm a woman, I'm talking biologically and as a person who was raised as female. Since I don't share either biology or socialization with a male-to-female transsexual, *what exactly do we share as women?*

I felt like the George Wallace of cyberspace when I didn't let Embraceable immediately in with just a phone call. How did the women of WIT feel about letting her in? Some didn't want her in there ever, with or without a dick. This was a problem. I've learned I can't make people like or accept anyone. That's up to the person to work out for themselves. When did it ever work, for instance, when we were young and someone was picking on you, to tell the teacher? It only made the kids hate you more.

Someone suggested starting a new conference for transsexuals. Shades of "separate but equal."

Topper: Here's my take on sex changes: clothes and/or surgery do not change who you are. Those that go that route for only that reason end up just as unhappy as they were prior to the change. And a transsexual will never be just a man or just a woman (depending upon which gender they chose), but just a transsexual.

Ding Dang Dali M.: I guess I don't have any problem with anyone who genuinely considers herself to be a woman, or is working to become one, being here (that is, as long as considering oneself male or female are the only two choices we've got). Here's one vote for Declines-to-state On ECHO.

Margaret: Interesting question. Dali says "anyone who considers herself . . . or is working to become one." I don't know about that, I guess my first instinct is to say that the person should already have gone through the physical as well as the psychological trans-formation. And even then, she'd probably forget a lot of items about PMS and such. But would be a real asset in terms of dis-cussing gender stereotypes and roles.

Plain Scarf: Wait a minute. Would you expect post-menopausal women to forget items on PMS, or rather assume any comments from them would be welcome, in light of their experience with estrogen fluctuations? Broaden the first assumptions, and the answer becomes slightly more complex.

Ms. P.: As far as having transsexuals in WIT—how would we know? Most of the women on WIT are people I only know online and maybe have met in person at a f2f [face-to-face]. I certainly don't know who is transsexual and who isn't and I don't care. If society is going to be so narrow as to say that there are only two genders then I think that those people who feel the need to change genders in order to be themselves shouldn't be punished for it.

Plain Scarf: Besides, the only identity which is verifiable under WIT is legal identity (which is mutable, after transsexual operations) and possible voice verification—that, and honor. Trust is what binds private conferences together, and that is a trait independent of present gender assignment.

Marian in a Storm: Guys are guys—op or no op. But I'd be willing to tolerate a post op only because they've got enough oppression and it's not important enough to add to it. But I don't like it.

Susanb: Me neither.

Shot a man in Perpetual just to watch him die: Aw . . . I can see where you nay-sayers are coming from, but it kind of seems to me that any guy who goes to all the trouble of mega-hormones treatments and getting his cock cut off ought to be welcomed. I mean—he's gotta want to be one SO BAD to go through all that, so . . . A for effort and all.

I'm beginning to suspect the line between male and female is even harder to pin down than I thought. "Some people think that sex and gender are the same, some people believe that gender is a discourse imposed upon biological sex. *I am beginning to believe that sex is a discourse imposed by gender*," this from Liza Cowan, known on Echo as Diamond. Liza nailed it. Sex, gender, it's all a discourse in cyberspace, and it is negotiated by who we believe we are and what the people around you agree to accept. From Allucquere Rosanne Stone: "Sex is not just physical, it's social." And cyberspace is a social medium.

"The post office can't find you, my mail is always returned," Embraceable Ewe told me whenever I begged her to pay her bill. (There's always a few people on Echo that never pay their bills. I try not to kick anyone off who wants to stay. There's always some service they can barter.) Ms. Ewe picked an unfortunate tactic. The post office and Echo are *like this*.

The first year we went into business a United States Post Office representative made a personal visit to my home to talk to me about the way I was sending mail. Business letters are so boring, one looks much the same as another, and I had imagined people all over the city tossing our mail into the trash like so much junk mail. To avoid this I made up rubber stamps; one that had a picture of a telephone and the words *SUBLIMINAL STAMP* underneath, the other a picture of a trout with the words *STUNT FISH*. Everything went out stamped with these pictures, front and back. Later, I threw a small toy in along with every bill and on the outside I stamped: *Toy Surprise Inside*. The U.S. Post Office representative showed me a memo that had been circulating throughout post office management—it had a picture of one of my envelopes on the first page! "The stamps are creating problems for the address readers," she explained. She gave me a diagram which pointed out where I could and could not stamp. "And the toys are jamming our sorting machines." I could mail toys but only if they were mostly flat. This ordeal brought Echo and the post office closer. The delivery guy, the people at the office, they all knew Echo and our earlier, machine-messing ways. They knew how to find me and anything addressed to me got to me.

Which is a long way of pointing out that Embraceable Ewe was not entirely honest and I didn't entirely trust her. It's not fair, but given my lack of sophistication on these issues at the time, this matter of trust was critical. In 1993 the idea of a woman with a dick was unthinkable to me.

I remember wishing that she had taken the decision out of my hands. If she had made friends with the women of WIT first and then come to me it would have been a done deal. My final decision was a cheat. "You can get into WIT when you have the operation," I told her. Three years ago, I knew little of gender issues. The extent of my opinion and understanding at the time was, if someone wants to go through all that trouble, I didn't have the heart to exclude her.

But I knew I was cheating. I had avoided making a real decision. And I can't help feeling that I behaved badly. I was raised differently than this. My grandparents were very strict about manners, Old World manners, good manners. My brothers and all my cousins and I had to behave just so in my grandparents' house, it was so civilized; I found peace there. It was different than how I had to be at home. Things were lovelier there, dark and delicate—we were lovelier there. In my grandparents' world I think it would have been considered only polite to accept that Embraceable Ewe was who she said she was. It would be unthinkable to insist to one of our guests, and Embraceable Ewe was so much more than a guest, "You are not a woman," when that was what she had presented herself to be. I also like the idea of mixing my grandparents' genteel manners in with the raw and exposed world of cyberspace.

You don't have any more guarantees that someone is who they say they are just because you can see them. We are as often fooled by appearances as we are informed by them. People misrepresent themselves all the time. They show you whatever side they choose. We get into trouble all the time making assumptions about people based on what they look like. In cyberspace it's the other way around: we get into trouble making assumptions based on what's inside. I'd say the chances of making a mistake online or off are pretty even.

There's some irony in this story of Embraceable Ewe, because for years I had been doing everything I could to get more women online. Here's what it was like for a woman on the Net when I started Echo:

Imagine a men's club. A huge men's club. Millions and millions of men, in fact. They built the place, they've been meeting for years, making improvements, the furniture is worn down to fit their shape—when a bunch of women walk into the room.

Heads pop up. Who's that? Who invited them? Some men immediately drop what they're doing and rush over to welcome them. Some flirt, some ask, "What the hell do you think you're doing here?" Most eventually turn around and go back to what they were doing as if the women weren't even there. Until the women start making changes. They don't do things the way they have always been done. "Now just one minute. You can't just walk in here . . ." and the struggle begins.

It's a natural response, I think. I'd do the same thing. Hey, we've been here for years. Why should we change how we do things for you? It's our place. We made it. If you want to join us you have to speak our language. That's how it felt for me when I first got online. I was either treated like an unwelcome guest or like some exotic creature. Everywhere I went, all-boys clubs and boy talk. "On the Internet, no one knows you're a dog," a famous *New Yorker* cartoon proclaims. Yeah, but they figure you're probably some white guy. In 1990, when I started Echo, women made up 10% of the online world. Cartoon metaphors popped up to describe the Net, the very word cyberspace (which I use, shoot me now), electronic frontier, information superhighway. Cartoon metaphors reinforce cartoon behavior.

In those days journalists wrote that I started Echo to provide a safe place for women on the Net. Bite me. I wanted to get more women on Echo to make it better. And safety is not an effective lure. Come to Echo, we're safe. That would be like hanging out a sign that said: BORING. Which is not to say that we tolerate the jerks and psychos that pester us elsewhere. It's just that we don't need protection from them. We can take care of ourselves. Not wanting to get in a discussion with some clueless idiot does not equal the need for protection. Some people make the mistake that free speech means they can say whatever they want whenever they want. Even the government gets to place some restrictions on speech.

Echo is 40% female. Because of that, some call us a women's online service. Let's see. The WELL is mostly men. Does that make The WELL a men's service? At 40%, we're still mostly men ourselves. I'll never forget showing a list of conferences and hosts to a man who was active on America Online. A third of the hosts on Echo were female at that time. He read the list and said, "Oh. Most of your hosts are women." Most! A third seemed like most to him. Not even half—most.

How did I get so many women online? It wasn't all that hard. Hell, back then I was the only one even trying. First, I have the home team advantage: I am a woman. Second, I really did want to talk to women. I went up to them at parties, at school, at bars, everywhere I happened to be. When I asked the women of Echo what they didn't like about being online, I was really listening and they told me the truth. I started a mentoring program for women, I gave women the entire year of 1990 for free, anything and everything I could think of.

Some early experiments to get more women online were disasters. When the editors of *Mademoiselle* magazine approached me about having a *Mademoiselle* Conference on Echo, I was a bit hesitant. *Mademoiselle?* Who reads that? But the people who had the idea were so normal, so smart—James Kim and the editor-in-chief at the time, Gabe Doppelt, and especially the woman they had chosen as the host for their conference, Amy McCutchin—that I decided to give it a try.

The response from the Echoids? What the hell are they doing here? Amy might have been able to pull it off, she gave as good as she got and Echoids appreciate that, but the new editor-in-chief took over the magazine not long after the conference began, and she said, "We want to talk about dating and makeup tips with the women on Echo." I tried to explain. It's not like the women on Echo don't date and wear makeup, and maybe they'll talk about it with you, but they want to talk about what they want to talk about and the best you can do is establish a tone and direction. A good host does not tell people what they can or cannot talk about. This is not a magazine. It's interactive. Blank looks from the editor-in-chief. "Think of it like a focus group," I tried. And even if they say *Mademoiselle* sucks, what an opportunity. Usually when someone says that you're not there to hear it—now you have the chance to persuade. Or change. Blank looks from the editor-in-chief.

The conference died. *Mademoiselle* pulled the plug, Echoids said, "We told you so," and I went back to the drawing board. For a full year afterward we got calls from *Mademoiselle* readers trying to give us their new address to mail their subscription. It gave us a real taste of their audience.

The phone rings.

Us:	"Echo."
Them:	"Is this *Mademoiselle* magazine?"
Us:	"Nope. It's Echo."
Them:	"Well I'd like to give you my new address so you can send the magazine here."
Us:	"Okay, well you'll have to call them, their number is . . ."
Them:	"Why can't you help me?"
Us:	"Because we're not *Mademoiselle*. We're Echo. We used to do business with them but we stopped. We're an online service. We're called Echo."
Them:	"This is not *Mademoiselle*?"
Us:	"No."
Short silence.	
Them:	"Can I give you my new address?"

It was not a good fit. The *Mademoiselle* readers do not want to discuss God, evil, not even "is a transsexual a woman," and the Echoids didn't want to discuss only dating and makeup tips. Okay, I fucked up. Which magazine would be a better fit? *Ms. Magazine*, I thought. That's where the smart people are. Echoid Rosemary Bray set up a meeting with myself and the editor. Smart woman— same editorial point of view.

The conference was put together by very young editors and assistant editors at *Ms.* and they were willing to take the risks that *Mademoiselle* cowered from. Along with responsible discussions on domestic violence and politics they had items such as: *To Shave or Not to Shave*, and my favorite: *The Menstruation item*. Girl after girl told stories of getting their periods, how they felt about them now, tampons vs. pads, all in the most graphic descriptions and all in a conference that was open to guys. Who weren't responding. Very unusual. This was perhaps the first public discussion on Echo that didn't include the contributions of men.

There is a command you can use to see who is actually reading a discussion. I took a look. The men were reading it all right. In shocked silence. A few older women stepped in to protest that discussions like this were private and belonged in WIT. You don't like it, don't read it, the girls responded, and went right back to their stories. Slowly the guys came out. They started asking questions that they'd probably been waiting years to ask. And they had some hysterical stories of their own. The *Ms.* girls answered. The spirit was so generous and infectious the women who protested took it back. Item after item had the same life. This is more like it, I thought. The smart girls are here. Conversations like the one about menstruation could never have existed anywhere except online. Nowhere else in life do we have a place that gives us just the right distance and time to negotiate such new territory. If this conversation had occurred at a party, the conversation would have probably ended with the initial reaction of shock and unease. Online, you've got the time and the distance you need to get past the first reactions of awkwardness and discomfort.

The *Ms.* editors called me into a meeting. I was sure it was to discuss our tremendous success. "They're discussing subjects we haven't raised," they complained. Well yeah, but nothing that doesn't have to do with feminism, I responded. The *Ms.* Conference was to be the feminist forum on Echo. Besides, didn't she see what was happening between the sexes? "Yes, but they're talking about things that we don't want to talk about," they insisted. I still don't get it. "As long as it has to do with feminism, what does it matter?" One of the editors looked at me as if I were completely dense. I felt completely dense. There was an uncomfortable silence. "Say you're having a party," I tried, "and someone over in another corner starts talking about a movie you haven't seen or a book you haven't read. You don't tell them to shut up, do you?" The same editor looked around the room and gave one of those "Am I crazy or is she?" looks to every member of her staff. I almost wanted to raise my hand to volunteer. "It's me! I'm crazy!"

She didn't pull the plug, but she pulled a lot of the in-your-face, unrepentant celebration out of it. It was on its way to becoming one of the more popular conferences on Echo and now it's an important but smaller, and much quieter place. Magazine people didn't understand and continue to misunderstand the medium. Having a presence, and thereby an influence, in the electronic discourse is what's important, not producing and editing it. You can establish a live, ongoing, evolving, and through this, more committed connection with your readers. They've made a personal and direct investment in the connection. The magazine metaphor is all wrong for cyberspace. It's closer to talk radio.

The most effective thing I did to get more women online was also the most controversial. I made sure that half the hosts on Echo were women. Cyberaffirmative action. The Echoids cried: Quotas! Tokenism! But I was beginning to suspect that it mattered less how differently men and women communicated. What mattered was that there were so few of us. If we were a force, our style, regardless of how different, would be incorporated into the discourse of cyberspace. The hosts have enormous influence over style on Echo. Again, style is content, especially online. Style fleshes out the picture that content alone cannot provide. It communicates feeling or nuance, it says something about the speaker. By having as many women host, the style of discourse is changed more naturally.

I once said in an interview, "Women are not interested in endless debate," and a journalist wrote, ". . . Horn's implication that all women are conciliatory creatures who shrink from confrontation." He got all that from: "Women are not interested in endless debate." As if debate is the only style of confrontation. Lack of interest does not equal fear. It's a common projection that some people make. If someone said, "I'm not interested in stamp collecting," would this journalist conclude that the person has some fear associated with placing stamps in books? And disinterest in debate does not lead to conciliation. Puhleeze. It frequently leads to dead silence. It's not that we don't want to talk about whatever, it usually means we don't want to talk to YOU. We'll just go talk to someone else.

Here is a perfect example of a clash of style. It occurred in an item about gender differences, ironically enough, and it illustrates how men and women sometimes communicate differently.

71:135) Garbled Uplink   **17-AUG-95 9:03**
Chromosomes determine gender.

71:136) Jane Doe Hates New York   **17-AUG-95 18:38**
<yawn>

71:139) Garbled Uplink   **18-AUG-95 8:38**
One in one hundred thousand births is a hermaphrodite.
XX chromosomes = female: gay, straight, bi, whatever. Female.
XY or XYY = male: gay, straight, bi, whatever. Male.
The rest is in the area of "How many angels can dance on the head of a pin?" and astrology.

71:140) Jane Doe Hates New York   **18-AUG-95 12:50**
Well, now that we have wrapped up the gender conundrum, lets close down the medical facilities and academic departments around the country and move on, shall we?

71:141) Garbled Uplink   **18-AUG-95 14:35**
If all they are doing is sucking up money that could be spent feeding little Jamal breakfast and teaching him to read involving themselves in vapid ideological debates about "gender", by all means, close them down.
It is a pointless bourgeois distraction. Do not be confusing identity with gender, and do not for a moment consider "gender issues" more important than nutrition and education.

71:142) Jane Doe Hates New York   18-AUG-95 15:37
Okay.

Let me state this in a less oblique way.

I find summary dismissals of inquiries on gender, in an item entitled SEX CHANGE to be counter-productive.

If you think you have all the answers (and I mean "you" to include
ANYONE) then you are certainly not in need of this forum.

I agree that hunger and education are important issues.

Perhaps the FOOD conference will provide you with a forum where
you can contribute to a dialogue, rather than stall it out mid-stream
with the Shell Answer Man routine.

I hope I have made my feelings clear on this. Others are free to disagree, of course. I just feel that statements along the lines of, "X is
this" coupled with observations regarding "little Jamal" don't open
up conversation, but rather close it down.

Unless of course what you are looking for is a flame war or Debate
Society.

There ARE other ways of talking to one another, and frankly, I grow
weary of the same old stand-bys.

Another gender difference in online style—men use the
instant, realtime methods of communicating more than women.
On AOL they're called Instant Messages, on The WELL it's Sends,
and on Echo we have YOs. This isn't necessarily a bad thing. That
would be like saying speaking up is a bad thing. There's a time and
a place. I have found though, that if anyone is going to lack that
kind of understanding and use these commands indiscriminately,
it's a guy.

When I teach I have a large-screen projector behind me to show
the students other online services. One night it was America
Online. I logged in before class and got everything ready. With
America Online on the screen behind me, class began. We were
going over some administrative details when someone sent me

America Online's equivalent of a YO. "What is your breast size?" Yup. Great line there, boy. I'm so hot.

"Hey," I typed back, "I'm a professor at NYU doing a demo here and a group of graduate students are all reading what you are saying." He thought I was flirting. "Oh teacher, teacher, punish me." No really, I insisted. I tried to get into a conversation with him. Who are you, where do you like to hang out online and why? No go. Okay, suit yourself, I told him, and he continued to flirt while the class and I discussed assignment details and makeup classes.

Another night I was teaching a group of NYU students how to YO. They were all sitting down together at a row of terminals. There was a mix of men and women. One by one, each woman's computer, not one man's, came alive with beeps as every last one of them received the exact same YO from some man logged into Echo. All the way down the line, the same YO over and over. HEY BABY HEY BABY HEY BABY, any baby will do. It was like a guy on the street calling out to any and every woman who passes by. Like a wolf whistle. Who still whistles at girls on the street? We had lost ground in cyberspace and had to revisit some rules of common courtesy.

A whole etiquette for YOs evolved. Would you walk up to a strange woman on the street and say that? Then don't do it in a YO. YOs can be thrilling, there's a whole subtext to Echo that takes place in the exchange of YOs, but it happens between people who have gotten to know each other first. And for God's sake, if a woman tells you to leave her alone, leave her alone. Like the real world, some people do not hear the word no, even though in cyberspace the word is recorded and saved—stamped in silicon. I finally added a policy about harassment. If someone tells you to leave them alone, don't email me, don't YO me, you must not contact them again.

Now when guys like that AOL freak wander onto Echo they're slapped down fast. No shrinking violets here. The men help. It's more effective when members of a community decide for them-selves how to behave, rather than making stringent rules. The men like having the women around as much as the other women do, and we've all relearned that, as long as you establish a connection first, the restrictions on your behavior in order to get along are actually very slight. You know how your friends can say things to you that other people can't? The same is true online. There are cer-tain ways a friend can YO you on Echo that a stranger may not. This is another common mistake that newcomers make: assuming an intimacy before it has been established. Just because you walked through that cyber-door doesn't make all of us your instant friends.

Men, for the most part, seem to miss the fact that when it comes to attracting women they are actually in a very good posi-tion. Just sit tight. Words are erotic. Speaking as a woman, we have always thought so. We buy pornographic books more than movies. It's intoxicating here. We swim in your words. Since it's all we have online, we can flit from topic to topic, coming again and again to revel in your words.

One early stylistic difference has since disappeared: men posted and women lurked. I remember how frustrated I was by this. Here were all these women and they were just sitting pretty. If you typed o, there they were, they just weren't talking. "Why are you lurking?" I asked them in WIT. When I look over our answers, I see that what we needed most was time. Time for our voices to be incorporated into the mix, and time for the men to get used to the change. When we began, men would stop conversations cold with one-line equivalents of a wet towel snapping at your butt. I don't get complaints about all the "electronic towel snapping" anymore. It all seems so quaint; women would lurk and defer, men would thump their chests and strut. I just ran a program to see who post-ed the most on Echo—in the top ten, five were men and five were women. In an incredibly short time, we learned how to talk to each other. And having as many women as men hosting these discussions contributed significantly.

Now women are all over the place and they are no longer shy. For a while everyone was changing their name to various slang terms for the female genitalia. It was a fad. Everyone was doing it, even a few men. One night, I was in front of a group of about 100 women from the organization New York Women in Film and Television, showing them around Echo. I type o to show them how at any time, half the people on Echo are women. The names scroll by. Any word that you can think of that was ever used instead of the word vagina was up there on the screen, in nice bold large letters so that even the people way in the back could see. I looked at the women in the audience. What could I say? "Okay, we're crude. I admit it." It wasn't necessary, they were all laughing. When are people going to abandon this delicate flower image for us? Molly Ker, my general manager, is having T-shirts made that say: *Echo. Where the girls have root and the boys have wood.*

Embraceable Ewe is gone now. Money was tight and she wasn't willing to barter. And she hasn't had the operation. Echo has had several preop transsexuals since Embraceable Ewe and last month we had another preop transsexual ask to get into WIT (only I've learned that the proper term is transgendered woman now, not transsexual). Like Embraceable, she still has a dick. But Echo has changed. And so have other places in cyberspace that have had to deal with this issue. We have a better understanding of gender politics now. I think mostly we just needed time to get used to the idea.

The transgendered people ask: Why should the medical establishment decide who is a man and who is a woman? Good question. What do they know? What training has prepared them to make this judgment? So they made a few cuts—what difference does that really make? What has really changed? Do I become a different person after cosmetic surgery? Although we are talking about pretty radical cosmetic surgery, I will admit. But then, is someone a different person if they lose an arm or a leg or more? They also argue that because the operation is so expensive, only rich people can be accepted as who they believe they already are. Another very compelling point.

This time, when I made my decision about letting someone who had not gotten the operation into WIT, I went back to lessons of my grandparents. It's not up to me to tell anyone who they are. I am not the one to decide anyone's gender. Transgendered women are welcome into WIT after they have been living twenty-four hours a day, seven days a week as a woman for at least a year, and after they have been on Echo at least six months. It's not entirely fair, I know. We don't place restrictions like this on anyone else. It's about establishing trust. It's what we do on Echo. The year is to make sure the person is really committed to this. This is a big deal to us. The women-only and men-only conferences are important and I need to know that it's as big a deal to our transgendered members, too. Since we have only someone's word about the year, the six months are about gaining that trust.

It's a compromise. We're more inclusive, but we're easing into it. Transgendered people do not necessarily have the immediate trust that is accorded traditional women (with respect to gender), but that's changing. Cyberspace helps. Three years ago, issues of transgender were foreign and unthinkable to me and many of the women on Echo. Now I feel like, "What's the big deal?" Perhaps in a year, when we've had a few transgendered women in WIT, the ones who were reluctant will also wonder what all the fuss was about.

It was a big deal at the time. We agonized over this. Even still, the Echoids were only able to reach a tentative understanding and agreement to give this a try through a lot of words, volumes and volumes, over years of time. And between people who have gotten to know each other. It's hard to say "you aren't who you say you are" to someone you have gotten to know—when you've heard the story of their struggles from the beginning. Which makes me wonder how people can possibly deal with these issues in any other arena, federal and state governments or the courts, for instance, where everyone doesn't necessarily get to know the life stories of the people involved the way we do online. When a friend tells you something completely outrageous, you listen to them because they're your friend. You hear them out. Cyberspace makes it easier to *hear people out*. I don't know anywhere else where you could recreate the kind of situation we have that allowed us to get this far.

Working through conflicts like this is what makes virtual communities true communities. I'm not saying we're working a lot out online. Right. I'd say our rate of resolution is, once again, the same as anyplace else: pretty damn low. Change or understanding is hard. More often we argue until we get sick of arguing and then we either learn to live with each other, the problems, the disagreements, or lay low until we have enough energy to resume those arguments, which we have over and over and over again. From Echoid Matthew Ehrlich, aka Oedipa: "On Echo, it seems that the largest subject of mutual interest is often killing another Echoid. And if that isn't proof of actual community, I don't know what is."

How communities deal with conflict is an important measure of that community, and gender differences are one of the oldest conflicts in the book. In cyberspace, we're forced to revisit our boy-girlness, we have no choice. We can't see each other. Whatever gender differences you believe or don't believe you have, if the differences are not apparent to anyone else in this new medium then you have to reassert them. Or, drop them. Which is why the online voice is evolving into one that is more gender neutral. Quite frankly, the online voice has become so gender neutral in these past couple of years that I can't tell someone's gender like I used to. Over time you learn, but that's only because gender is one of the things you find out about a person when you get to know them. Content is now a more obvious indicator than style. For example: "That brand of tampon sucks." Personally, I love when you can tell, when a voice has girl or guy written all over it. But that's just me.

With only words, what is the difference between men and women?

Whatever we say.

I HATE MYSELF CONTINUED...

606:287) Miss Outer Boro 1991   02-FEB-92 9:15
I hate myself for having so little enthusiasm about anything except sex with inappropriate people.

606:294) SuZin   26-FEB-92 0:37
I hate myself.

606:295) Neandergal   26-FEB-92 0:38
I hate myself for wanting to know all of the reasons, including lurid details, why SuZin hates herself.

606:296) praam   26-FEB-92 0:43
She don't hate herself.

606:297) SuZin   26-FEB-92 0:49
Oh yes she does.

606:306) Spingo   26-FEB-92 1:28
I hate myself for being too weak to stomach others' self-hatred.

606:309) Miss Outer Boro 1991　　　　　**26-FEB-92 8:08**

I hate myself for being happy that the Spingoid Monster is taking baby steps on the Great Dance Floor of Self Hatred.

606:372) Icky Joey　　　　　**03-MAR-92 20:27**

I hate myself for cancelling plans so I can do laundry, and then falling asleep and the laundromat closes and I can't do laundry and I have no clothes and I hate myself and I hate the world and I hate everyone who has clean clothes.

606:389) SuZin　　　　　**04-MAR-92 20:59**

I hate myself for having to mine for clean clothes.
I hate myself for biting the hell out of my lip while chewing gum (even if it WAS sugarless).

606:601) Miss Outer Boro 1991　　　　　**06-APR-92 8:31**

I hate myself for fucking up the ONE thing I really wanted to do in ages so I couldn't do it. I REALLY hate myself this time, I'm not kidding around!!!

606:606) Kiwi　　　　　**06-APR-92 15:47**

I HATE MYSELF for letting my life not go how I want it to.

606:607) Xixax　　　　　**06-APR-92 16:02**

I hate myself for thinking I have control over my life.
Handing over control of my life to Kiwi.

606:621) Icky Joey　　　　　**07-APR-92 19:08**

I hate myself for a lunch of pizza, goldfish crackers, and licorice.

606:674) SuZin　　　　　**10-APR-92 21:47**

I hate myself for a multitude of reasons. First of all, I hate myself for spending beaucoup delores <tm Jeff Spicoli> getting my hair highlighted when a) I have no money and b) it is exactly the same color as it was before. Secondly, I hate myself for pissing people off. Thirdly, I hate myself for not making my bed for days on end. Fourthly, I hate myself for not being able to cook pasta properly. Fifthly, I hate myself for still being in my apartment at this hour on a Friday night. Sixthly, I hate myself for being self-indulgent and posting more than my customary two lines. And lastly, I hate myself because I JUST DO, OK? Mind your own business.

606:696) Jim Baumbach   **13-APR-92 15:23**

I am considering not hating myself as much.

606:720) Icky Joey   **16-APR-92 21:33**

I hate myself for drinking so much last night that I became JoJo, stick boy vomit machine to the stars.
I hate myself for almost pullin' an Elvis last night (dead and naked in the bathroom).

606:722) SuZin   **16-APR-92 22:35**

I hate myself for not drinking more beer so Joey would have had less.

35:18) Miss Outer Boro 1991   **19-JAN-92 8:47**

I hate myself for grinding two of my teeth down really far and in a year or so they will both disappear and I will be a gap-tooth hag with no friends.

35:21) Jim Baumbach (another item to forget)   **21-JAN-92 20:01**

I hate myself because I expect to be devalued and want to get a head start.

35:58) Miss Outer Boro 1991   **28-JAN-92 21:06**

I hate myself for not being able to tolerate being employed for more than a few weeks at a time.

35:59) Miss Outer Boro 1991   28-JAN-92 21:06
What am I talking about?
No I don't.

35:84) Chameleon   02-FEB-92 1:14
I hate myself. Or at least my life. My friends all would rather hang out with my vapid roommate. I hate myself for thinking she's vapid when she's just more popular than me.

I am bitter, depressed, unambitious, boring, shallow, vindictive, self-pitying scum, and I hate myself for all of that. I want to quit everything and disappear completely, that way people won't have to listen to me whine about my bullshit life.

I don't know why I keep taking up responses (like breathing air) put to better use by some more worthy being.

35:88) jneil   02-FEB-92 1:43
I hate myself for feeling that my self-hate isn't even in the same league as Chameleon's.

I am unworthy of sharing an item with such exquisite self-loathing.

35:95) SuZin   04-FEB-92 21:32
I only slightly hate myself today, but I will hate myself far more when them chickens come home to roost, and it's only a matter of time.

35:96) Bartleby the Programmer   05-FEB-92 1:41
If I'm careful about what I think about, I can avoid hating myself today.

35:122) SuZin   14-FEB-92 0:53
I hate myself for being immature and irresponsible. (Normally, I love myself for this, but not right now.)

35:190) Victor Immature.   06-MAR-92 10:10

I hate myself for fucking everything up.

35:191) jneil   06-MAR-92 10:35

Not everything. I fucked up some stuff too. And boy do I hate myself for it.

ECHO POLL

Source: From an online survey of 368 members of Echo, January 1996.

Margin of Error: That 33% that said no—do they hate us?

Do you go to any of the face-to-face events?

67% said yes.

ECHO POLL

Source: From an online survey of 267 members of Echo, November 1996.

Margin of Error: Keep this in mind: Echoids like to mess with your head.

Do you ever see other people from Echo offline; either at work, socially, or at Echo events?

83% said yes.

IN THE FLESH

A user once asked me if I would please post monthly management reports on Echo the way Steve Case does on America Online. (Case runs America Online.) I'll tell you, the very idea of monthly management reports makes me put my head down on my desk, groan, and go into a *Night of the Living Dead* state. It's not that I didn't want to tell him. "Look," I said to the guy, "I'm about as likely to issue monthly management reports as Steve Case is to start hanging out in chat rooms on AOL talking about who he lusts after in the movies or have a drink with you at the Art Bar." I'm right here, online and in-person, talking about what I'm up to night and day. Sit down, have a beer. I'll tell you what our plans are. I'll tell you to your face.

The strongest virtual communities are not strictly virtual.

* * *

I'm curled up on a chair that is more like a couch. I'm sitting so the hole in my jeans that shows everything *doesn't*—I really must pick up my laundry so I can go out without revealing more than I would to someone on the first date. I'm in a club in Soho, the room is dark but packed with Echoids; you can't spit without hitting an Echoid. The band is White Courtesy Telephone, an all-Echoid band—for better or worse, this is how I see the world now: Is an Echoid involved or not? Rob Tannenbaum's velvet pants are a nightmare. Only he could pull an outfit like that off. I hope Garbled isn't too drunk—when did Maggot Boy shave his head and grow a goatee? I think that makes every guy on Echo that has had a goatee at one time or another. Bucky is wearing one of the AND NOW? T-shirts that Binky made; I elbow Marianne, "Bucky's wearing an AND NOW? T-shirt," I say, all excited. Hugh's guitar looks funny. I would get up and say hello to everyone, but I have this hole in my pants and it's too hot to walk around in my winter coat to cover it. It's a few days after Christmas and we all need to hear songs like: "Eat What You Kill," "Stephen Hawking's Wheelchair," "Killing Spree," and "I Wanna Be Your Prison Wife."

Rob throws a small stuffed Santa at me halfway through the set. "Christmas can fucking blow me," says Clem, now known as Echo Boy because Kevin wrote a program that told us who posted the most and Clem won. Marianne (aka MR Petit, aka Marianne Petit) is looking very much how she looked when I saw her in her show, *The Mutant Gene & Tainted Kool-Aid Sideshow*—all dark eyes and shiny, Day-Glo clothes. Bucky and Hugh, whom I think of as the High Times Mag boys only Hugh doesn't work there anymore, look typically serene. Practically everyone in this sardine palace knows each other and no one in this room knew each other before Echo. No one in the band knew each other before Echo. And the virtual community of Echo just wouldn't be the same without this. The f-t-f. Face to face. I want to see whom I'm talking to. And I love to hear them sing.

*   *   *

For most of my life I've been trying to get to Potter's Field. In cyberspace, you get to know people's obsessions. The Echoids know mine is death. New York's Potter's Field is located on Hart Island, an impossibly small island for the final resting place of nameless thousands. It sits in the Long Island Sound, just east of the Bronx. As soon as I heard of it I wanted to go. I imagined it, I wrote about it, I couldn't get to it. You're not allowed on Hart Island. Convicts bury the dead, perhaps it's a matter of safety. "I can take you there," Echoid Nick Rosato told me. A group of us had gone out to Nick's to go sailing one day. We had planned lunch on City Island, but when Nick heard of my Hart Island obsession he immediately offered to sail us there instead. No one else objected so off we went.

Nothing grows on Hart Island, nothing much anyway. Scrub pine, some grass and weeds, everything gray-brownish. It was as empty and barren as I dreamed it would be. A storm comes in, of all things, and to take my mind off the fear of going into the Sound on this cold, cold day Nick teaches me to sail as we continuously tack back and forth between Hart and City Islands. Josh Chu, aka Slacker, doesn't look in the least bit nervous. He's going to be a daddy this winter. Mention that and you'll see him get nervous. He met his wife, Magdalen, on Echo, at a bowling face-to-face we organized our first year, only her name was Lee-Ann then. Her Magdalen persona emerged online. It was more real and more true to her soul than Lee-Ann had ever been, so she had her name legally changed and married Josh, whom I hired three years later. Shark also looks perfectly at ease. I think it must be me until I turn to see the face of the person who knows best about these things, the guy who has been sailing for thirty years, and he looks decidedly nervous. This cheers me up. I mean, I was right after all, we are in trouble. I'm soaking wet, my hair is whipping my face (that's it, I'm cutting it), and I smell like seaweed. Cyberspace got me to Potter's Field.

*   *   *

It's a lovely day. I go to Central Park to watch the Echo softball game. A bunch of Echoids play there every Sunday and I've never gone before. It takes me a while to find them. They're on some back, dusty field, no grass, and they're all drinking beer, audience and players. Jaime Levy, who's pitching today, takes a hit of hers, puts it down behind the mound, and strikes out the batter. Spingo pulls a cigar out of his mouth to shout, "Blow me." I have no idea if he is talking to the pitcher, the batter, or the umpire. In any case, he's ignored. The players are filthy because sliding into base is everyone's favorite part. They make a big show of it, and if they do it well, both sides applaud. It looks painful. "How are the teams picked?" I ask. "Have a beer," someone says.

"No thanks. What's the score?" No one knows. Then they argue about who was to supposed to keep track. "Sure you won't have a beer?" "No. Thanks." It doesn't take long for both sides to amicably agree on what the score may have been if anyone had been paying attention. Beers are raised, more cigars lit—the game goes on. A new member of Echo closed her account one summer because she got a bunch of her friends who had a real team to come all the way out to play and the Echoids wouldn't play seriously. "You all have such low esteem," she told them. "You might win if you tried." "Well," I started to explain. She interrupted, "And one of your dogs bit my friend."

Seeing these people in the flesh is important. You go to Potter's Field with someone and it changes everything. It does something to the electronic discourse. We weren't sure what to make of Garbled Uplink until we met him. Yes, he's a bit of a nut, but he's our nut now. Okay, it makes sense that meeting someone would change things, I know: duh. But what changes exactly?

In the beginning, we were very naïve about the nature of cyberspace and what was going on. We had all sorts of problems with communication and community to work out. It goes back to the lack of visual clues. Because we couldn't see each other when we were talking, we were projecting all over the place and making incorrect assumptions about who we were. We thought that to know someone inside so thoroughly, what they were really thinking and how they felt, was to truly know them. It's not that we thought that this was all there is to a person. We thought it's what counted. We thought if we fell in love with someone online it was because they were the man or woman of our dreams. We thought if we couldn't stand someone online it was because they weren't a particularly likable person. But a look can change everything. It can make the love of your life someone you never would have even considered going out with in the first place, or an annoying person tolerable, perhaps even a friend. By the time you get to be an adult you've learned a million times that you can't judge someone by what's on the outside. What we don't have down is that, strangely enough, the opposite is true, too. Knowing someone from the inside is not the whole picture, either.

The most important thing I have learned about communities in cyberspace is that it is frequently impossible to have tolerance, something absolutely essential to keep a community going, without some face-to-face connection. For a community to work you have to accept imperfection. Like I said, we're all assholes from time to time. On Echo we get all kinds. Contrary to frequent reports describing cyberspace as communities of common interest, any one place in cyberspace is not filled with only the people you like or who share your interests. Wherever there are people there's going to be conflict. And people who don't like you. You have to overlook some of everyone's shortcomings, or rather, you can't get so bent out of shape about them or the community won't hold together. It is hard to accept what bugs the hell out of you in people you haven't met. You can tolerate a wider range of behavior once you look someone in the face. I don't think it's that you know them better once you've met them, necessarily, it's that when you get back online, you project less. You know how you can tell what a friend or someone you've met means when they say something to you on the phone? You don't have to see them to understand what they're trying to tell you. That's why meeting people helps hold a virtual community together. Fewer misunderstandings. And, once you meet a person, it's harder to dismiss them thoughtlessly. You cut them just enough slack to get over the rough spots.

Not everyone has to meet for the virtual community to work. A person may seem a bit off online and we'll ask each other, "What's the deal with so and so?" If enough trusted members of Echo say, "Oh yeah, we met him, he's all right," then everyone else will be okay with him, too. Everyone meeting is also not important because it's not essential that every member of a community have the same depth of involvement or relationship to it. People participate in different ways, just like any city or town. You have go-getters, people who sit back and watch or play, and people who are essentially loners. "You go meet that freak," someone might say. "Let me know what you think."

Some people say the relationships in virtual communities aren't real—usually some disappointed Utopian who wasn't looking for real, but better. They are unhappy with how dismally real it can be. They're pretend relationships, they say, because you can just turn off your computer and the people there, and you can't do that to your neighbors or your coworkers or your family and friends in the physical world.

First, yes, you can. I go home from work. I shut the door on my neighbors; I don't always pick up the phone when people call. I go into another room; I take a walk. The need and the ability to "turn off the computer" exists in the physical world. I can't always be on and connected to the people in my life. We're just talking about taking a break, and the need to be alone sometimes. The ability to turn off the computer doesn't necessarily imply a lack of commitment. Besides, we have a variety of depth of commitment to the people around us in our physical life, too. Many of these relationships are "pretend" relationships, if you're going to look at people that way. We just chat about whatever, the weather, the Yankees, the Mayor or the subway, then I move on and don't give them another thought until the next time I run into them. I value the casual relationships of my neighbors in the physical world, just as I value my acquaintances online. I can't be close friends with everyone. I love the people in my life where we just talk about baseball, or music, or the landlord.

Second, we're surrounded by people that we never really get to know at all. There are people we see every day at the office, on our street, or in our apartment building, who remain essentially strangers. It's such a complicated mix of knowing and not knowing, that real or not real just isn't useful. I don't think my chances of forming a more close, intimate and important relationship with someone depends on how or where I first met them. It depends on us. I've got a small number of people I'm truly close to online and off. And because I do, I don't always get to choose, either virtually or physically, when to "turn off the computer." If a friend or family member or neighbor needs me, whether it's online or off, I'm turning that computer back on. And even when I do turn the damn thing off, I only do so for a time. I don't want to take a break forever. I always come back. I care about these people.

In the most successful virtual communities, and especially local services like Echo, the people who are members of a virtual community *are* also neighbors, coworkers, friends and family in the physical world. On Echo, we get together at the drop of a hat. 83% of the people who responded to our poll said they get together with Echoids offline.

For years we've been getting together every other Monday night, it's our most enduring face-to-face gathering, and it grew out of our utter lack of ambition. We were talking about cliques on Echo, are they a good thing or a bad thing, do we have them or not, and someone suggested that if we didn't we should. A group of Echoids had been meeting regularly at the Moonstruck Diner to discuss their accomplishments from the previous week. They called their group the Cultural Coffee House. Richard Newsome decided to take a stand for the slackers of Echo. He and Bob Knuts suggested a gathering for the rest of us who had accomplished absolutely nothing. It was January 1991. Bush had recently given Saddam Hussein until midnight January 15th to get out of Kuwait. On the evening of January 14th, a small group of Echoids got together at the White Horse Tavern for what they called an Eve of Destruction send-off. We figured the place where Dylan Thomas drank himself to death was as good a place as any to celebrate the accomplishment of *nothing*. It quickly became known as the White Horse Clique and we continued to meet every other Monday except one week when we moved it to Tuesday so no one would miss *Twin Peaks*. (You must remember this was the summer of 1991, VCRs weren't quite standard operating gear back then, and we had our priorities straight by God.)

These gatherings made Echo better. Whenever there's a problem that we can't work out online, we can try to have it out at the White Horse—except now it's at a place called the Art Bar; we outgrew the back rooms of the White Horse Tavern several years ago. If we're unsure about someone we try to check them out there. Sometimes we plan things. The members of Panscan, a conference hosted by artist Mark Bloch, known on Echo as Panman, came up with a project. They would rubberstamp a phrase on every piece of paper money they could get their hands on. They took a vote. The phrase that won: *Is it worth it?* They pooled their money, went to my stamp guy, had dozens of rubber stamps made up with this question and gave them away at the White Horse. So if you ever get a dollar bill stamped with *Is it worth it?*, it's one of ours. Another good use of the Art Bar—if you develop an electronic crush and you want to see what they look like, you can try to get a glimpse of them there.

Or at any number of places we get together. There's an item in our Central Conference (that's where we make announcements mostly) called *Shameless Self Promotion*. Echo has a lot of artists online, and musicians and playwrights and actors, and they're always doing something or other that they want people to go to. If they have a gig, a book signing, or whatever, they post about it there and a crowd of Echoids are bound to show up. I doubt a week goes by that there isn't something to go to. Echo has several official ongoing events. Because there are so many writers online we started a reading series called READ ONLY. It's a geek term. It refers to a certain type of device for storing information. You can't write to a read-only device, you can only read it. I swear most of the time I do my best to avoid geek slang, but I couldn't resist using this term for our reading series. We hold them at a neighborhood bar in the East Village called KGB. Every month, one published and one unpublished writer on Echo gets up and reads from their work. Our Open Mike nights are often the most interesting. One guy got up and sang instead of reading, but it was so entertaining and so strange (something about his mother) that I didn't stop him.

We also cosponsor an ongoing series with the Whitney Museum of American Art called Virtual Culture. (I talk about a lunatic I inherited from this series in the chapter called *Banished!*) Several times a year we pick a topic having to do with virtual culture and then we invite a panel of experts to Performance Space 122, also in the East Village, to speak about the topic. The audience question-and-answer period was always the best part, so we made the entire thing audience question and answer. It was like recreating what happened online in person. Miss Outer Boro and Neandergal, with *WORD*, the webzine, are putting together a similar thing called Dinner Theatre of the Mind. It will be a monthly gathering where people will discuss topics like consciousness, death, and beauty. And for me, because I'm a movie fanatic, we're producing an independent film series called

Alt.Film. I can satisfy my movie lust *and* give Echoids another opportunity to meet.

Any excuse to get together. We've had dances, jam sessions, tea parties, cigar parties, and baby showers. And I've rarely felt, "God, you're nothing like I pictured you would be," when meeting Echoids for the first time. In the beginning, though, more than a few people said that to me. What did they expect? Tall and blond. Almost without exception. Where did that come from? What in any of my writing says tall and blond? (I am short and brunette.) Talk about projection. Anyway, Echoids, for the most part, represent themselves fairly accurately. There are several reasons for this. (And not one of them is because we are more honest or "real.") New York is small and the people on Echo live close to each other, and a large percentage of us go to the face-to-face events that are going on all the time everywhere. I think people on Echo know in the back of their heads that there is the distinct possibility that they are going to meet a fellow Echoid eventually. Echoids are also running into each other all the time either professionally or socially at some non-Echoid event or other about town. The few times I've been surprised was when meeting people from other online services. Their online personas didn't quite match what they were like in person. People who are gregarious online turned out to be quiet in person. One woman who was this incredible sex goddess online was not the least bit flirtatious in person.

But meeting people doesn't eliminate the need for the electronic connection. It enhances it. It always cracks me up that whenever we get together, and we could have spent an entire evening together, the very first thing we do when we get back home is log on. Half the fun of doing something is talking about it afterward. I remember how I used to get home from dates or parties and rush to the telephone to talk to the people I'd been with about what happened. We'd deconstruct the entire evening. "Did you see so and so?" "No! Tell!" Or, "And then what did he do?"

This face-to-face component weaves the virtual community through people's day-to-day lives and so creates stronger and more meaningful bonds. It's a delicate balance that takes time. But it's a critical process in the development of any online community. The more anonymous the system, the more people flame. When people don't know whom they are talking to, where there is no account-ability, they'll say *anything*. (This is not always a bad thing.) People are less likely to fly off the handle at every little thing in places like Echo or The WELL, where everyone knows who everyone else is. On Echo, because we know your name *and* we know your face, we're just that more tolerant. It's the difference between Echo and most online communities that is crucial. It give us a depth that few places achieve because most places online are still anonymous, and because people get together in person less. For a community to work it has to accept the flaws of its members. Again, it's harder to dismiss someone once you've met them. Or rather, it's easier to be tolerant. A pearl is formed, coat after coat, around something that was originally an irritant. On Echo, each coat is longing: longing for sex or love, a job, entertainment, friends, or something that we can't name, a reminder that we are not alone and here, and longing has become a thing—a place.

I HATE
MYSELF
CONTINUED...

35:280) chameleon   24-APR-92 15:10
I hate myself for putting all my eggs in one basket and then dropping it (without even coloring the eggs or nothin.)

35:302) SuZin   24-MAY-92 12:02
I hate myself for being in here when I could be out there.

35:340) Neandergal   02-JUN-92 22:09
I hate myself because there are things I should be doing and sort
of want to do and want to have finished, but I lack structure and
direction so I keep forgetting what they are.

35:348) SuZin   04-JUN-92 21:27
I hate myself. Period.

35:379) I ate Jim's brain   18-JUN-92 9:10
The usual.

35:380) Kilgore Trout   18-JUN-92 22:20
Make that 2.

35:388) SuZin   23-JUN-92 21:39

Hate myself for crying at work even though only Keith saw and he's
cool.

35:415) Miss Outer Boro 1991   11-JUL-92 16:49

Actually I'm a pretty ok gal.

35:716) jneil   30-NOV-92 13:46

I hate myself to make it unanimous.

35:723) Laze-A-Bed Topper   09-DEC-92 0:18

I spent a good deal of time at work yesterday ordering from cata-
logs.
I do not hate myself for this, though, so I will leave.
Thank you.

35:794) SuZin   22-MAR-93 22:50

I hate myself for having bursitis.
BURSITIS!
Can you believe it?

35:799) jneil   23-MAR-93 0:06

There's a little note at the bottom of the Mac 'n Cheez box that sez:

Makes 5 Servings

I hate myself for proving them wrong.

35:860) SuZin   28-MAR-93 11:56

I hate myself but not for the same reasons everyone else hates me.

17:15) Gabriel   24-MAY-93 21:56

I hate myself for feeding my fish on an irregular basis.

17:42) Tumbleweed Topper   15-JUN-93 13:09

I hate myself just like my momma taught me.

17:53) The Strange Apparatus   20-JUN-93 22:52

I hate myself for immersing myself in Echo on a Friday night of a
holiday weekend, when I could either be dancing my shinbones off
in some clubatorium, or leaving NYC for some beachy climate, and
all I can think about is Trapper John, MD.
I hate myself for my shameless devotion to Loni Anderson, through
thick and thin.

17:65) S. Berg   26-JUN-93 11:32

I hate myself for sitting in front of this damned computer when I
should be on my way to the mermaid parade.

17:66) What should my new name be?   26-JUN-93 11:37

Where the fuck is this parade anyway? I hate myself for not knowing what everyone else seems to know. And don't say Coney Island.
It's a big fucking place.

17:67) S. Berg   26-JUN-93 11:44

I hate myself for not having been to Coney Island since I was a
child, and being unable to direct jimb to the location of the parade.
I hate myself for the wide-eyed "I'm-a-tourist-please-kill-me" look
I'll have should I go to Coney Island today.

17:72) The Strange Apparatus   28-JUN-93 10:27

I hate myself for dressing like a mermaid 5 out of 7 days a week.
Then not going to the parade.

17:73) Scottso (Liquid Light) Connor   29-JUN-93 7:56

I hate myself for not going to the Mermaid parade and not taking along the world's largest Popeil Pocket Fish Scaler <tm Ronco Industries>.

17:75) Key Lime Zin   29-JUN-93 20:15

I hate myself for . . .

Dang, I can't think of anything. Will you all please hate me for this? Thanks. It would mean a lot to me. No, really.

17:119) Phiber Optik   28-AUG-93 3:45

I hate myself. I'm just a passing fad.

I'll be out of style real soon now.

You in the mirror, fuck off.

17:123) cafephreak   28-AUG-93 23:21

I hate myself for not being able to come up with a witty response in an item that was built for me.

Fuck all of you, anyway.

17:132) S. Berg   29-AUG-93 14:36

I hate myself for realizing that Topper's post reminds me of the writings of Paul the Apostle.

I hate myself for the Sundays of my youth being spent in church instead of watching Abbot and Costello on channel 11.

I hate myself because that's what they taught me in church.

17:146) SuZin   31-AUG-93 2:15

I hate myself for being up at this hour.

17:149) SuZin   31-AUG-93 17:38

I hate myself for being up at this hour.

ECHO POLL

Source: From an online survey of 121 members of Echo, December 1995.

Margin of Error: Very few people answered this one!

Do people like or dislike you more online than in person?

10% said people liked them more.

13% said people disliked them more.

23% said they were liked or disliked the same.

24% didn't know what people thought of them.

5% of the women said: I don't know.

19% of the men said: I don't know.

Face-2-Face   And Now?   Mystery Button

IN CYBER-
SPACE... THE WE
ARE... THAT WE
WE TALK...
ABOUT...THE

THE FEAR

We dread it, we're drawn to it: The Fear. Every once in a while someone logs on who gives us The Fear. Someone no one likes. Joey X brought this term to Echo. Like Miss Outer Boro, Joey X's posts are a constant reminder to me to swallow my coffee *before* reading what they've written. Beautiful and with a dark sense of humor—why, oh why can't he be ten or twenty years older—Joey X is an expression of the twisted heart of Echo. In an item in Plain Wrapper about new people on Echo, Joey X posted: *Can't live with them, can't set them on fire and watch them run down the street screaming, "For the love of God, they've set me on fire!!!"* The Fear came from Joey X's college days. A roommate of his was famous for never putting the milk away. Out of that sick, bored curiosity we all had (or have) in our school days, Joey and his roommates decided to leave the milk out to see just how long it took before the guy finally put it back himself. Days went by. The sides bowed out. The smell was unbearable. It became the carton o' fear and from then on they used the term The Fear to describe anything gross or creepy.

No, cyberspace is not filled with just the people you like. You're also going to run into people who give you The Fear. People who are angry without a trace of humor, downright crazy, or, more often, simply oblivious to their effect on others. Because of this, they go around repeatedly saying just the things that alienate everyone else. They're creepy. They're like someone walking down the street, stopping to talk to everyone they pass by but never staying long enough to notice anyone's reaction or listen to their response. Or they pretend to. Very creepy. Longtime Echoid Eric Hochman divides them into three categories: people with authority issues, provocateurs, and high school debate team refugees. Miss Outer Boro says they're people with something to prove. "They tend to stick to arguments long after everyone else is bored." I say the defining characteristic of this particular class of user is their utter inability to get along with anyone. You can be angry or crazy or whatever and still find a place here if you have some ability to get along with people. If you can't be sociable, you're screwed. Simple basic things, like appreciation of nuance. It's essential. Those who lack this skill are the social clods of cyberspace, just as they would be anywhere else. Like those who can't appreciate that there is a right time and a wrong time to say something, these people are in for it.

When someone like this appears on Echo, the word goes out on the Echo underground of YOs and email: *I have The Fear*. A small group of Echoids formed what they called The Fear Network. Through email, they privately broadcast the scariest posts they come across. We even had a rock band called The Feartones for a while. (When they played at the going-away party we gave for Phiber Optik, they changed the spelling to The Pheartones.)

In person these people are just as prickly. It's not like perfectly decent people get online and suddenly turn into creatures who make you want to run screaming from the room. A couple of them literally make my hair stand on end. I avoid them—I'm human—and invariably they complain that I have snubbed them. Stacy didn't talk to me at the Art Bar! That's because you SCARE ME. These people are as creepy in person as they are on Echo. (Oh God, I just heard the chorus of a thousand people asking WTAM? *Was that about me?*) Take Railman (not his real pseudonym), who was going to sue me by the way. I've received this threat so many times I was going to include a chapter called People Who Have Threatened to Sue Me. Another common characteristic of people who give us The Fear: It's never their fault. And, for people like Railman, it therefore must be *mine*. Railman would bait people and then exclaim, "See! See!" when people finally responded.

Here are Topper's (my conference manager) impressions of Railman. She is the voice of reason on Echo.

> "He looks normal. You wouldn't necessarily be able to pick him out of a crowd and say 'that guy is weird.' It's more just a sense that one gets when talking to him that he's not quite socialized.
>
> "You know how disconcerting it is when you're talking to someone and their eyes don't meet yours but instead focus somewhere over your head? He doesn't do that, BUT it's as if his brain/being/person is doing that.
>
> "Or, how about this: have you ever been high on drugs and then you found yourself in a situation where no one else was high and you had to keep telling yourself to 'just act normal, just act normal' only suddenly you had difficulty remembering what 'normal' means.
>
> "Well, it's something like that."

Lana Tuna, Host of the Love Conference, brought him up while we were talking about another fear provoker entirely.

"He attended the New York Subway F2F and was completely inoffensive, friendly and normal, which is MUCH more than one can say about Railman, who was weird both on and offline.

"Railman was VERY drunk the first Art Bar I saw him at. Then he was a player in the Dating Game [a game they play in the Love Conference] before he revealed his weirdness. Way before. Shark was chosen. They had an OK date, and she kindly offered to show him around the Art Bar since he'd been 'lonely and drunk' the first time <tm Victim mentality>. According to her, he was again, drunk and weird."

Alcohol is frequently the explanation. People sometimes post drunk. One Echoid calls us occasionally to leave long, rambling and ugly messages on our answering machine about how much she hates us. The first time it happened I called her back the next morning, scared out of my wits, to ask her what the problem was exactly. The message wasn't clear, except that we sucked very much. She had no memory of calling us. As I hung up the phone I realized my mistake. Her words on the machine were slurred, barely comprehensible. Everyone who works for Echo now has instructions to never return her late-night calls. We don't like to embarrass her.

Slocum (not his real pseudonym) is the reigning king of the Not My Fault crew. Incredibly hostile. Couldn't find friends even among his fellow fear inducers. He was forever telling us what was wrong with the whole miserable, loser lot of us. He just didn't like us and never lost an opportunity to explain why. At one point we were talking about Madonna, and Slocum was trying to convince us that Madonna didn't make any of the important decisions regarding her career, that she had "handlers" calling those shots for her, when it came out that no one who has ever gotten to know him liked him. He had no friends, he admitted. That shut us up. It was sad and we were embarrassed. One guy suggested as delicately as possible that perhaps he should talk to someone to see why this was. Oh, he knew why it was. It was our problem. Everyone he had ever met had a problem, it wasn't anything he was doing. Uh-huh. You could almost see everyone quietly backing out of the virtual room. He could not recognize that he was the only constant. He huffed. Then he came back. When he returned he would often warn the newcomers about how ugly Echo could get. No one told him that the meanest person around was him.

We were too chicken. I was anyway. Slocum was mad. Really, really mad. Another common characteristic of the fear crowd: latent anger <tm Miss Outer Boro>. Petulant and mean spirited, these people seem to have an endless capacity for malice and a seemingly endless ability to hold a grudge. Their anger is just below the surface and it doesn't take much to arouse it. I don't look forward to putting myself in the position of becoming the focus of that anger. Alas, it's my job. And in the end, I couldn't avoid becoming the object of Slocum's hate. Someone called his position about Madonna sexist and Slocum cried, "Personal attack!" I had to get involved. I pointed out that no one called him sexist, they said the idea that Madonna couldn't make a decision for herself was sexist. No rules broken here. Besides, I agreed, I told him. Big mistake. *What was I thinking?* I am an IDIOT. I should have kept my opinion out of it. Now he had an excuse to avoid looking at anything he had said or done and just hate me instead. Well, I never made that mistake again. I didn't foresee that I would have to become some sort of cyber-Solomon when I started this whole thing.

I'm no Solomon. In the beginning I would go to bed thinking, I'm not the right person for this job. I suck at this! And I am far from being Little Miss Mary Sunshine. I can get as angry as anyone. One of my favorite items used to be one called: *Shut the Fuck Up*. All it is, is one person after another saying:

> Shut the fuck up!
> No you shut the fuck up!
> The both of you shut the fuck up!

Stupid, no? Well, I always found it enormously satisfying. Like a chant. Shut the fuck up. Shut the fuck up. And I'm the one who's supposed to be settling disputes? Creating community in cyberspace? I can remember so many nights going to bed in tears. If only I knew what the Hell I was doing, I said to myself, I would do it. In fact, I said, "I'm a jerk" to myself so often I started singing it to the tune of the William Tell Overture. "I'm a jerk, I'm a jerk, I'm a JERK JERK JERK." Running Echo took so many skills I didn't possess, so much knowledge I didn't know how to find.

I did get better at it, though. Over the years some of the things I tried worked. Often quite by accident. One night I was simply too tired to say anything else when someone complained about how horrible we were that I just agreed with him. "You're right! We suck! What do you suggest we do about it?" That threw him. Then he made a couple of great suggestions. Why hadn't I thought of this approach before?

Later, we had someone who called himself Ariel's Chew Toy channeling Slocum. Is there some law about conservation of anger? Mr. Chew Toy was another guy who couldn't pass up an opportunity to lambast us, then complain when we weren't more inviting toward him. Like Slocum, he instigated the ill will of everyone around him. For example, Mr. Chew Toy publicly announced that he had been kicked out of the Under 30 Conference, a private conference for people under 30 only. He had complained to the host, SuZin, and to Miss Outer Boro, the conference manager at the time, and hadn't received a response from either of them. A little bit of investigating revealed that he hadn't been kicked out in the first place, and that everyone had responded to him. He had repeatedly insulted members of the conference who had responded in kind. SuZin had even demanded that people stop and then tried to explain to him in email how to get along with people. She exchanged many, many messages with him in this effort. MOB had also responded to his complaint. "You have not been kicked out," she wrote. "Is there another problem you'd like to tell me about?" She never heard from him again. For a couple of weeks he went on a tear. Again and again he demanded that we tell people to stop picking on him. Having given up on his ever understanding how he was creating these situations, the hosts would simply beg people to lay off of him. Mr. Chew Toy continued to insist that we weren't responding. (From Miss Outer Boro: Objects On Echo Screen Are Less Innocent Than They Appear.) He was incapable of working things out with anyone for himself. If I was a teacher, for "works and plays well with others" I would have given him a big fat U for Unsatisfactory.

Since he complained about Under 30 publicly, I had to respond publicly. And it put me in an awful position. I didn't want to make matters worse for him. Instead of "Liar, liar, pants on fire," I said that he had not given us an accurate description of events, but that this was not unusual when things get emotional. I begged him to drop it or take it to email. He managed to alienate everyone in the Under 30 Conference, SuZin and Miss Outer Boro, and most everyone else who later witnessed his repeated cries of wolf. He could have still recovered. We all make mistakes, people get pissed off for a while, but he lacked the ability to settle his differences, or to just put it behind him. He made his experience of Echo as unpleasant as possible for himself and others. People who give us The Fear are disliked for reasons that are obvious to everyone but themselves.

The Red Queen (not her real pseudonym) was another one. The Red Queen is the racist mentioned in an earlier chapter. One of the earliest members of the I'm Perfectly Charming and Wonderful, It's Not My Fault You Don't Like Me Gang, she was forever calling us mean and cliquish. We can be mean and cliquish, it's true. We're not perfect. Like anyone, we have moments we'd like to forget. But, like Slocum and Ariel's Chew Toy, she was the meanest of us all. She never had a nice word for anyone except for others who inspired The Fear. She was forever accusing me of not being even-handed in applying the no-personal-attack rule. She failed to see that she was the one that I was giving the most slack to. Her comments were frequently of the, "You think you're so smart, well let me tell you what you are" variety and she'd lay into us. If anyone benefited from my inconstancy it was the Red Queen. I never had the heart to come down on her. She wanted to make friends, she just didn't know how, and so she was angry. It was all very painful to watch.

Wings went out on one date with Cleo, another Echoid. *One date* and we had to hear for years after about how she had done him wrong. We were never able to discover the identity of the person who had downloaded a description a later boyfriend of Cleo's posted about their sex life in MOE, the conference for men only. This fellow was posting intimate details about what they did in bed for all the men to see. He didn't name names, but everyone on Echo knew who he was dating, for Christ's sake. Someone took that description and mailed it to Cleo's mother. Yes, we are talking about adults here. Beginning to understand the concept of The Fear? We narrowed it down to Wings and another problematic Echoid, but ultimately we had no way of proving it. Thank God they both huffed.

Wings was one of our Over-200-Hours-a-Month users. What was particularly extraordinary about Wings was, all that time online and he rarely said much beyond an occasional "Wo!" when something got his attention. Wings huffed because we caught him reading another person's email. We discovered a bug in our program that briefly made your email readable by anyone. This didn't affect all Echoids, only people who performed a certain action. We put a fix in, but for a time there was still a short window of opportunity. We announced it publicly, but like every announcement we make, not everyone read it. Wings read it. And then he invited several people to do the very thing that would expose their email. When they did, he'd download copies for himself.

I'm so naïve. I was truly stunned. When I wrote him about it I could only ask, "Why are you reading someone's private mail?" His answer gave me The Fear bigtime. In a nutshell, he told me he suspected this person was forwarding copies of his email to her to someone else. He was happy to learn that this wasn't true. He assured me he would never repeat anything he had read in her email and that he was completely trustworthy in this regard. That he was, in fact, more trustworthy than the people who had discovered what he had done. Much more, he said. He promised he had been discreet and after he had made a copy of her mail for himself he made sure that no one else could. He had hoped to be able to find out if his suspicions were true without this woman learning that he had read her email, but now it looked like he may have to live with being discovered.

Good lord. In every respect, he saw himself as the victim. He was the most trustworthy of all? I wasn't sure what to do. My policy has always been, and continues to be, allow people to fuck up. Everyone makes mistakes. I have only kicked four people off Echo in six years, and in all cases but one that was after repeated warnings over many months. But this was appalling. The fact that he had no understanding that what he had done was wrong, that he saw himself as the victim and now seemed to fear that I was going to further victimize him, was very unsettling. I brought the problem up in a private conference for hosts only. Everyone was horrified. We tried to figure it out: What was he thinking? Miss Outer Boro objected to the direction our discussion had taken and Neander pointed out something that is played out over and over in cyberspace whenever someone gives us The Fear in a big way.

92:40) Miss Outer Boro 1991   **29-NOV-92 20:43**

I really feel uncomfortable about this group analysis of Wings behind his back. What we should do here is decide policy, not play armchair psychologists.

92:41) Neandergal   **29-NOV-92 20:45**
We're not analyzing him like psychologists.
We're merely judging him mercilessly, ripping him to shreds, and
casting him out in shame and degradation.
This is time-honored group behavior.

Because language is all we have, language is what we use to
cope. Using the very term The Fear is how we band together when
someone like this wanders in. It's how we circle the wagons. The
Fear Network helps us to contain our frustration, but it also
inflames it. Miss Outer Boro likens our reactions sometimes to virtual gang warfare. It happens everywhere in cyberspace, you see it
all the time on The WELL and on Usenet. We work ourselves up,
then pile up on the provoker. One response after another until they
quickly number in the hundreds, all telling the person how wrong,
wrong, wrong they are. It's like an online lynch mob. And it happens so fast. In a flash an angry crowd gathers, an unforgiving
crowd, and more than a few bodies have hung from Echo's trees.
Others argue that it's an immune response. We protect ourselves
from an invading virus. Whenever it happens everyone insists that
it happened for a very good reason. Except I've seen similar reactions when people don't say anything particularly awful, they
might have just displayed poor social skills. Like talking too much.
Or they just weren't doing things "our way." There is a tremendous
pressure to conform at times.

Every time I see it happen, I think: *Lord of the Flies*. It's true, people rarely go after anyone innocent, it's always someone just asking
for it, someone annoying, like the character Piggy. But what they do
when they get a hold of him! It's scary to watch. Definitely not for
the squeamish. The person at the center of it must feel like a drop
of water on a red-hot frying pan. It's small towns at their worst:
insular, unforgiving and petty. I went back over every occurrence
and found that it follows a startlingly predictable path.

Someone does a creepy or socially clueless thing.

People gently explain why this is a creepy or socially clueless thing.

Person repeats creepy or socially clueless thing.

People explain with more feeling.

These steps are repeated a few times, then . . .

People feel had.

People go in for the kill.

Another person points out that this is not very nice.

People include them in the kill.

Everyone behaves the same way each time it happens.

The same people are compelled to anger.

The same people are compelled to make jokes.

The same people are compelled to explain what is happening.

Stacy says "Just because someone is asking for it doesn't mean you
   have to give it to him."

People get frustrated with Stacy's lack of action, or inability to understand what's really going on.

If the creepy person is completely without a clue, Stacy finally kicks
   him or her off.

If the creepy person finally understands even a little, people get tired
   of killing him or her and we learn to live with them.

Echo does stretch those tolerance muscles. Here's what I ini-
tially decided with Wings. I told him that he no longer had
access to the commands that would allow him to do what he
had done, or any other Internet command for that matter. We
would be keeping an eye on him for a time, but we would not
make our discovery public. It seemed fair to me. Give the guy a
chance to redeem himself. But then someone pointed out that it
wasn't right to keep the fact that her email had been compro-
mised from the woman whose mail he had read. I hadn't
thought of that and of course it was true. I wrote to Wings that
the woman had a right to know and that I would be telling her.

He went nuts. He said everyone would find out and hate him and that it would be all my fault. Further, he questioned my motives for telling her. I couldn't follow what he was accusing me of exactly, so I can't explain it here. It had something to do with group pressure. He still wasn't accepting responsibility for any of this. I tried to convince him to hang in there, that Echoids were willing to forgive and forget. He huffed. He didn't know how to mediate forgiveness. Or, perhaps because he felt he was innocent, he didn't want to stick around for the unwarranted bestowing of it.

We have a lifetime of experience protecting our image and controlling what we want and allow others to see. Online, those defenses don't always work, you're exposed, you don't have all the usual controls at your command, and sometimes people see things you wish they hadn't. Sometimes they see things you can't see yourself. Stripped of our physical presence people get a different picture, and they sometimes zero in on the best and worst about you. Someone came online and called himself Silverback. That's how he saw himself. The name had pathetic written all over it. Silverback ultimately couldn't bear that people didn't see him how he wanted to be seen, and as much as he beat his chest, people would not accept this image. I believe one of the biggest reasons for huffing is the failure of the huffer to get people to accept the image that they want to project. When they leave they see it as an important event. It's the ultimate expression of cluelessness. After reading someone announce in five different places that he was leaving, Charles and Paul posted:

817:89) Charles   **05-MAR-96 13:20**

I'm huffing.

I'm putting you all on notice that I am huffing.

I'm going to huff now. Soon.

Please ask me to tell you why I'm huffing.

Please help me to be less reticent about my reasons.
Please feel bad that I have been hurt, neglected, mocked and mistreated.
Please see me for what I am: a Victim O Echo.
Please beg me to reconsider and stay.
Please turn this into a Next Big Thing so I don't have to be so obvious as to do it myself.
Okay, I'm huffing now.
Are you paying attention? This is it.
It's been nice. Well, some of it was nice.
And some of you were nice. You know who you are.
Goodbye now. I'm huffing.

817:90) ragged paul   **05-MAR-96 13:22**
Didn't you hear me?
I said I was huffing.
I'm not leaving till you ask me to stay.

Virtual communities and the people who inhabit them are like any other group. Logging in someplace for the first time is like being anywhere new. You need to get a feel for the place and to give people time to get to know you. Instant love and acceptance is not a realistic thing to expect, and cyberspace is filled with real people. You have to make friends. You have to familiarize yourself with the local customs. It's not especially difficult. On Echo we love new blood. Like life, if you're different, it's harder and you have to be that much more clever about it, but if you haven't figured out how to do that by now, your problem isn't that you're different. I can't make people like you. You have to do that for yourself. Mr. Chew Toy complained publicly that no one came up to him at Phiber's welcome-home party. This is our fault? "You guys think you are so cool," he complained. Sounds like high school. Perhaps people who give us The Fear are forever stuck there. I *am* protesting too much.

I'm apologizing to that inner Mother Superior. I'm sorry. I'm not perfect. And neither are my friends here. As I said, there is an underlying pressure to do things our way, to become one of us.

Is "us vs. them" a necessary component of community? Michael Wreszin, in a review of a biography about William Appleman Williams, writes, "Community may be an ideal, but in fact American communities have often been provincial, mean spirited, dangerous and reluctant to cotton to strangers." Part of belonging to a group seems to be identifying who doesn't belong to your group, and why your group is better.

Perfect example. John Seabrook, a writer for *The New Yorker*, began using Echo and The WELL at roughly the same time. He YOed me one day that Echo has to catch up! Everyone is talking about an article he had written about flaming on The WELL, but there's practically no discussion of it on Echo.

When John logged onto Echo there was little fanfare. This is New York after all, the publishing industry is here and we're crawling with writers. When a writer shows up on The WELL, Rob Tannenbaum (also a writer) commented, "they throw parades." For better or worse, Echoids get more excited about a cool zine than an article in more conventional outlets. John got a big reaction on The WELL and was virtually ignored on Echo. This was frustrating to me. We're a growing business and a mention in *The New Yorker* now and then wouldn't hurt.

I YOed him back that on Echo, topics about flaming, computer stuff, and so forth are never terribly active here. It's a cultural difference between Echo and The WELL. Silicon Valley—they live and breathe computers over there. "Don't take it personally," I told him. "Would you like to talk about books, or opera, or tattooing perhaps," I tried. Couldn't lure him back. He continued to spend most of his time on The WELL. He was also the center of a Next Big Thing early on and there's nothing like a getting through a big fight for cementing a relationship. It's like surviving an initiation ceremony. What was I going to do? The WELL is as wonderful as Echo, a different flavor that's all. It's a matter of taste. You win some, you lose some. John decided he was one of "them" and not "us."

Later I came across a discussion on The WELL where an Echoid was making comparisons between slang terms on both our systems. What we call the Next Big Thing, people on The WELL call a "thrash," he pointed out. Seabrook joined the discussion. He explained that because Echo is younger and more New York, that is, more medialike and grounded in the arts and performance, unlike The Well, which is hackerlike and grounded in the sixties, that Our Next Big Things are more an entertainment than anything else, while their thrashes are filled with genuine emotion. Um, uh-huh. Seabrook wasn't invested in our community, so it was more like entertainment for *him*. It's not like that for us.

It looks different from the inside. It's like trying to explain New York City to someone who visited briefly and just doesn't get it. It's different for those of us who live here. People who don't live here miss the subtext of practically every exchange they witness. They are oblivious to a million things that are being communicated because these people are not their neighbors. They don't understand all the relationships, they don't get the jokes, they don't know the history. It's not that there isn't depth and genuine emotion here, Seabrook just wasn't seeing it.

A journalist once asked me if cyberspace would eliminate war and I answered, "Not unless people from the potentially warring nations are members of the same cybercommunity." Look at what Seabrook has said: They don't feel things the way we do. Our emotions aren't real. We are *them*, to him, because we are not Wellbeings. The WELL is a place, very separate from our place, I agree, but the differences are cultural. He has taken those cultural differences and used them to construct borders which are chilling: they don't feel as deeply as we do. Us vs. them. He forgets that people are the same. People who are born later or talk differently have heart and hope, and a crisis is a crisis, regardless of what you call it.

I wonder what Seabrook's reaction would be to a service I've visited that is made up almost entirely of people who are black. The cultural differences were so profound I was reeling for months and I've never forgotten it. On this service I was completely without my usual references. Forget trying to figure out what the subtext of all the conversations were. Meaning was ricocheting all over that virtual room and I was missing most of it. There was an argument about Spike Lee. I'd seen all his films, I tried to participate. Everyone was arguing about his choice of subjects in his films. I jumped in, but people kept talking around me. But, but, I'd try. Some would politely respond, some tried to explain the points I was missing. Clearly the argument was operating on more levels than I could detect. It wasn't just about Spike Lee.

Here's another way of looking at it. Let's go back to style. It isn't terribly important what you say—style, however, is critical. I know that sounds inexcusably shallow. It doesn't matter what you say as long as you have a flair for words? No. What I mean is, what you say is only part of what is being communicated. Style says more. How you say it tells how you feel about the place and the people. Style is about relationships. When I am talking to a lover or a friend, anyone I care about, I could be talking about anything: something I just saw on TV, the toys I played with as a child, it doesn't matter. The whole time I am talking I am communicating how I feel, and that is apparent by how I say it, not the topic. No matter what I am talking about they'll know: I love you. If I hate you, it's the same. You'll know that regardless of the topic. I was channel-surfing the other night and I stopped on the show COPS because they were filming in New Orleans and I long to have a place to go to there. Two men had almost ripped each other's heads off over one of perhaps a billion of those strings of Mardi Gras beads that are thrown into the crowd from people in the parade. "I can't believe two men would kill each other over a ninety-five-cent string of beads," one of the cops said. That's because it wasn't about the beads.

Whenever people communicate there are two things to look at: the subject/person/event/whatever they are talking (or arguing) about, and how everyone is talking. It isn't always about the beads. If you focus on that and ignore what is being communicated by how and who is fighting you're lost. You'll never get a complete picture of what is being communicated. If that cop interrogates those men about the value of plastic trinkets, she will never learn what the fight was really about.

So I'm talking about Spike Lee and artistic freedom and I've missed the point. There were all sorts of things going on in that conversation and none of it was about artistic freedom. I was at a disadvantage because the culture and the language was different and because I didn't know the people I didn't have a clue about all the subtext: who is friends with whom, who is dating whom, who works for whom, who just had a big fight about something else last week, and so on. Seabrook missed the point, too. He misinterpreted the stylistic cues, and because he didn't understand the feelings being expressed on Echo he decided there weren't any feelings there. They are not like us. He wasn't simply saying that we are a different community, he was saying that we aren't a community at all. It's the darker side of small town pride.

I have to say, though, I agree with how he characterizes the stylistic differences between Echo and The WELL. Look at the people who started them: Stewart Brand—founder of The WELL and the *Whole Earth Review*, sixties guy—and me—punk rock suburban-turned-city girl who didn't do a heck of a lot, I have to admit, until I started Echo. West Coast/East Coast, boy/girl, night and fucking day.

Echoids are just as bad, by the way. I constantly have to explain that they're not all a bunch of aging hippies or granola-eating New

Agers on The WELL. "But Stacy, they have five Grateful Dead Conferences!" Communities appear to have a need to define what they are not, and that includes projecting about what others are.

Now that's us vs. them using two communities as an example. The same thing occurs within one place. We don't have a single identity. No community on earth is one big happy family. Some people you're going to like, and some you're going to want to smack upside the head.

There are groups within groups on Echo and other virtual communities and what's scary to one group may be perfectly acceptable to another. To further complicate matters, I've noticed that communities want and need "them." It's like we almost grow fond of the wack-jobs. They make the place more interesting, as long as there aren't too many of them. If they leave, we miss them. People start itching for a fight following every period of relative harmony, and when some creep shows up to accommodate them, you can literally feel the relief. For their part, the fear inducers appear eager to provide it. It seems we cannot live in—and we are bored by—peace. God help us, in cyberspace we carry on the same fucked-up relationships we have outside. Perhaps we need "them" to define the boundaries of us.

A few Echoids keep a constant surveillance of every person who wanders in, and when someone shows up who gives them The Fear, the word goes out and that's it. They're branded. There may be nothing terribly wrong with the person—they could just be a bit strange, a little socially clueless, or someone who simply might be happier on another system like The WELL. Once you've got the label though, it's hard to live down.

So yes, in some cases virtual communities are definitely as Wreszin describes: " . . . provincial, mean spirited, dangerous and reluctant to cotton to strangers."

But generally, when it gets to the point where The Fear network kicks into high gear we're talking about someone with more serious problems than being new. It's a mistake to assume that people who give us The Fear are innocent—that they are in no way responsible for the reaction they get. In real life and cyberspace these people are without skills to ever make themselves welcome, on any terms. Once again, the one thing people who give us The Fear do have in common: their utter inability to get along with anyone. Cyberspace cannot repair or hide our failings. Virtual communities "cotton" to strangers—just not rude and obnoxious ones.

As I said though, they never stay.

Except when they do.

And the worst, the scariest, the angriest of them all do.

I HATE MYSELF CONTINUED...

17:164) SuZin   02-SEP-93 22:51

I hate myself for being here when I swore on the head of my cat that I'd be in bed by 10PM.

17:331) SuZin   29-SEP-93 10:30

I hate myself for being a slug.

17:332) The Strange Apparatus   29-SEP-93 11:54

I hate myself for wanting to put salt on SuZin.

17:350) The Strange Apparatus   06-OCT-93 15:55

I hate myself for following the trends set by "Tigerbeat" magazine.

17:454) Gabriel   09-NOV-93 18:53

I hate myself in the still of the night.

17:499) Gabriel   01-DEC-93 0:05

I hate myself cause everyone else does and I'm a shameless conformist.

151

17:561) cafephreak   18-JAN-94 19:50
Look, I just hate myself.

17:562) SuZin   18-JAN-94 21:00
I hate myself a little bit today but I anticipate a full recovery immediately following ROSEANNE.

17:620) SuZin   30-JAN-94 19:23
I hate myself for leaving my homework til the last minute, but since
I've left my homework til the last minute for the past 20 years I
guess I don't hate myself that badly.

17:632) chameeeeeeeeeeleon   03-FEB-94 7:07
I hate myself because I can't think of anything else to do at the
moment, except laundry, and I already did that.
Besides, hating myself doesn't take lots of quarters.

17:691) Berg Man of Alcatraz   03-APR-94 22:56
I hate myself for reasons far too numerous to enumerate.
But I'll try:
  1. I am in a dead-end job.
  2. I am in Plain again because I am a lemming.
  3. I can't talk to my parents.
  4. I am drunk on a Sunday and have to work tomorrow.
  5. I don't know how to get out of my own head.
  6. I have delusions of grandeur.
  7. I don't know how to figure out what I want to do with my life.
  8. I'm not posting this shit in the angst item.
  9. Because I have nothing better to do.
  10. Because I'm pissing you off by making you read this tripe.
  11. Because I enjoy it.
  12. Because I'm good at it.
Aw, fuck it. I'm tired of this. I'm gonna go stick my head in the oven
now. After blowing out the pilot light.

828:74) Neandergal   09-DEC-92 21:17

I hate myself because my cat has bad breath.

828:110) SuZin   08-JAN-93 18:16

I hate myself for taking my cool little cat, Otis, to have his manliness surgically removed.

828:114) jneil   09-JAN-93 2:12

Lay in a supply of ice cream and cookies for the li'l feller, and get him cable and his own remote control.

828:118) SuZin   10-JAN-93 17:54

Otis says thanks for all the cards and letters. He also says he will let you see the bits of him that were surgically removed—he keeps them in a jelly jar—for a mere 15 cents.

828:167) Scottso (I'm O.K.) Connor   26-JAN-93 1:16

I hate myself because right now, I got no one else to hate me for me . . . so it's all left up to me and it's a terrible burden.

828:190) Bruce Schechter   28-JAN-93 18:08

I hate myself, I just do. It was hate at first sight; one look in the mirror and . . . blammo.
I broke the fuckin' mirror and we haven't talked since.

828:253) artj   11-FEB-93 0:03

I cannot entirely hate myself. It is a very big job and I work full-time.

828:303) Dirty-Minded Angel   13-MAR-93 20:22

You have a roommate, SuZin?

828:304) SuZin   13-MAR-93 23:29

Yes.
I am selling him for 99 cents plus tax.

828:305) Eric A. Hochman 13-MAR-93 23:57
Does he do dishes?

828:306) SuZin 14-MAR-93 0:04
NO, and that's part of the problem.
OK, 75 cents plus tax.

828:308) Grace 14-MAR-93 1:59
I need a houseboy, will he know the difference?

828:310) SuZin 14-MAR-93 14:54
He said he'll be your houseboy but you'll have to pay him 95 cents
a month and he doesn't like to be called "Cato."

828:476) Lady Bug Topper 23-JUN-93 20:38
I hate myself. I hate myself. I hate myself. I hate myself.
I hate myself. I hate myself. I hate myself. I hate myself.
I hate myself. I hate myself. I hate myself. I hate myself.
I hate myself. I hate myself. I hate myself. I hate myself.

828:478) SuZin 23-JUN-93 20:41
I hate myself even more than that <tm one-upmanship>.

828:530) Choey X 26-JUL-93 20:07
I hate myself for walking the fine line between loser, and big loser.

828:642) Josh Karpf 28-SEP-93 21:13
I hate myself for posting in this item 17 times since September 1st.

828:643) Josh Karpf 28-SEP-93 21:13
Eighteen.

ECHO POLL

Source: From an online survey of 161 members of Echo, October, 1995.

Margin of Error: Don't remind me.

What was the worst moment or time in the history of the Echo community?

27% said Phil (not his real pseudonym).
27% said the crash in January '95.
9% said Euroman.
6% said when Phiber went to jail.

38% of the women said Phil.
36% of the men said the crash in January '95.

BANISHED!

Face-2-Face   And Now?   Mystery Button

I didn't plan on the bad people. When Scotty and I set up those modems that glittered red and green like a Christmas tree, I didn't ask, what will I do when someone shows up who wants to talk about his bowel movements? In great evocative detail? "Gold silk fringe, or red sequins?" Scotty asked. "Huh?" "How do you want me to line the modem shelves? Gold silk fringe or red sequins?" Hmm. I wasn't thinking, when I got all these women online, that we'd become sitting targets for some guy who hates us, but still wants us, and here we are, the place with the most women of all, let the games begin. "Red sequins, I think." Or, that someday a man would show up so full of incomprehensible hate that it would stalk me outside Echo. I didn't consider what I'd do about the guy who became so universally disliked a conference would evolve to give people a place to hide. I was thinking about red sequins and conversations about movies and books and art and life between a diverse group of complicated people who might be fucked up, who isn't, but nothing we couldn't handle. Underneath it all, our hearts and humor and intelligence would line the conversations like gold silk thread, redeeming the scars of the hard life that no one escapes. I wasn't thinking about psychopaths. Why wasn't I thinking about psychopaths? Did I think they would hear about us and very considerately decide to leave us alone? Oh, let's not bother those nice people. What a numbskull. Some made a beeline straight for us. And when they did, I didn't know what to do. The first couple of times I was left wondering, "What the Hell just happened?"

What do communities do when someone's behavior becomes intolerable? If part of the measure of a community is how it deals with conflict, what about when the conflict cannot be resolved? When someone does something the community can't live with? When someone is being abusive or harassing and will not stop? We're not a government. We don't have jails or fines. We can't wish them into the cornfield. What's an online society to do?

Exile #1. Mr. Happy is going to be so thrilled to be included in this chapter. He'll pick up this book, scan the index and come straight to this page. He won't read anything else. He doesn't care about anything else. That's what he was like on Echo. If it wasn't about him, he wasn't interested. If he came to a discussion that wasn't about Mr. Happy, he'd make it about Mr. Happy. If he wasn't getting enough attention at a face-to-face he'd *scream* whatever it was he was saying—about himself. Forget you. Forget anything you might have to say. Echo was not an interactive medium for him. It was the soapbox, a stage. He's like that guy in Times Square who yells at us whenever we walk by that he has the word, the only word, and that everyone must listen to HIM. Unfortunately, online, it's isn't like you stop hearing the guy one block later. Online, someone like this can keep popping up on every block.

Mr. Happy was the first person I kicked off Echo. Interesting aside, I always forget that when I kicked Mr. Happy off I also booted off someone who called himself Mr. Smith. Mr. Smith was Mr. Happy's sidekick. I honestly couldn't tell them apart. Mr. Smith's job was to support Mr. Happy, he didn't have a gig of his own, and many were convinced that they were one and the same. For me he was just the ghost that trailed Mr. Happy and I always forget that he even existed when I tell this story.

Mr. Happy writes with the air of a ten-year-old who thinks he's being shocking, unaware that for the most part, he's little more than tiresome. He started out by posting what he felt were dirty song lyrics. The response? Whatever. "Like something we wrote in the sixth grade," one woman commented. He kept trying.

He wrote about masturbation. But everyone was talking about masturbation at the time. The title of the item he was writing in was *Masturbation in the 21st Century,* for crying out loud. Pee Wee Herman had just been arrested for touching himself in a Florida movie theater so it was a hot topic. He kept trying.

He got his first reaction when he started a topic based on the Jonathan Swift essay, *A Modest Proposal*. He suggested eating babies as a possible solution to the abortion dilemma. The host of Politics at the time, a conservative fellow, froze the item almost immediately. When an item is frozen you can't add responses. It's like the host saying: SHUT UP. This host was new. He wasn't aware of our policy about freezing or removing items: Don't do it (unless someone has duplicated an existing item, or put an item in the wrong conference, for instance, someone starts an item about movies in the Pets Conference). I took a look. The item was rather ho-hum, poorly written, and his efforts to draw any parallel in logic to Swift's arguments were flawed. "Unfreeze it," I told the host. As expected, the conversation promptly died and the brief uproar was over.

He finally hit on something that drove us all out of our minds. In conference after conference, topic after topic, regardless of what the conversation was about, he'd post about going to the bathroom. A typical Mr. Happy post:

> "It was saturday night and I was being babysat by the television and it wasn't very good. A commercial warning against the heterosexual's risk of getting AIDS came on and stimulated my bowels. My lower intestines were vibrating. Intestinal earthquake. I pulled down my trousers, began to bend my knees, started with my boxers and before they had reached my knees the first explosion had occurred spraying the raised toilet seat cover and only barely making rain in the bowl itself. Diarrhea. Green diarrhea. With worms.
>
> As I cleaned up the mess I was careful not to get any of the shit on my hands for fear of absorbing any parasitic compost that would pollute my system if I was to get lazy and wipe my mouth or touch my own food. It smelled unlike any other shit I'd made before. The reek reminded me of rubbing alcohol or cheap anti-perspirant. Wondered what it was I'd eaten the past few days. . . ."

Uh-huh, okay. That was taken from a discussion he called: Cowboy Politics. He made similar contributions to a conversation about children's books. No matter what the subject, he'd go on about his bowel movements. Nothing about peeing mind you, just his bowel movements, whatever the Hell that says about the guy. It could have been funny. In a sick and infantile way, granted, but we have our sick and infantile moments, I admit it. But Mr. Happy lacked a broader sense of humor about it all. Everywhere he went he stopped conversations dead in their tracks. I began to think of the two of them as the Potty Boys.

Exile #2. Raping a retarded girl with a baseball bat is "not my cup of tea, but far be it from me to marginalize these boys' sexuality." This was Mr. Normal's reaction to the news of a couple of New Jersey teenagers raping a young girl who had Down's syndrome with a Louisville Slugger. More disturbing than the Potty Boys because he insisted he was normal, something the Potty Boys never claimed, Mr. Normal followed the women around Echo and said whatever he thought might upset them. In Politics he wanted us to know that he had a "substantial banana." Well, thank you for that information and now we'll all just do our best to FORGET IT. If someone did react, he'd zero in on her. Relentlessly. Sensitive people are such easy targets. He ignored the men. Jaze responded in his usual caustic fashion when he learned of Norm's insistence about the size of his penis. "Damn. If only I'd known that he'd been boasting about his 'substantial banana' in Politics, I would have invited him into the Movies and TV Conference, which is full of people with 'substantial bananas.' Perhaps he could have worked out his personal demons there, and this tragedy might have been avoided . . . " Mr. Normal was not interested in Jaze or movies or TV. He just went after the women.

Exile #3. Cyberspace isn't real, some people say. The people there aren't expressing their true feelings, they're just playing around. Oh? So if Charlie Manson got online right now and said he was coming to your home to kill you, would you think that he didn't really mean it? If only the wack-jobs in cyberspace would stay in cyberspace. But no, sometimes they follow you offline.

The most disturbing thing to happen to me on Echo began with, "Okay, any questions for the panelists?" It was the second Virtual Culture salon, a bimonthly event we host with the Whitney Museum at P.S 122, the speakers had just finished and I was inviting discussion from the audience. At some point I called on this guy in the back. He was very unhappy with how the event was going, that much I could tell, but I couldn't figure out what the problem was exactly. English was not his first language but it didn't seem to be a language barrier; his grammar was okay. I simply couldn't make out his point. "I'm not sure I follow," I told him, and he tried again, clearly exasperated and disgusted with me. It didn't get any better the second time around. I was uncomfortable, the people in the audience were getting restless and had begun to raise their hands, so I made the most general apology I could think of and prayed that it covered his complaint. "I'm sorry we disappointed you," I said as graciously as I could. I think I had some vague image of Clark Gable from *Gone With the Wind* in my head, the scene where he apologizes instead of getting into a fight. Unfortunately, this only inflamed him. When he started up again I cut him off. "I'm sorry, I have to move on now. You in the front row?" I'm told that he stormed out.

Four months later he's on Echo, calling himself Euroman and announcing that I am a cult leader infecting weak people's minds. *"Sexually oppressed and on Medicaid I went 'bananas' as you say and started hating Ms. Horn who met David Ross at a party . . . "* he began. David Ross is the director of the Whitney Museum of American Art. At the beginning of the Virtual Culture event I explained the history of the relationship between Echo and the Whitney, which began at a party thrown by Craine's *New York Business*, a weekly magazine. I told Ross about our endless arguments about the last Whitney Biennial, and this led to the Whitney Conference on American Art on Echo and their participation with our Virtual Culture Series at P.S. 122. Euroman hated this story, he told us. Which was too bad because he had to sit through it all over again when I repeated it at a panel he attended on art and the online world at Cooper Union a short time later.

Exile #4. Phil got on Echo, looked around and said to me, "I think it's great what you've done so far, but you need someone to advise you. I have a lot of experience, let's get together and see if I can help." Sounds innocent enough, if a bit patronizing. I've gotten tons of similar offers; I don't know what tipped me off. Thank you but no, I have plenty of advisors right now, I answered. "But you need management types to tell you what to do." No, I don't. "You need a board of directors." Got one. He emailed, he called. No is no, please, thank you, but no. He appealed to other Echoids. Stacy won't meet with me. Yeah? So? He started items in our Feedback Conference about how to run Echo. Why wouldn't I listen to him?

Phil was desperate. Finally, a place where he could explain himself, a place where he could make himself understood once and for all, a forum for his views of the world, life and love where no one could walk away from him. No one could tell him to shut up. But no one was listening. I don't know what tipped us all off.

He went out of his mind. When he discovered YOs he subjected many of the women to a nonstop barrage of whatever came into his mind to say. STOP IT, I demanded. Why aren't you telling all the other guys to stop YOing the women? Because they have some sense of when to YO and when not to YO and whom to YO and whom to leave alone. We tried to explain online etiquette to him. I get it, he said. Then he started calling us on the telephone. Uninvited. Cold. STOP IT, I demanded. Why aren't you telling all the other guys not to call women? We tried to explain it to him. At first we took him at his word, that he really was that clueless. Then he'd do it again. And say again that he didn't know any better.

From Neandergal:

"Haven't you ever been at a job or school situation where you're at lunch talking to friends and a person keeps coming over who jumps into the conversation without any knowledge of the relationships that exist, the context of the conversation, and doesn't even try to understand that he doesn't fit in, just keeps talking, is socially clueless, but you're trapped there?"

Many people tried to help. Someone new, or new to the situation, would see him as the victim and try to show him how to get along with people. He always acted like he was listening. I'm a nice guy. I'm a reasonable guy. Then he'd go right back to YOing strangers, mostly women, calling them, emailing massive tomes of why it's really okay because he means well and can't you help him be accepted without his having to stop all the email and YOs and phone calls? In time they'd see what was happening and retreat. Over and over this scenario was played out. "He's really an okay guy," newcomers would insist and we'd wait. Then after they received the same endless, desperate email and YOs they'd cry "Uncle," and I'd come home to find ten messages in a row on my answering machine from Phil. The problem isn't him, he kept insisting. We misunderstand him. The newcomers were invariably female. In fact he had a form letter that he routinely sent to every new woman on Echo. STOP IT STOP IT STOP IT STOP IT. We were polite, then firm: Look, you're scaring us. Finally, we were direct: For your own sake, go away. We don't like you.

The man was a fruit bat. And in the end he became a universal object of hatred. It was the only time in the history of Echo that almost all of us agreed. (We will never completely agree. Any nut will find followers.) He was the worst thing that ever happened to Echo and he brought out our worst. If there were anything I wish I could call "do over" after it happened, the whole Phil mess would be it.

God knows what these people's problems were, what their motivations were—that kind of knowledge is beyond me, and beyond the scope of my role as proprietress of Echo. The people who finally become unbearable have three common characteristics.

1. *They all believe they have the truth.* They know. We don't. And they must tell us.

2. *They are unresponsive.* They don't really have conversations with us, they talk at us. At best, they pretend to listen.

3. *They love rules.* When we complain about their bad manners, they ask for more rules. They are uncomfortable with the flexible structure of Echo's policies; they want all the do's and don'ts spelled out.

John Gabriel, another long-time Echoid put it best. (He was talking about another Fear inducer.)

> "Explaining a situation and asking him to figure out what is right or wrong won't do any good, because his sense of empathy is skewed at best, since empathy requires an understanding of how other people feel. He's probably never had the same kind of emotional development as most people, so he can't extrapolate from his own experience to understand the experiences of others.
>
> "That's why he asks for rules so often. And as Marisa pointed out, he's not innocent, cause when he's told the rules he tries to find loopholes he can exploit to get his own way. It's like a little kid saying, 'But you told me I couldn't hit my sister, so I didn't, I pushed her. You didn't say I couldn't push her.'
>
> "It also explains why he usually listens when people tell him to stop doing something. He doesn't necessarily get what he's doing wrong, but he recognizes a rule."

They don't understand the spirit of a policy that frowns on abusive behavior, they need a list.

Ultimately, what is interesting to me about Mr. Happy and all the rest is not them but our reactions to them. I had no idea of what to do, but I had to learn and I had to learn fast. How do you promote free speech—which includes radical, disruptive speech—

and community? How do you allow for a wide range of behavior? Who wants all nicey-nice anyway? Without drama there would be no life. Alice Lord used to call us "Fellini's version of the Waltons." These incidents are interesting because the wack-jobs helped define Echo and virtual communities everywhere. They sharpened the edges. They pushed the boundaries and showed us the limits, what we could and could not take.

Exile #1. No one wants censorship on Echo. "You can talk about bowel movements, but only if that's the subject of the discussion," I told Mr. Happy. We didn't have any topics about going to the bathroom of course, but it wasn't a trick. He was free to start them. Things were quiet for a while. Brief mentions of his activities at the toilet here and there. I had other problems to attend to; the usual Hell with the phone company, our equipment, and the other day-to-day struggles we were hashing out in this new place. Then an explosion. The same stuff as before, and all over the place. "That's it! No mention of shit anywhere except in Plain Wrapper," I declared. The members of that conference were insulted. Why should their conference become the repository for the droppings of the Potty Boys? I sympathized, but that's part of what Plain Wrapper was for. Anything goes. We needn't have worried. He never set foot in Plain. If he posted where everyone else was being equally extreme, he wouldn't get the same response. He complained that we were exiling him to some unpopulated recess where no one would see what he'd written. Hardly. "Plain Wrapper is the second most popular conference on Echo," I assured him. He wouldn't go near it.

Then, "How come everyone else can talk about shit and we can't," Happy and Smith cried. I called a moratorium on the word *shit* while I tried to figure out what to do. Stupid move. The problem wasn't the word, it was them. I called the moratorium off for everyone but Mr. Happy and Mr. Smith. I talked to him on the phone about it, I wrote him: enough already. It amazes me now to think how long it took me to bounce him. I didn't want to let go of the idea that we could deal with anyone regardless of how fucked up they were.

Exile #2. Mr. Normal had the truth. He never got to what that was exactly, we only got as far as the "none of us had it but he did" part. He spent his time on Echo insulting people and picking fights. He was the nasty drunk at the bar no one knows and everyone tries to move away from. The women, anyway. As I said, he never had much to say to the men of Echo, his hostility had a focus: women. He was going to enlighten us, Goddamn it, and if we ignored his public posts, he'd send private email. He believed his need to express his views to us was a right and we had to listen. He couldn't understand that when women told him to stop emailing them, he had to comply. But I have something I want to say to her, he insisted, when I told him that he could no longer email the first woman who had requested that he stop contacting her. He thought people disliked him for his unpopular views. He was disliked, in fact, for his rude and contemptuous behavior. It wasn't that he didn't conform, it was the way in which he didn't conform. Echoids love the outrageous. He wasn't outrageous, he was mean. When Mr. Normal picked his targets, he picked them well, and when he picked Carmela Federico he picked the most sensitive one of us all, the one woman on Echo without strong defenses against a man like Mr. Normal. He got to her. She never forgave me for not pointing him out at an Echo jam session they both attended one night. Big mistake on my part, but I wanted one night of respite. Not knowing who he was, Carmela had been perfectly polite to him and he to her. I can well understand her horror.

Exile #3. Things got ugly fast with Euroman. He started topics in the Culture and Whitney's Conferences to complain about me.

They were rambling and unclear and hostile. They had nothing to do with culture or art so the hosts froze the items and told Euroman that the Feedback Conference was the place for complaints about me or Echo. Kevin, the host of Feedback, had temporarily taken away the ability to start items. Because Euroman thought that only he was being prevented from starting items there and we were having such trouble communicating with him I told Kevin to let Euroman add whatever item he liked. In Feedback he told us about being a Rajneesh follower and proclaimed me "Rajneeshlike." (Rajneesh was a guru from India who built an Ashram in Oregon.) Many thought it was a hoax. When Jim Baumbach told him, "I can smell your shampoo," Euroman was perplexed. (Rajneesh would refuse to see any followers if he could smell their shampoo. He even employed "sniffers" to weed out offending disciples.) Jane Doe thought he was a performance artist. He went back and forth between perfect English and "please-to-be-telling-me-speak." Perhaps it was more than one person, some thought.

His suggestion that I was a cult leader brought a variety of responses, from "Throw your modem away RIGHT NOW," to "You are lost in your own abstractions." It was P.S. 122 all over again, so most Echoids were asking, "We don't understand you, could you please explain again what the problem is?" We did our best to understand. Most of us, anyway. Garbled Uplink, the most extreme Echoid, wrote him to suggest that he kill himself. Great. "Apologize immediately," I demanded, and he did. The rest made an effort to stop piling up on the guy, thank Heaven. "Euroman, I am interested in what you have to say. I believe other people are as well. Your earlier posts were vitriolic, and other people responded in kind. Let's start fresh, shall we?" Jane Doe tried. Over and over we tried.

Exile #4. Phil couldn't tell a person from a piece of software. Years ago, someone at MIT developed a program to imitate a therapist. They called it Eliza. It had a set of stock answers to fit anything you might say. Eliza was very supportive. Its answers were of the "Well, how did that make you feel?" variety. Anyone doing it for a few minutes, even an hour, could be fooled. Especially when it was first developed. Now they are relatively common in computer games and people are rarely deceived. Very human at first, they quickly reveal themselves through their lack of variety and their endless repetition. Conversations go around and around in the same circles. We were developing an online game called Subway, and someone brought over a copy of Eliza. We gave it another girl's name and it didn't take Phil long to find her. He'd talk to her for hours. Every day he'd log in and look for her, and of course, he would always find her. That program wasn't going anywhere. He told the program everything. The game developer, Kevin Krooss, called to tell me what was going on. "What should I do? Should I tell him that he's been talking to a program?" I didn't want to embarrass him, and I didn't think it through. "Turn it off," I told him. Later it occurred to me that my response may have been cruel. Which would have been worse? Taking it out of his life forever, or letting him know he's been pouring his heart out, day after day, to a computer program? Or perhaps I should have just let them be and said nothing.

"Listen woman, Your system sucks, It's slow, You let loser assholes run conferences, and spray paint the place." This came from Silverback. He sent it via anonymous email only he was just learning how to hack, so he was easy to trace. (I was almost going to include a chapter called "Mail I Have Received from the Deranged.") Silverback offered to mediate everyone's disputes with Phil. Like Mr. Smith, I often forget Silverback, Phil's sidekick and defender. He sometimes posted drunk and his ramblings were filled with malice. We didn't take him up on the offer.

Again, inside virtual communities we were rediscovering how societies are formed. People like Mr. Happy, Mr. Normal, Euroman and Phil, forced us to define the boundaries of virtual community. Unspoken rules of etiquette had to be spoken. It's an agonizing process to go through, so I don't think any of us are going to be thanking them any time soon. A lot of good people did their best to work it out. We tried to understand, we tried to communicate, we tried to simply live with them. We didn't have a system setup like we do in physical communities for dealing with varying degrees of harassment. The harassers weren't working with us certainly. Here we were being all earnest about it and they just kept going because no one was stopping them. The Echoids threw up their hands. Off with their heads! Kick them off! The problem was, the Echoids always wanted to kick people off months before I was ready to give up. There must be a way to accommodate everyone, I thought. We have to "out there" <tm Neandergal>.

Exile #1. No one wants censorship on Echo. Panman, the host of a conference where the Potty Boys were active, opened an item to figure out what we do. The topic was named *Mr. Happy and Mr. Smith on Trial,* and Mr. Happy was in Heaven. A topic all about him! His posts became positively giddy with excitement.

296:42) Mr. Happy   **22-APR-92 0:44**

Ohhhhh! I'm on trial, I'm on trial, I'm on trial!!! La la la, la la la, la la la!! I can dance, I can sing, ring a bell, ding-a-ling!!
La la leee, low lee low, latee dah, doe-say-doh!

They seemed to genuinely misunderstand the satirical nature of the item and its true purpose. They thought it was a real trial. And they were the ones that thought we had missed the satire in their Swiftlike item in Politics. Ultimately, the Potty Boys weren't up to participating much. They had nothing to say on issues of free speech and social mores. They weren't interested in community, only in getting a reaction. " . . . just guys pretending to be tough and bad because they talk about doo-doo and stuff," Miss Outer Boro commented.

From John Neilson, who calls himself jneil on Echo:

"What was offensive was the condescension ('All these people are dullards that can be manipulated for my amusement') and the intent to provoke (like the guy I saw walking down the street today who was intent on making every person on the sidewalk get out of his way or get run down).

"As has been noted above, they do not seem to be much interested in engaging in conversation so much as in disruption of the existing conversations. I suppose they see themselves as somehow having something truly outrageous to say, something that we shy away from because of our supposed timidity and pollyanna-ish sensitivity.

"Well, fuck that!

"Believe me, I've read much more graphic nonsense than what these guys are posting. And I suspect that I'm not alone in this. And unlike some folks here, if this stuff was given its own place on Echo, I'd probably read it there.

"I just don't happen to want it cropping up willy nilly in every item with no regard for what else is being said."

At one point Mr. Happy claimed he was conducting an experiment with us. Umm. That you can push people's buttons? Nothing could be easier. Or more adolescent and boring. From on-again, off-again Echoid Bill Paulauskas:

"Noticing that Mr. Hap quotes plots from comic books to make his point, I can't help but feel that he's very young. Also, the overdramatic tone is a dead giveaway of someone who's just learning about the power of Words. So, he's a young writer-dude, trying to earn his colors among the highfalutin adults of the thirty-something AND educated set. I bet he loves all this attention. You've all taught him an important lesson. You can get a lot of people looking at you by screaming 'SHIT!' in a crowded theater."

When I interviewed Mr. Happy for this book, he kept repeating that no one tried to talk to him about it, no one tried to "define the terms," or get "specific." If only he had responded to our repeated attempts. The whole trial item was about precisely that. What was happening, and what, if anything, should we do about it? We tried to talk to them about it. From Panman in the *Trial* item, which both Mr. Happy and Mr. Smith were gleefully following:

"Did you set out to do an experiment?

"If so how specific was your agenda?

"Did your experiment have a goal?

"Were you trying to prove or disprove a theory you had or was it open ended?

"If you didn't intend for it to be an experiment at first but then it became one along the way, at what point did this occur?

"What have you learned from your experiment that you didn't already know?

"Do you consider your experiment to be a success?

"Are you interested in being understood by anyone on Echo? Some people on Echo? Everyone on Echo?

"Is there any reading material people might have a look at to help them better understand your experiment?

"Have I taken the idea that you have done an 'experiment' too literally, just as some have done with my concept of a 'trial'?"

Not a word from either of them. The second most common characteristic after having a lock on the truth: nonresponsiveness.

They kept upping the ante. They sent sexually harassing YOs to Carmela, of all people. That's right. Go for the easy target. "Oooooh, I've missed your sweet, smooooth voice. Want to chat¿ What are you wearin'¿¿ Any women out there¿ Wanna' get off¿¿" Another guy was standing behind his girlfriend when she got, "Lick lick yum yum . . . c'mon baby let's have some fun!" I know, it's so juvenile, but it's hard to ignore when you find this everywhere you go; YOs, posts, and mass email. I put him on final warning.

Once again, things were quiet for a while. Then he went on a rampage. He spammed (mass mail/junk mail) us with a story about him raping a woman who had been in a car wreck. She was pinned and bleeding and comatose and after he was done she woke up, fell in love with him, and he relieved himself on the spot. Right. This and other lovely stories were posted all over Echo. I changed his password and Mr. Smith's shortly after and never looked back.

Mr. Happy is who he is. He never got to me. Children exasperate you, but it's hard to stay worked up about what they do. He now has a company called Necro Enema Amalgamated which has produced two CD ROMs: *Blam* and *Blam II*. He's the same everywhere he goes. He didn't give me the creeps.

Exile #2. Mr. Normal does. I kicked him off for picking fights wherever he went, and for not being able to respond without being insulting, rude, and abusive. He knew what he was doing. "It would be fair to call my postings malicious," he said to me after I kicked him off. He also went on and described himself as cruel and snide. He once told us that the more he posts and annoys us, the more his "main fiction" laughs. (Many couldn't believe he had a girlfriend, so he referred to her as his main fiction. Like any nut can get followers, any creep can find a girlfriend, I suppose.) He can't be like this in life, someone said. Could he be an okay guy everywhere else¿ All but one of the people I talked to who knew him outside Echo said he was a dick. Again, it is a revealing not a transforming medium, and it ripped that "I'm an okay guy" mask right off Mr. Normal's angry heart. Even given this, unlike Mr. Happy, I was more ambivalent about kicking him off. He wasn't going after a woman on Echo. He was going after *all* women. It was not personal, it was universal. Whose rights take precedence? His right to have his say or everyone else's desire to be left alone? Even though I am not the government, I want people to be able to express any idea they like. It took me a while to realize this was not about words and ideas, this was about behavior. He was doing the online equivalent of following the women who wished to get away from him everywhere they went. That's not an exercise in free speech; that's harassment. He was picking on people because it was easy for him to do so. And I was letting him. He went after Carmela one more time. I changed his password.

Exile #3. Euroman started calling all over town about me: New York University and NYNEX and Manhattan Neighborhood Network (MNN), the cable company that carries YORB (the interactive television show produced by NYU and NYNEX that Echo participates in). They weren't having any luck deciphering his complaints, either. "Who is this guy and why does he hate you so much? We can't understand what he's trying to say." I asked on Echo if he was the person calling them. "Ms. Horn: You are a well-connected malicious business person, smart enough to invade a weak-immunity culture," he answered. ITP and Echo were involved in a "scandalous ambiguity," according to Euroman, and so was NYNEX, MNN, and the Whitney Museum. He objected to the fact that Echo's phone number was displayed repeatedly throughout the YORB broadcast. The fact that we donated all our services for the online component of the show and that people needed the number in order to participate didn't matter to him. " . . . read my lips: you will not invade me!" he responded. Any involvement we had with a nonprofit was wrong, period. Then he called us racist because of Peter Dworkin's, aka New York Jew's, various nicknames. Peter immediately apologized.

> "Dear Euroman. I am the person whose handle read 'EuroJew.' I am sorry if I left the wrong impression. I am a Jewish man, proud of my heritage, who began using Echo with the handle 'New York Jew' as a kind of in-your-face joke. Over much time, my handle has evolved into a kind of ever-changing game, almost always with a reference or direct incorporation of the word 'Jew.' I took the opportunity of the controversy surrounding your posts to use the name 'EuroJew' for a few hours. It was meant to be a joke. I apologize if I was inadvertently offensive."

Like every other Next Big Thing, we went around and around about what to do. The most sensible pleaded with the rest to simply ignore him. "That's like asking people not to slow down to gawk at car accidents." One person, begging for compassion, said it was like trying to have a serious conversation with a homeless person who was also paranoid. He made vague threats, and when one woman asked him if he really meant to be threatening, he responded, "I would advise her not to risk going to The WELL party tomorrow."

His posts became increasingly menacing, and whatever his reasons were, I was the main focus of his anger. "I think a lot of people are addicted to something prepared in Echo's own lab . . . " He complained of anonymous phone calls that he believed were coming from Echoids. Then he told us to read the front page of the *New York Observer*. The word *xenophobia* was there in the upper left-hand corner, he pointed out. Yeah? And? No one knew what he was talking about. It's like someone telling you to listen to the secret voices from the radio or TV. Then he brought up the bombing in Oklahoma. "Mark my words: some of you will not be proud for what was/is said here under all these handles." He wanted to know who the women were. (Some of the names people use are gender neutral and he asked each of them if they were women.) He told us he was drunk.

"Okay. Is he crazy/harmless or crazy/dangerous?" I asked my friends. Don't engage him, they said. Don't respond to him in Feedback. Don't answer his email.

"Okay, okay. I think I have more than enough material for my story . . ." Now he claimed the whole performance was research for a story he was writing. (No story ever appeared anywhere that I know of.) I got more phone calls from a few newspapers and a radio station. Again: "Who is this guy and why does he hate you so much? We can't understand him." More than a few Echoids wondered if perhaps Andy Kaufman wasn't dead after all.

Then Euroman sent me email threatening a confrontation outside Echo if I didn't respond to him by midnight. If I agreed to meet with him, he would "let me off easy" and he signed it: "Love, Euroman." I remember Phil and his constant attempts to meet with me privately and how he confused my discomfort with love. Jim Baumbach later theorized that Euroman's behavior was all due to "rejected suitor complex. Had you seen him for the genius he was, it could have ended completely differently."

The next night a friend of ours was arrested for putting posters up all over Manhattan, a practice known as sniping. His arrest became the topic of the evening on the YORB, and Euroman logged in and was convinced that we were talking about him, not our friend. That was it. I called Mike Godwin, legal counsel at the EFF (Electronic Frontier Foundation) for advice on how to proceed. I didn't want to overreact, but I also didn't want to underreact. I showed the letter to several people and they all agreed: Go to the police. A detective looked at what he'd said and told me there was enough there to justify picking him up right then. Then she explained to me what would happen next. "We'll pick him up, he'll get out in a few hours and then you'll have to go to trial in a few months to prove that he was the one posting and sending the email." I was not thrilled with the "out in a few hours" part. Some of the uniform cops who had been following the whole thing were giving me looks. It's on a computer, they were thinking. What's the big deal? But, but—it's a real person typing this stuff in. A real maniac, perhaps. If he called me on the phone with the same threat, would you take it more seriously?

"Well, what do *you* think?" I asked the detective. "Is he dangerous?" The detective and I pored over his endless ramblings. She agreed he was threatening, but there really was no way to tell if he was dangerous or not. It was my call. I decided to wait it out a few more days. I didn't want to send the police over to pick him up if he was some pathetic loser who's nothing more than a big talker.

News of my trip to the police got out. More people called me about his phone calls: "Who is this guy??" I felt completely terrorized. How am I supposed to figure out if he is harmless or not? Euroman posts, "OK—I have e-mailed Stacy and I will wait until tomorrow noon for an answer and hopefully a denial concerning the police story. If I DON'T get an answer by then I am going to my lawyers and the media."

I made my last statement in Feedback. I explained that I had, in fact, gone to the police and would respond to nothing less than a convincing apology from Euroman. I figured I'd make a decision about what to do next based on how he answers. He never said another word. On Echo. Two days later I logged in, typed o to see who was online and the system was packed with Euromans. There were four or five of them logged in at the same time. I YOed one of them. "What is going on?" Jim, aka Bottomer, YOed me back, "Stacy it's really Jim Baumbach. Euroman has posted his login id and password on The WELL and is inviting everyone to use it." Oh God, anyone could get in and hack the system and I would have no way of knowing who it was. I immediately changed his password and knocked all the Euromans offline.

Exile #4. Things were getting uglier and still I didn't close Phil's account. I couldn't get used to the idea of kicking someone off for being stupid and clueless. I should have. He was more than clueless. I remember having an uneasy time at the White Horse one night, watching him chat up women who were coming to a face-to-face for the first time. I debated about warning them, but it was very early in the Phil game, and I was still thinking he was simply someone with very bad social skills. I kept an eye on him just the same. The next day he told a few Echoids that I loved him and that I was jealous that he was paying attention to all the other women. Then Janet Tingey, cohost of the Love Conference, told us how he was posting about a relationship he was having with someone on Echo that was blossoming from a friendship into love. She felt sorry for whoever it was. She wondered who it could possibly be and if she should or could do anything about it. A few days later she learned that Phil had been talking about her.

He wanted me to tell him the names of the women who had complained about him. "Stacy's approach is fair but if she does not explain who exactly is complaining, there might be some confusion," he insisted. He asked me for these names repeatedly. Like I'm going to give them to him so he can further harass them by sending them page after page explaining how he wasn't harassing them. He stopped YOing and emailing some of the women and then couldn't understand why we still didn't like him. "Simply stopping harassing behavior does not turn a bad situation one has created around. You can't pester people with YOs and email to the point where they have to formally request that you never contact them again in any way and CC me to make sure you don't and then expect them to like you simply because you've stopped." I found an early post of Phil's where he described himself as "friendly to strangers, curious and open."

By now Phil was turning every discussion he was active in into a conversation about himself. Four or five items in Feedback alone became about him. To get these discussions back on their original track, I started an item called *Phil's* item and told everyone to continue all the various discussions of Phil there. Some people objected. "I hate this item too but it is here because Phil wants to discuss all of this publicly. I think it's the electronic equivalent of a kick me sign," I answered. He felt he had been wronged and was convinced he would be found innocent in the court of public opinion. The situation was unrecoverable. I should have kicked him off.

People were hiding out in an older conference that had been closed and abandoned and expressing their anger there. The conference came to be known as X. The first topic I saw when I stumbled into the place was called simply: *Fuck Phil*. One of the responses from that item:

63:22) Gabriel   **20-JAN-94 16:58**

I'm sick of this shit. He's just gonna come back and give us screenfuls of speeches telling us how to behave.

screenful after screenful after screenful after screenful after
screenful after screenful after screenful after screenful after
screenful after screenful after screenful after screenful after
screenful after screenful after screenful after screenful after
screenful after screenful after screenful after screenful after
screenful after screenful after screenful after screenful after
screenful after screenful after screenful after screenful after
screenful after screenful after screenful after screenful after
screenful after screenful after screenful after screenful after
screenful after screenful after screenful after screenful after
screenful after screenful after screenful after screenful after
screenful after screenful after screenful after screenful after
screenful after screenful after screenful after screenful after
screenful after screenful after screenful after screenful after
screenful after screenful after screenful after screenful after

screenful after screenful after screenful after screenful after
screenful after screenful after screenful after screenful after
screenful after screenful after screenful after screenful after
screenful after screenful after screenful after screenful after
screenful after screenful after screenful after screenful after
screenful after screenful after screenful after screenful after
screenful after screenful after screenful after screenful after
screenful after screenful after screenful after screenful after
screenful after screenful after screenful after screenful after
screenful after screenful after screenful after screenful after
screenful after screenful after screenful after screenful after
screenful after screenful after screenful after screenful after

(Paragraph break)

screenful after screenful after screenful after screenful after
screenful after screenful after screenful after screenful after
screenful after screenful after screenful after screenful after
screenful after screenful after screenful after screenful after
screenful after screenful after screenful after screenful after
screenful after screenful after screenful after screenful after
screenful after screenful after screenful after screenful after
screenful after screenful after screenful after screenful after
screenful after screenful after screenful after screenful after
screenful after screenful after screenful after screenful after
screenful after screenful after screenful after screenful after
screenful after screenful after screenful after screenful after
screenful after screenful after screenful after screenful after
screenful after screenful after screenful after screenful after
screenful after screenful after screenful after

(Little homily)

screenful after screenful after screenful after screenful after
screenful after screenful after screenful after screenful after
screenful after screenful after screenful after screenful after
screenful after screenful after screenful after screenful after

screenful after screenful after screenful after screenful after
screenful after screenful after screenful after screenful after
screenful after screenful after screenful after screenful after
screenful after screenful after screenful after screenful after
screenful after screenful after screenful after screenful after
screenful after screenful after screenful after screenful after
screenful after screenful after screenful after screenful after
screenful after screenful after screenful after screenful after
screenful after screenful after screenful after screenful after
screenful after screenful after screenful after screenful after
screenful after screenful after screenful after

(Self-deprecating joke to show us what a cool guy he is who can laugh at himself.)

screenful after screenful after screenful after screenful after
screenful after screenful after screenful after screenful after
screenful after screenful after screenful after screenful after
screenful after screenful after screenful after screenful after
screenful after screenful after screenful after screenful after
screenful after screenful after screenful after screenful after
screenful after screenful after screenful after screenful after
screenful after screenful after screenful after screenful after
screenful after screenful after screenful after screenful after
screenful after screenful after screenful after screenful after
screenful after screenful after screenful after screenful after
screenful after screenful after screenful after screenful after
screenful after screenful after screenful after screenful after
screenful after screenful after

(Paranoia)

screenful after screenful after screenful after screenful after
screenful after screenful after screenful after screenful after
screenful after screenful after screenful after screenful after
screenful after screenful after screenful after screenful after
screenful after screenful after screenful after screenful after

screenful after screenful after screenful after screenful after
screenful after screenful after screenful after screenful after
screenful after screenful after screenful after screenful after
screenful after screenful after screenful after screenful after
(Pointless accusatory self-analysis, eventually coming to the con-
clusion that it is all your fault for not being communicative enough.)
screenful after screenful after screenful after screenful after
screenful after screenful after screenful after screenful after
screenful after screenful after screenful after screenful after
screenful after screenful after screenful after screenful after
screenful after screenful after screenful after screenful after
screenful after screenful after screenful after screenful after
screenful after screenful after screenful after
AAARRRRRRGGGHHHHH!!!!!!!!!

Marianne Petit posted in Feedback:

"I think this is one of those instances where too much has
happened for 'resolution.' Too many very nice people have
been pushed to a point where they simply have no more
patience, no more tolerance."

Nick Scheer agreed:

"Phil, anyone with the slightest shred of dignity would not
encourage further discussion of this topic. They would have
quietly resigned from Echo many months ago. The only con-
ceivable reason I see for this lurid spectacle is that it provides
fodder for your persecution complex and serves as a forum to
exhibit your doomed attempt at online martyrdom."

Silverback complained that we were plotting against Phil.
Lizbet responded:

"There is no hidden conspiracy against Phil. We are not getting together in a private conference, via e-mail, telephone, or f-t-f, to endlessly discuss how to get Phil off of Echo. This is painful, ugly, and frustrating as hell to watch.

"This isn't 'mob rule.' It's a collection of disparate individuals who have experienced 'Phil behavior' in some degree or another. It may be a groundswell of public opinion. Those usually signify something worth listening to."

Silverback's reply:

" . . . don't think that I buy your lines of shit for a minute. If I can be of anyone's assistance in this matter email me. I will attempt to resolve this matter if there are interested parties."

From Daniela:

"Your offer to help is quickly becoming most uncivil. Thus, I fear your offer would not likely be helpful."

One night Phil left a ten-minute message on my machine which went something like this:

"Stacy, I've been really bad. I know I've been bad before but this time I've been really, really bad. Please call me. All those other times, even though they seemed bad, they weren't really bad but this time I've been really bad. I'm scared. Call me back please. I don't blame people now. I really went too far this time. This time I was truly bad. Please call me."

On and on it went. I was sure there was going to be a body at the end of it, but he never got to what the bad thing was. I still hear about him from time to time. A woman who ran a forum on CompuServe told me he telephoned the women there if they didn't respond to his email quickly enough. I'm ashamed to say that I never made a decision. I closed his account when he stopped paying his bill.

I hate kicking people off. It was agony each time and each time it happened they didn't want to go. "Be merciful, say 'death,' For exile hath more terror in his look, Much more than death" (From *Romeo and Juliet*. Romeo's response to banishment). A psychologist would probably be able to explain, but even though they continued to do precisely what they knew would get them booted, they were upset when it happened. Whatever the reason, they were every bit as attached to Echo as anyone. They always try to come back. After Mr. Normal's removal, a woman named "maria" opened an account. "Please let me into WIT," Maria asked. You know where this is going. It was Mr. Normal. We discovered this rather quickly, the super cybersleuths that we are, because "maria" logged in one day, YOed another woman on Echo, and said, "Hi! This is really Mr. Normal!" We changed the password. "Maria" wrote us asking to get her account reinstated and when I called her to talk to her about it I was told that she no longer worked at the number she had given us. I asked for Mr. Normal (using his real name of course) and was told he was not in at the moment. Would I like to leave a message? Snagged! I offered to post his response to being kicked off, and he sent us a note where he compared Echo to: Stalin's Soviet Union, Hussein's Iraq, Khomeini's Iran, Peron's Argentina, and Mao's China. He compared himself to: Dostoyevsky, Lenny Bruce, and Arnold Schwarzenegger. Uh-huh.

Mr. Happy cried when I closed his account, according to Mr. Smith. You have no feelings, he YOed, Mr. Happy has had a hard life. If it's gotten to the point where I've closed someone's account, it's too late for tears. Closing someone's account follows months and months of abuse. I'm like the Prince from *Romeo and Juliet* when he banished Romeo. "I will be deaf to pleading and excuses. Nor tears nor prayers shall purchase out abuses." Mr. Happy now says they laughed and toasted their banishment over beers. He still emails me from time to time. When I interviewed him for this book he gave me a long letter he had written shortly after being kicked off but never mailed. Fifty-nine pages of how he has the word, we missed our chance, and what a bunch of losers we all are. After Echo he was kicked off another service in New York and America Online. Phil also still writes us about getting back in. And he still hasn't paid his bill.

Euroman tried to open an account a year later and this was after a pretty dramatic parting gesture. When I changed Euroman's password, he didn't protest, he had found a new home on The WELL and he was busily replaying all my sins for the Wellbeings, who weren't having any luck figuring out just what those sins were either. It was essentially a duplication of what had happened on Echo with a few cultural differences in the reaction from the community. Our initial response was "fuck you" until we figured out he was nuts. Then we were kind. The WELL's initial response was to be kind. One Wellbeing offered to pray for him. Then, when they figured out he was nuts, FUCK YOU. Like us, they wondered if Euroman was, in fact, more than one person, or one personality.

It didn't end there. One month after changing his password, Euroman appeared at my door with two New York City policemen. The police were there to serve papers requesting my appearance at the Manhattan Mediation Center—Euroman had complained that I was harassing him! It had been many months since my brief encounter with him at P.S. 122, and I didn't recognize the small, nervous, sixtyish man standing behind the police. "Are you Euroman," I asked him. "Yes," he answered, without ever looking up. Sue, Josh, and I were dumbfounded. My lawyers looked into the matter, I called the detective from the Sixth precinct and she did her own checking. It turned out that he had not filed a complaint with the police. The Manhattan Mediation Center, where he filed his complaint, is a free service run by the city for settling disputes. They didn't know I had filed a complaint about him with the police (something they might want to put on their standard to-do list in the future). It's all strictly voluntary, I was under no obligation to attend. I declined. My lawyer then sent him a letter explaining that his account has been closed because he publicly posted his password, and in so many paragraphs, he was told to leave me alone.

Euroman continues to complain about me wherever he goes. He recently referred to me as a "nymph and a lady who is protected by ex-lovers." His description gives weight to the theory that he experienced my dismissal at our Virtual Culture Series like a rejected suitor. Thankfully, he has turned out to be crazy/harmless and not crazy/dangerous. So far. Last month he sat five feet away from me at our most recent Virtual Culture event and again we weren't sure if it was him. Josh Chu (Slacker) and I stared and stared, but for the life of us, we couldn't remember what Euroman looked like.

No one thinks about Mr. Happy, or Mr. Normal, or the others anymore. Okay. I still occasionally hear, "I miss Euroman," to this day. God we're shallow. But these periodic upheavals do have their entertaining side, I have to admit. *In some cases.* Mr. Happy seems rather tame now. Essentially they all used Echo to act out in ways they wouldn't dare to in person, or, in some cases, even on other online systems. Mr. Happy went straight to The WELL from Echo and not a single post about his bowel movements appeared there. Generally, if their names come up at all we don't talk about them, we explain what happened and I think we like to do this because we didn't know at the time. But we figured it out. Yeah, I may not have planned on what to do when the bad people came, but I got plenty of advice from the Echoids. Everyone has an opinion. Thank

God, because I didn't know what the Hell to do. Besides, it's not like I have any control over the Echoids, it's more like I'm in constant negotiation with them. What am I? President, owner, mayor, what? Anyway, it was all so new—we were making it up as we went along. Let's try this. Uh-uh, bad idea. How about this? Better. On Echo it was a mediation of our humanity—what we could and couldn't live with. There is a small-town demand for conformity here, it's true, but it is tempered by the fact that Echo is filled with typical New Yorkers and, once more, like most New Yorkers, we wouldn't be here if part of us didn't love the wack-jobs. So we do our best to gracefully accommodate people on (or over) the edge. This place is daily coauthored and created by the consensus of the sometimes glorious and generous and sometimes petty and mean-spirited community. In time we learned what kind of behavior online was beyond the pale and our experiences are not all that different from what is happening in other virtual communities. You'll find few places online that welcome spamming, harassment, or threats.

Incidentally, just in case you think we all live in happy agreement about these matters, there's always one person who thinks we should never kick anyone off no matter what. The last time someone expressed this view, Kevin Krooss posted, "If anyone misses him I suggest you get in touch with him and invite him over to your house and continue your conversations there." To the best of my knowledge, no one who has complained has ever invited Mr. Happy, Mr. Normal, Euroman, or Phil into their homes.

*   *   *

We will argue until the day we die about the power of words. Words. Action. Some desperately try to separate the two. "Sticks and stones," they say. As if the kind of pain that doesn't leave a mark is nothing and must be endured. The line between words and actions is not as clearly drawn as some long for it to be. This medium points that out more dramatically than any other. It has been and continues to be one of the most important struggles of the new virtual communities—trying to establish a balance between the right and need to express yourself and how to behave in a world of mostly text. Is it personal expression or art? Bad manners or harassment? It's ironic to me that writers of all people, when defending free speech, try to deny the power of words. "It's only words," I hear over and over. Only words? Like words are nothing? Just because we don't entirely understand the effects yet doesn't mean it's nothing. Cyberspace makes it as clear as day: sometimes words are expression *and* action. A pretty good rule of thumb I've found for cyberspace: If it's unacceptable "out there," it's generally unacceptable in here, and if someone is a jerk online, they're not going to turn out to be a perfectly decent person in person. What kind of person gets online anyway and starts harassing people just because they can? Not anyone I want to talk to.

I HATE MYSELF CONTINUED...

828:690) Singer   11-OCT-93 21:00

I hate myself because I, Singer, have gotten so fat that, were I a lady, it would be over.

828:703) Josh Karpf   12-OCT-93 22:52

I hate myself for not hanging in sports bars, possibly the only places where I could meet a woman who likes red meat. Or any kind of meat.

Till then, life will be an endless replay of "Yes, I'd LOVE the mixed vegetables!"

828:889) Josh Karpf   06-NOV-93 17:05

I hate myself for not pouring hot bacon grease down the little hole in the floor when the downstairs neighbor plays her piano.

828:891) SuZin   07-NOV-93 10:54

I hate myself for wanting Josh to come over to my house and pour hot bacon grease on the woman across the courtyard who has the worst "operatic" voice I have ever heard in my life.

404:28) Lana Tuna   26-FEB-95 13:39

I hate myself for giving a shit and I hate myself when I don't. There is no pleasing me, is there?

404:37) Miss Outer Boro 1991   27-FEB-95 7:55

I hate myself for having a messy apartment, for ordering the *NYTimes* and not reading it except the article about the Whitney Biennial, when I swore to myself I wouldn't pay attention to art any more, and I hate myself for getting a haircut partly so it would be more convenient to exercise, except ever since I got the haircut I've had the flu so there goes that idea, and I hate myself for only reading stupid books when I finally do make time to read, which I almost never do, and for being curt with my mother even though I love her, and for being mean <tm> to anyone, ever, even when they drive me crazy, because I should know by now that anybody who behaves strangely or nastily is only acting out their problems and I shouldn't let it get to me or cause me to be mean <tm>.

404:108) geekboy   28-FEB-95 23:31

I hate myself for not having Plan B.

404:112) Miss Outer Boro 1991   01-MAR-95 8:02

I hate myself for vague, yet pressing, reasons.

404:149) Jane Doe, Darling of the Phlegm Set   09-MAR-95 23:52

I don't hate myself right now.
Stay tuned, though.

404:173) Kitten/Cham/Prosciutto   15-MAR-95 10:16

I hate myself for metaphorically running away from big icky monstas, and kind of succeeding, but then tripping and falling and letting the big icky monstas catch up with me.
I hate myself for living the great B-movie of the psyche.

404:299) OpPhantom   23-MAR-95 13:37

While I had successfully suppressed my self-hate throughout most of this morning, it is Fucking Blooming right now.

404:300) Sit mir helfen vie a toiten bankis.   23-MAR-95 14:08

I hate myself for Never Learning <tm my mom>.

404:304) Neandergal   23-MAR-95 18:00

I hate myself but I'm too tired to remember why.
Oh, I think it has something to do with thoughts and feelings.

404:319) False Bottomer   24-MAR-95 11:13

I hate myself because if I don't hurry up, I won't get all the hate in before I die.

404:439) Was it good for Jew?   18-APR-95 8:53

I hate myself. I haven't made enough money in the last three weeks even to cover my child support, much less all my other expenses, and this at a time when I am in court with my ex over visitation and custody issues. I have some stuff I wrote which editor pals of mine say might even be publishable and I can't even get up the nerve to submit them to someone. I live in a dream world. I live in a world of blase entitlement. I'm too proud to go out and get a burger-flipping job, which is what would really suit a fuckin loosah high-school dropout with no Curriculum Vitae and no prospects. I hate my fuckin guts, and you have permission to shoot me. Oh, yeah, and I'm a fat fuck, too, but does that stop me from eating fatty brisket by the quarter ton?

404:444) Neandergal   18-APR-95 15:24

I hate myself for not being able to get things together properly and being ver' ver' confused.
I hate myself for thinking taking care of a two-year-old is a job,

when clearly all the Career Gals out there balance family AND career. I hate myself for using the child as an excuse, when in fact I was a Career Loser before he was even born.
And eating too much and stuff.

404:472) Jane Doe 24-APR-95 22:12
I hate myself.
I hate myself.
I hate myself.
I hate Derrida.
I hate myself.

404:645) SuZin 03-MAY-95 15:01
I hate myself for seeking out people with George Costanza-like qualities because they are entertaining.

404:682) Batwerdlechamdoofus 04-MAY-95 20:47
I hate myself in a general purpose, blanket-bombing sort of way. Tomorrow, I may hate myself in strategic strikes.

404:843) Alice, Part of A Complete Breakfast. 18-MAY-95 23:30
I hate myself because when the cashier at Coliseum said "Enjoy the book!", I chirped, "You too!"

404:874) SuZin 19-MAY-95 13:25
I hate myself for spilling duck sauce on a spot uncomfortably close to the fly of my jeans.

404:875) Trash 19-MAY-95 13:35
I hate myself for not getting the "A" chocolate and deciding to get Oreos instead.

404:878) Yooey & hugh's army   19-MAY-95 15:19

IHM for not being as good as Jaco Pastorius was in bed.

404:879) ragged paul   19-MAY-95 15:40

IHM for not even knowing who Jaco Pastorius was.

404:882) neandergal   19-MAY-95 17:32

I hate myself for knowing that JP was a famous madrigal composer.

I hate myself for buying a Big Organ when I can't even afford to pay the Con Ed bill.

I hate myself for believing that I can light candles and hold High Mass in my apartment and am above electricity.

404:912) SuZin   21-MAY-95 9:34

I hate myself for staying in bed after my radio came on this morning because I wanted to listen to "Wouldn't It Be Nice" and "Build Me Up Buttercup."

ECHO POLL

Source: From an online survey of 209 members of Echo, October, 1995.

Margin of Error: Well, let's look back at the answers to the lying question.

Have you said things on Echo you wouldn't say to anyone or only to your closest friends?

42% said yes.

ECHO POLL

Source: From an online survey of 228 members of Echo, February 1996.

Margin of Error: Bad typing skills should figure into this.

If I ever see <fill in the blank> I'm leaving!

16% said ads.
7% said censorship.
7% said Newt Gingrich.
5% said my parents.
3 people said God, Pia Zadora, or Yanni.

WHO LET THE NAZI IN?

I met Parzival at the Art Bar. Perfectly nice fellow. This was before he started ranting about the Jewish sickness that was infecting us all. No, he'd been on Echo a couple of years before that came out. At this point he was still just some quiet schleppy looking guy I didn't know much about and who did his best to be liked. I read that he had donated books to the East Harlem school where Echoid Carolyn Hahn worked. When he learned that I used to work at Mobil and loved gas station memorabilia, he sent me reproductions of two 1950s gas station signs. One was from Texaco, and the other was from Sinclair. The Sinclair sign had a picture of that green dinosaur they always used to use, Dino I think he was called. I remember they had a big, huge Dino at the 1964 World's Fair. I was there. I was eight at the time and I will never forget how I felt. I walked around after my mother in stunned joy. I wanted one of the hats with the long pink feathers that my older cousins Chris and Barbara bought and wore, pirate-like, all over the fair. The signs Parzival mailed to me brought me back to one of the better memories from my childhood and I was grateful. I loved them. I planned to hang them up if I ever got Echo out of my stupid apartment.

Then: Jews are selfish, materialistic, and devious. This is what he told us. And they are way too sensitive to criticism about it, he added. We have all been conned into believing the Holocaust is unique by Jewish propaganda when the only thing singular about the Holocaust is that the survivors are media savvy. There is a lot of truth buried in anti-Semitic writing. We know it. We just won't admit it.

The second we hit cyberspace, the struggle of free speech was resumed. When you give people a place to talk, sooner or later they will argue about what they can or cannot say. Once more we were faced with a problem that forced us to examine what kind of place we were. Is this a real community? And if it is, what kind? The kind that welcomes Nazis? I talked about the idea that cyberspace isn't real because people can always simply turn off the computer—they don't have to stay when the going gets tough. Except they do. On Echo, when we had to decide on a policy about hate speech, they called and participated more than ever before. They didn't have to stay and resolve the conflict. They stayed because they wanted to work it out. (Okay, they probably stayed for other, less noble reasons, like they can't resist a little virtual bloodshed. But that only makes cyberspace even more just like anyplace else.)

Parzival, whom I think of as the Mr. Normal of anti-Semitism, gets his name from Arthurian legend. Parzival (aka Parsifal or Percival or Galahad) is the pure knight who saves King Arthur and the kingdom when he finds the Holy Grail. Marian, one of our hosts, tells me that neo-Nazis love grail mythology. They see themselves as heroes, God help us. I keep seeing the Percival from *Excalibur,* the John Boorman film based on the same story. The actor Paul Geoffrey portrayed him as this lovable, innocent galoot.

That's how I'll always see him. How could anyone with so much hate identify with that? The Parzival on Echo longed for the return of National Socialism. His time. The time where he could play the role of the White Knight and rescue modern society from the Black Knight of "Jewishness." It was coming, he told us. Once again, someone had the truth and we had The Fear.

I knew what I wanted to do about hate speech, but in November 1991, I threw it out to the Echoids. You decide, I told them. Bruce Schechter posted: "The only remedy for bad speech is good speech. A community, especially one the size of Echo, should be self-censoring. This is not a crowd to let hateful or thoughtless comments slide, as has been shown many times in the past." The rest of the Echoids agreed. "I'd rather know than not know about someone's bigotry," Margaret Segall added. There was not one dissenting opinion: We will not censor hate speech. "Sunlight is the best disinfectant," a supreme court justice once said. I remember thinking, "Phew. That was close." I did not want to get into what people could and couldn't say.

It's one thing to make this decision when hate speech was extremely rare. Before Parzival, there was one truth about bigots on Echo and that was: bigots huff. Now we had someone who wasn't going anywhere. He was in our face, day in and day out getting nostalgic for the sound of marching boots and ranting about the "immoral aspect of what Jews do and how they conduct themselves in society" in a discussion about the Roman Catholic church. Now what?

In November 1995, exactly four years after the Echoids decided they didn't want to censor hate speech, things changed. Echo had a Nazi, and Visigoth, aka Doug Cooper, an Echo regular, decided enough was enough.

"I propose that this BBS act to rid itself of its resident Nazi.
"I am posting this in the 'Censorship' item, simply to draw

attention to what it is that I am not about to propose: that is, censorship, as it is classically defined. It is not censorship for a publisher to refuse to publish a certain author. The First Amendment does not protect a writer whose manuscript is turned down, for instance, by Knopf; he or she can always take it elsewhere.

"I think it's time Echo revoked Parzival's account. He is, by his own admission, a National Socialist. He posts routinely in defense of Hitler and the Third Reich. Given that a vast majority of Echoids are Jewish, black, or gay, what this means—in blunt terms—is that Parzival would like to see them, and their families, thrown into the ovens.

"By permitting Parzival to continue to use Echo, we are giving him a platform for his views. It is by no means our responsibility to do so. Like Knopf, or Random House, it is entirely within our rights to say: post your words elsewhere.

"He can always take his enthusiasms to Usenet. Or AOL. Clearly, he might not enjoy posting there as much as he does on Echo, where his words are guaranteed to cause maximal outrage and pain, but again: I do not think it is our responsibility to provide entertainment to this Nazi.

"I understand that what I am proposing will make liberals—I am one, by the way—nervous. And I welcome the thoughts of others on this matter. But, given the current geopolitical situation, I think we all have to think hard about whether we want to offer a platform, and community, to the Parzivals of this world.

"It would be censorship if the state were to step in and regulate what can and cannot be said on our BBS. As you well know, many politicians are suggesting precisely this kind of intervention. An alternative to censorship is to demonstrate that we ourselves, as a responsible community, can take care of such matters. If someone were uploading pedophilic GIFs, for instance, we'd have no trouble asking him or her to leave.

"I suggest that Parzival is considerably more evil than your average pedophile. It is time we asked him to go elsewhere."

As of this writing, 1,015 posts have been made in response to Visigoth's proposal. Six people publicly supported the idea; two people seemed to like the idea with misgivings; and two more expressed support privately.

I was torn. Part of me also wanted him off. Nazis were not part of the plan. I never thought, Now! How can I make this place more welcoming to Nazis? I didn't want to deal with it. And it just seemed unspeakably insensitive to the members of the community to keep him around. Echo is a local New York service. It's packed with Jews. Parzival once joked that he thought of New York as Jew York. Funny guy. On the other hand, Parzival was also the biggest traffic accident we had ever seen and I wanted to look at it. Was there a safe distance anywhere in the world, anywhere on Echo, to peer into the head of a Nazi? And what is the best method of combating hate and bigotry? Repression or the light of day? I certainly didn't know. No one on earth can answer these questions definitively. It was Embraceable Ewe all over again. I had to make a decision without facts or wisdom or experience.

Our first hint that there was something wrong with our buddy Parzival came one summer evening when we announced that we had invited AIDS activist Jim Fouratt to be our guest for a live chat. Parzival's response: Jim Fouratt is a faggot who is lucky he didn't die from AIDS. The summer of 1995, the summer Berg had dubbed: The Summer That Will Not Suck, also became the summer our Nazi made himself known.

When people objected to his comments about Fouratt, Parzival cried that he was guaranteed his right to refer to people any way he wanted to by the United States Constitution. He could have said worse, he assured us. Asterix responded, "And I'm sure we're all very, very grateful to you for not sharing with us the 'more descriptive words' that you might have used, you First Amendment crusader, you." Asterix is one of the cigar-smoking softball players I mentioned in an earlier chapter. He has to play infield because he's a little nearsighted. Jack Taylor, aka The Strange Apparatus, and cohost of the conference where these comments were made, stepped in with, "Please try to drop your personal bigotry at the door to this conference. This is not a publicly-owned medium; I am not the government; and your right to unlimited speech in this conference is only guaranteed by your decorum." Then he opened an item titled: *Freely Speaking About Civility & Censorship.*

Jae Cen was amused at our distress over Parzival's post about Jim Fouratt. Lonesome Drifter asked him, "Jae, would you prefer that remarks about 'lucky faggots who didn't die of AIDS' become part of the normal order of discourse around here—accepted without a ripple by the community because after all, it's only words?"

Parzival refused to apologize and Jack stepped in again. "Offensive posting for its own sake is only intended to injure the feelings of others. When it comes wrapped in a flag, and delivered on a First Amendment platter, it's intellectual fraud if it can't be responded to in kind. I'd hardly call the result useful, much less adult debate. While this conference invites spirited arguments from all sides, let's keep it clear of invective."

Parzival promised to post with the "express intent of offending you all." "Could you moon us while you're at it?" Molly Ker asked.

Parzival's answer:

" . . . how about a nice burning cross?"

IN HOC SIGNO VINCE

(Which translates to: In this sign, conquer. "By the way, it's 'In hoc signo vinces,'" Michael Peck corrected him. "I'm dyslexic," Parzival responded.)

Then it all came out in Politics. Out of nowhere he started talking about "Jewish sickness" and the "eternal Jew" in an item about social class, Margaret Segall, the host of Politics told us immediately in the private conference for hosts. Our virtual jaws collectively dropped. "What the fuck . . . ?" Since we had decided not to ban hate speech I didn't even consider removing his comments, but I wanted to contain them. At our request, Parzival opened a separate item and called it: *National Socialism, Beyond Hate and Race.* That way, people who did not wish to read the things he was saying could avoid the discussion altogether. The Echoids responded with anger, heart, and humor. From Guru Stu: "Perhaps we can stop the spread of Jewishness if we take Seinfeld off television?"

Parzival explained that he didn't have a problem with Jews per se, but with Jewishness, and that, he told us, could be possessed by anyone. That was one of the mistakes the Nazis had made, he went on. The problem wasn't with National Socialism but with how it was applied.

Nottinghill: "A rational discussion of National Socialism is one thing and I think the notion of German policy during WWII as a crazy aberration is a dangerous one. However, since that's the case—we all agree with that—it still doesn't have anything to do with Parzival's ugly anti-Semitic posts which brought this discussion on.

"If it's all so human and understandable, why engage in those vile little rants. No discussion of comparative historical theory diminishes those remarks which he hasn't apologized for and continue to rankle me."

Slag me: " . . . you have to understand that when somebody calls Jews 'media-savvy,' it's like calling blacks 'musical' or calling Russians lazy or calling Germans obsessed with order or calling Muslims fanatical or calling Irish dumb. It's a description of the group which has in the past been linked to attempts to exterminate us. So if people call you an anti-Semite when you say that, don't respond that you're only speaking the truth as you see it. You ought to know that you're saying something your audience regards as vicious and insulting; anyone of genuinely good will ought to be able to get their point across without saying those sorts of things."

Words and action. Parzival complained that our responses were liberal claptrap and Jewish propaganda and that we were violating his rights. "It is the liberal interpretation of the rights of Echoids which has allowed your belligerent and nasty racist garbage to continue to exist at all here," Luce snapped back. The Echoids struggled to find the proper response.

Ike Nahem: "The response to Parzi should be anger and fighting determination not pain and hurt."

Nottinghill: "To say you feel pain and hurt doesn't preclude anger and a fighting spirit. I said that because I sometimes get the impression that when people say ugly things, because they have depersonalized the object of their hate, they don't realize the plain, straightforward human reaction it might produce.

"What all you theoreticians of the left and right tend to forget a lot of the time is that much of human activity has a lot to do with that yucky stuff called emotions and it doesn't hurt to inject that into a discussion every once in a while. And I really don't like being told what a correct response to something is. This item is making unpleasant people out of us all."

After all the racist slurs, a tiny virtual gesture brought it home for me. Parzival posted a long, endless invective and broke it up with "Hi Janet's," an old Echo custom.

I'll explain. It's hard to read text on a computer. If you're saying something that goes beyond one screenful, it helps to break the text up into smaller pieces instead of posting it as one long block. Longtime Echoid Janet Tingey, whom I can't see without remembering her dancing on a platform in a short black leather skirt as one of the go-go girls at Phiber's going away party, frequently posted that she simply would not read beyond a screenful unless you broke up the text. People did not like being ignored by the lovely Ms. Tingey. One night, soon after, someone broke up a long post with a blank line, then a "Hi Janet" on a line all by itself, then another blank line and on with more text. It made it genuinely easier to read. Soon we were all breaking up longer text like this.

Hi Janet!

It became a tradition. (Then there's Neandergal's version: *"Hi Janet, how the fuck are you?"*) We called it the Tingey 10 because Janet claimed she wouldn't read beyond ten lines. To see something as sweet and as intimate as Hi Janet, and so personal—it was ours—sprinkled throughout the twisted ruin of Parzival's heart! It was like watching Janet herself being trapped and used to voice his hate. Their time will come, he warns us. He insists on the error of our liberal, Jewish ways. He shall "fight all people who do not and cannot embrace the romantic principles of NS [National Socialism]." National Socialism is " . . . something deeper, truer and higher calling on one's soul. It is a battle with the forces of evil and nothing will change that." He really does see himself as the lone, brave Knight on Echo. " . . . rest assured I am not alone and I do believe that time will vindicate us and restore what has been lost." *Hi Janet.*

Three weeks later the item was frozen. Iced. No more responses could be added. Everyone agreed, Parzival included, that the conversation had run its course. Every participant had their say, they were just repeating themselves now. Margaret then called for a policy banning hate speech. "No," I told her. We tried to draft a policy about hate speech at one point, as a result of some other, less dramatic bigot, and we had to give up. Try it: Define hate speech. If the definition is too broad you choke the place. For instance, a few Echoids were going after the Catholic church with a sledgehammer in the Culture Conference. These were former Catholics who had strong feelings about their treatment by the church. Sure it's rough, but shouldn't they be allowed to voice their resentment? If it's too narrow though, such as specifically banning anti-Semitic but not anti-Catholic remarks, people might quite rightly complain that the policy is biased. "Oh, so it's okay to bash Catholics?" Is all hate evil? "Ban hate speech in your conference, if you like," was my response. Individual hosts can set any restrictions they like within their own conferences. If Margaret didn't want hate speech there, I would support her and find another place for it. After the item was frozen, Parzival was quiet for the most part, but he still made an anti-Semitic remark here and there.

Not good enough said Visigoth and a few other Echoids.

Remove him. We don't want to be in the same place with the likes of him.

Then we really had it out. The thing to remember is—like the cop in New Orleans who wondered how two grown men could fight to the death over a string of cheap Mardi Gras beads—this isn't just about the beads. There is subtext to every human exchange and especially among people who have been sharing their lives for years.

Even a topic as straightforward as *Are Nazis welcome on Echo* is about more than Nazis. Hell, if only it could be a debate over ideas. That would give us less to think about, less to have to understand. A lot of people argue that we can only address the ideas, such as Nazis, because we can never know all the subtext. I say if you pretend that it's just about ideas you'll never stop arguing. Just because we can't understand it all doesn't mean we shouldn't make an attempt to understand it better. You can't separate people from their ideas. It is by understanding people that you get to the ideas.

The struggle over the right thing to do about our Nazi was also a struggle about the place and ourselves: how we felt and related to it and each other and how we resolve a difficult conflict. It really is about that as much as it is about the source of conflict itself. Every place that has people in it, cyber or otherwise, is continually defining itself through its conflicts. Who are we, what is this place, and what will we tolerate? The subtext, our relationships with each other—it all factors in. But it's almost impossible, when you are in the thick of it, to realize that people aren't exclusively reacting to what you are saying, they are also responding to *you*. Also, people tend to agree with and support their friends, and fight the people they dislike on every point. We can't always know the subtext (but as good hosts we do pay attention to the lives of our guests), but awareness of the fact that this is part of the conflict helps you from continually banging your head against the brick wall of content.

In cyberspace, where words rule, the question of what you can say takes on greater urgency. The question is reintroduced relentlessly, everywhere. And it will never stop. We will always have to revisit this issue because people don't listen to each other and they rarely agree. I've reproduced part of the battle over our Nazi here. A very small part. The entire discussion took up hundreds of pages. What can I tell you? You've been to PTA meetings, or any kind of community board meeting, family meetings, what have you. It's all the same. People feel as strongly here as they do elsewhere. The conversation was long, sometimes inflamed, sometimes tender. People took sides, fights broke out, people were misunderstood or understood all too well. It was a long, hard summer for us. When you care, it's never easy to resolve these things. So here is what some of us had to say that one particular summer about one particular neighbor, our Nazi.

Some began by laying out the issues. Goat Noise said, "Disallowing Nazis on Echo would be a symbolic gesture, a declaration of the managements values," but " . . . there is the argument in favor of dialogue as the real work. And then there is the 'know your enemy' notion . . . " Mono added: " . . . the question is: are there things outside the realm of human decency. For me, Naziism is." Then Marian posted:

> "For me the measure of safety and community on this BBS is:
>
> "1) The Echo civility standard. No, you cannot post 'I want to see your mongrel baby roast over a spit,' or any other brutal verbal attack.
>
> "2) The Echo community rise to my defense when somebody says something intolerable.
>
> "Pleaser [Parzival's login id] with no rebuttal—with a lazy tolerance by the community—that would scare me off this board.
>
> "But if we start pulling the ticket of all the people who are

offensive in their sincerely held convictions—I'm not sure
where that stops.

"This puts more pressure on the well-meaning Goth . . . to
hunt, refute and set himself off from the Pleasers where he
finds him. But it's not the Pleasers who make me run.

"It's the Goths who make me stay."

Then they came up against the same problem I had when I
tried to craft a policy about hate speech. Where do you begin?

Jojo: "Why is anti-semitism worse than killing fags? Is it just
because fags are worse than Jews? Why get so incredibly operatic
about Parzival, when it's clear that anti-semitism as a political
stance has zero chances of success here. Why go on and on and
on about his inflammatory and 'dangerous' presence when it's
clear that politically more Echoids are in danger of falling to official
and unofficial anti-queer pogroms, such as those praised by the
Church and neo-cons like Podhoretz?"

Lazy J. Cooley: "You know something? It's this debate, it's seeing so
many people willing to get rid of this person because he destroys
our happy comfortable environment, that makes me want to leave
Echo. This is most definitely not Stacy's living room, it's a public
space. Does Stacy ask people's beliefs before handing out Echo
accounts? Then it is a semi-public space, and we've all joined it
because of that. There's a lot of people here who make me sick. We
all disagree on stuff. But we want to make a special case out of
Parz. Because he spouts stuff that's in a special category of hate-
fulness. Oh! and also! Some of us want to sound like we hate Nazi's
more than the rest of us because we're MADDER than the rest of
us! Bullshit, bullshit, bullshit. I don't want to be online at a fucking
country club where people don't have to be made uncomfortable or
angry. If you don't understand the chilling effect of violating free

speech, you are far more frightening to me than Parzival. And if you see one of his anti-Jewish posts and get a sick angry feeling, you can rant right back at him. Or you can come in here and agitate to get rid of him because he makes you angry and uncomfortable. Well, that's the world. Toni once posted that she heard anti-Semitic remarks at a coffee shop near her home. She was angry and uncomfortable, and shouted at them. If it's out there, it's in here. Go ahead, work to create your little online world that gives you that warm fuzzy feeling all over."

And where do you stop? Someone says kicking him off will make us as bad as the Nazis. Edward Hutchinson, aka The Lonesome Drifter, disagreed.

The Lonesome Drifter: "The 'Watch lest ye become what ye hate' argument seems to me based on a type of mysticism, at least insofar as it's being applied to this issue. It's a premature rush to absolutes. Maybe—though I don't believe it—there exists some transcendental cosmic karmic accounting house where all divergences from the ideal of nonjudgmental omnibenevolence are toted up and found equal, but practically speaking, in this lifetime, I see no likelihood that one who starts out doing his or her small part to make their communities inhospitable to Nazis is going to end up engineering the murder of six million in gas chambers."

Then Marian asked the question we should have asked before we asked any other. Why didn't we ask this question first? What took us so long to get to the heart of the matter?

Marian: "Okay, now I am curious. Pleaser [Parizival]—you've been a member of this community for quite a while now. What does the fact that you have clearly upset and hurt so many other community members suggest to you? Do you think they should get out of the kitchen? Do you think you should be more careful about casually dropping your more incendiary opinions?

"Do you care about our feelings at all?"

While he said that he did not join Echo specifically to offend anyone, nothing in his response indicated that he did, in fact, care about our feelings at all. The Echoids argued whether feelings should even be considered. Feelings are tricky. Others wondered what else there was to consider.

Topper: "Ideals are nice. Support free speech. Invite anyone you like here. But this place isn't so much about Free Speech as it is about socializing. And somehow socializing isn't so much fun when I know that the person I'm socializing with is a Nazi. It makes me feel bad. It makes me think about things I don't want to think about. Yes. There's something wrong with me. I'm not able to overcome my feelings. When I come home dead tired and beat from work, I'm not sure that I have enough energy to be vigilant and post against views I see as despicable. (Are viewpoints 'dangerous?' History has shown that some ARE!)

"Well, maybe what it all comes down to, is I'm just not the type of person suitable for a BBS system because sometimes I just can't measure up to the Goodness & Tolerance necessary to stay. So what usually happens: the 'nazis' stay and people like me leave.

"I had stopped reading this thread because it was clear that all the 'free speech' people cared about Parzival and his rights to be here. But few of those same people cared for my rights.

"So for those people I would ask: Whose rights are more RIGHT?

"Maybe it's because mine are tied up with feelings. That's too girly for this board, ain't it? Let's only respond to words written on a screen. Logic is good. Feelings are bad."

Jane Doe: "Garbled Uplink had told me that I wasn't taking up the 'challenge' of dealing with speech I find abhorrent. Perhaps that which doesn't kill me will make me stronger in the long run. But in the meantime, I spend my valuable hours surviving (or fighting for my right to exist) rather than thriving.

"Combatting this kind of hatred extracts a higher price emotionally from some people than it does others. I think people should be able to at least articulate that much in this forum, and not be told to 'get over it,' or be pistol-whipped with the metaphysics of the First Amendment."

The Lonesome Drifter: "If there were another member whose favored scapegoats were not Jews but African-Americans, and who persisted in dropping little zingers in this conference or that, indicating his allegiance to the Klan and his contempt for 'niggers,' or, excuse me, 'niggerishness,' then yeah, I think it would be appropriate to at least take up the question of what he thinks he's contributing to the community here and whether the community wants to continue accepting the gift."

Once again the wack-jobs forced us to examine what we had and what we could live with. This is how communities are formed—not by creating a place and putting out a welcome sign. They are formed and strengthened through the resolution of conflict. You could say the heart of a community can be found in these conflicts—the struggle, the outcome, what is created, *is* the community. It's tremendously satisfying when the Echoids manage to work something like this out. You know how you feel after successfully getting through a terrible fight with a good friend? You're closer. The fight gave you history. You went to Hell and back together and you're still friends, you're still here. That is what is at the end of each of our Big Things: the bond that comes from working something out that almost tore you apart.

Eric A. Hochman: "To those who have said it's not fun reading or posting in this item: It's not fun for me either; in fact it has required a lot of time and thought, and has been rather draining. But I'm in it, because I feel the principles behind this discussion are important, both in themselves, and in defining what Echo is. We're not an oasis from controversy, and I doubt that we can be without making online life really, really, boring."

Senor Voce: "It gives us a rare opportunity to see and examine who we really are. Sometimes it's a very unpleasant task."

Alto Artist: "That we're a community without a definition, that we can evolve our own definition, is a rare and exciting thing. We couldn't do so without this kind of difficult discourse."

Can we negotiate a fair and civil response? You've been to those PTA meetings, or co-op board meetings, or any other meeting where people who don't necessarily have a lot in common try to resolve even relatively simple issues. Try free speech. We can't even agree as a country about this issue. However, one idea kept returning throughout the discussion. From Visigoth: "If we had a Holocaust survivor on Echo, I think it would be very easy to demonstrate how each Nazi post constitutes a direct personal assault." And Maggot Boy: "I think that one of the reasons that people may be upset is that they feel that they have been personally attacked by Parzival by his generalizations about groups that they are a part of." And David Green: "Echo has adopted one restraint on Free Speech, and of course, that is the 'no personal attacks' rule. However, one alleged Nazi has so far maligned Jews under the cover of 'political speech.' I believe quite strongly, that those statements are as close as one can get to a 'personal attack.'" Others suggested leaving it as it was—let the hosts decide if hate speech is or is not acceptable in their individual conferences.

Now what? Everyone had valid points, arguments for each position were compelling; the time had come for me to make a decision. A single response to a range of issues in a place like Echo, which has such a variety of voices. A single policy that will suit everyone and every occasion. Come on, Stacy. We're all waiting. And one of us is a Nazi who doesn't like your liberal, Jew-loving ways.

We revised our policy concerning personal attacks.

Echo believes in freedom of expression. However, personal attacks are not acceptable behavior on Echo. Remember: discuss the idea, not the person. Similarly, attacks on groups of persons based on such persons' race, sex, ethnicity, religious beliefs or sexual orientation are not acceptable. Repeated attacks may lead to the user being placed on read-only status, or, in extreme cases, the closure of your account.

This was going to get me into trouble. The no personal attack rule had always been problematic. It's an imperfect solution. Sometimes we attack. Sometimes it's called for. I'm not convinced that repression is the best response to hate speech. This policy did, however, allow Parzival to continue to sing the praises of National Socialism, he just had to do it without reference to "Jewish sickness." Like the personal attack policy, he still could, in so many words, say fuck you to all the Jews everywhere if that was what was in his sick, sick heart, but now he had to explain just what he meant when he made an attack. He had to think first. And I didn't think he could. We have yet to hear what "Jewish sickness" means and that's because he can't explain it. And because he can't, he hasn't brought it up since. I know some people may not like the fact that he is still here, and that he and other Nazis can still open topics praising the Third Reich, but it covers us for the people in the future who may say horrifying or frightening things that we don't want to or shouldn't censor. It's compromise that gives us a measure of civility that protects both ideas and community.

So we didn't kick him off. And it didn't kill us. The struggle that a society goes through as it defines itself is a painful, and frequently heartbreaking, one. A virtual community doesn't get to short-cut this process. I can't guarantee people's Echo experiences will always be wonderful. Life is not always wonderful. And Echo doesn't happen outside of life. This is what we went through that summer. But it wasn't the only thing. If it was, we would never have survived the season. Why would anyone go through such a difficult struggle if it offered nothing but heartache?

Why don't people hang up the phone or turn off the computer when they can? Because, while we were fighting heat and the worst hate we could imagine, we still managed to get through the business of day-to-day living and find joy in our virtual community. The Summer That Will Not Suck, the summer of our Nazi, and the summer of the worst heat wave in years, where the temperature routinely broke one hundred degrees and made the already humid, sultry, New York City sometimes unbearable—as Parzival made Echo sometimes unbearable—was all over the map in activity. This is Echo and this is cyberspace. It's life. Where you can battle hate and ignorance and still find grace in a poker game. So we didn't hang up the phone when we could. We stayed online and fought to define and preserve this place because it was something worth fighting for.

But we weren't fighting for Nazis. We were fighting for this:

After being turned down two summers in a row, one of KZ's paintings was selected for the Boca Museum of Art's All-Florida juried exhibition.

Liz L., Perpetual Dawn, Bottomer, and Neander and their son Max, watched fireworks from the U.N. Terrace rooftop of a friend of Marian's, an Echoid who lives outside New York.

The Strange Apparatus got a new job, a kamaka ukulele, and partied at Jane Doe's home on Nantucket with MP, MP's fiancé Renee, and MoNo. They ate, drank far too much, and declared MP to be "The Beach Master."

Shrink moved back to New York from North Dakota, but she sent her cats home first. Elkay picked them up at Laguardia and dropped them off at Carolindas', who took care of them for two weeks until Shrink arrived and found a place to live.

We went to the Mermaid Parade at Coney Island and Jackie Blue posted, "Coney Island is one of the most wonderful places on this earth. I'm so happy I was raised there and consider it home." Neander said, "My mother and my first analyst were raised there, so I consider it my ancestral home."

Garbled Uplink and his wife Yankee Roses' dog Zac died. He was six years old.

Joro put the finishing touches on a CD-ROM version of the movie *The Blob*. He worked with the movie's original producer, Jack Harris, and Joro was Ed Wood to Jack's Bela Lugosi.

The softball players argued the merits of weeknights vs. weekends and Berg posted, "It's become a Sunday tradition, and a good way to fight the Sunday-is-the-lamest-day blues." They decided to stick with Sundays.

Maggot Boy went to get a permit to play ball and was told that *"The Conan O'Brien Show* has the permit for 12–5." The permit guy said that they haven't paid yet and that if they don't we can have it.

They decided to show up and play anyway, and Null posted, "There were two fields; one was filled with little kids, the other was filled with us. If it comes to it, I say we let the kids and the Conan O'Brien folks fight to the death for the remaining field."

When someone said that Molly Ker volunteered to ump, she responded, "This is in fact a gross misrepresentation of what actually happened; he and Spingo told me that if I didn't 'volunteer,' they'd strap me to the bar at the Art Bar and pour Glenlivet down my throat until my eyes turned blue. If the consensus is that we need an ump, I'm happy to do it as long as I don't get excessive lip from anyone who disagrees with me. I also want a tiara with rubies that spell out Queen Molly."

On June 25, after scoring the home run that won the game, Steve Berg whirled around and whacked himself in the knee, dislocating it and thereby forcing him to take up two seats at the movies for the rest of the summer.

Susanb immediately posted in an effort to assure her monthly poker game guests: "I would like to add for the record that no one has ever dislocated a knee at the Echo poker game."

Lana Tuna brought salad to every poker game that summer except one.

Tonik had to miss the August poker game because her grandmother died.

Marisa Bowe, aka Miss Outer Boro, didn't see the light of sweltering day while she worked 100-hour weeks to get *WORD Magazine* out on the World Wide Web.

Coyote and Fourway Flytrap got a new puppy named Jesse, who later peed on the carpets of Echo's brand-new office, but we forgave her.

SuZin spent two days in the mountains with a friend from the office who "can only be described as a jewel." She also got a new job and became secretly engaged to a chemist from Ohio. He's not an Echoid but we forgave her.

Girl Next Door and Squeaking Cat met on Echo, fell in love, got married, and moved in together all in the space of that one summer.

Nottinghill fell in love for the first time in twenty years. She was also "professionally disgraced but financially rewarded beyond my wildest dreams" when she was hired to produce the BBC's weekly coverage of the O.J. trial.

Pavia got a love letter via registered mail. "Life is better than good; it's grand," she said. "You're like a lady in white gloves at a tea party in an asylum," MG Lord told her.

Oh, let's just call it the Echo Summer of Love, shall we? Jackie Blue went to an Echo softball game and fell in love with Jaguar, aka Ivan Nahem, even though he is bald and she doesn't normally go for bald guys, she told us.

On the second anniversary of Clem's mother's death, Spingo, who had also lost a parent, invited Clem over after midnight, where they drank and told stories until dawn.

"*Central Park West* is taking over my block for filming," Spingo told us. "I wrote FUCK OFF TV SCUM on the flyer announcing this in my lobby."

Camel passed the bar.

Chow Bella and Jaze cooked filet mignon and crème brûlée on the "record-breaking, hottest day of the year in July" without an air-conditioner.

Tank Grrrl quit smoking.

We all watched *Casablanca* in Bryant Park, behind the New York Public Library, on a very, very small patch of cement, and we sweated the whole time.

Oshma won a trip to Jerusalem on a game show called *Inspiration Please* by correctly answering this question: What country was the current Pope born in? Oshma swears there were other, much harder questions.

Bite the Wax Godhead's wife Cynthia had some trouble in the third and fourth months of her pregnancy. (The new baby is fine!)

Amy R. graduated from law school.

Phiber Optik's mother sent a birthday prayer to his ex-girlfriend, Cafephreak.

Oedipa woke up at 7 A.M. for two months straight and walked the streets before it got too hot. In July he became the poster boy for bisexuality when his face appeared on the cover of *Newsweek*. His grandmother was not thrilled.

Alice, Part of A Complete Breakfast, posted:

"I bought a Frozen Lemonade today from a vendor, and I asked for a spoon.

"He held up a straw and he said, 'Spoony Straw!'
"And so it was.
"How could life NOT be good,
   with spoony straws in the world?"

Marianne received the following note from one of her young students:

I love you so much
you are so beautiful to me
I see and I hope that you see you are the bester
teacher I had.

Slacker, aka Josh Chu, spent his last summer as a nonparent. He also took a deep paycut to come and work for me.

Jerry Garcia died. Some Echoids mourned, most made jokes, and we all argued about whether these jokes were funny or not. We have this argument about fifty times a year.

I HATE
MYSELF
CONTINUED...

404:913) OpPhantom   21-MAY-95 10:25

I hate myself for passing out drunk in the fully reclined La-Z-Boy <tm> and not waking till 5:00 a.m. to find every light in the house blazing and some weird ass fucking movie blaring and my hayed pounding and my eyes impossible to keep open because my contacts are drier than dust with no rewetting drops at hand and the cats passed out on top of me resisting every effort to move them and for how long it took to stagger around looking for aspirin and the Sensitive Eyes <tm> Drops and wasting one of my precious Vernors <tm> stash just to hydrate myself because there wasn't anything else worth drinking and finally collapsing into bed.

404:937) aeonflux   21-MAY-95 23:23

I hate myself for comparing myself to the successful artists in the Biennial who were born in 1970 like me.

404:939) gail in cleats   21-MAY-95 23:46

I hate myself for realizing people born in 1974 are 21 years old now, and very possibly further along in their careers-of-choice than I.

221

404:958) jneil   **22-MAY-95 15:31**

I hate myself because I am eating chicken with a spoon.

404:963) jaguar   **22-MAY-95 19:40**

I hate myself for my motivation, desire, and most of all, commitment. Oh, and earnestness. What an ugly word, and I brought it up.

404:1014) Bang!   **25-MAY-95 0:57**

I hate myself because I got a pathetic 5 out of 20 score on this weeks Name That Tune contest. I hate myself because two of the ones I got right were Paula Abdul and Right Said Fred.

404:1015) Rob Tannenbaum   **25-MAY-95 0:58**

Both Canadians.

404:1016) Bang!   **25-MAY-95 1:03**

Not! Mommy! Rob is teasing me again.

404:1017) Rob Tannenbaum   **25-MAY-95 1:05**

Are!

Paula Abdul told me so, off the record, when I interviewed her. And that scary bald fuck in Right Said Fred was Visigoth, [Visigoth is also a tall, bald guy] before the home-correspondence courses.

404:1027) lilac breasted visigoth **25-MAY-95 17:36**

I hate myself for the secret pride I feel, being outed, finally, as Right Said Fred.

404:1028) SuZin   **25-MAY-95 17:37**

I hate myself for having a renewed interest in visigoth.

404:1029) lilac breasted visigoth **25-MAY-95 17:39**

I hate myself for wondering if I can parlay this into a blowjob at the Art Bar.

404:1030) SuZin 25-MAY-95 17:40

I hate myself for wondering if blowjob is one word or two.

I hate myself for thinking that maybe it should be hyphenated.

404:1033) cafephreak 25-MAY-95 18:39

I hate myself for always wondering if women can receive blowjobs or if only men are blown.

I hate myself for only recently figuring out that a woman can say that she would like some head now, please.

I thought only men got head because I thought the head folks were talking about was the head that guys got down there.

I hate myself for being almost 31, and all I can say STILL is . . . please kiss me down there.

404:1034) neandergal 25-MAY-95 18:42

Women don't get blown because it gives us embolisms.

I hate myself cause I'm 44 and I can only say "mouthal activity."

404:1041) MRPetit—aka Marianne 25-MAY-95 21:51

I hate myself for thinking that I should use the expression "feast on my cootchy pop" more often.

404:1050) Jane Spridle Doe 26-MAY-95 0:03

IHM for never having a problem yelling LICK ME NOWWWWWWW!

404:1123) The Strange Apparatus 31-MAY-95 11:52

IHM because Hane says my cat is not a "working" (AKA mouse-slaughterin') feline, but a "living plushie."

404:1251) ragged paul 05-JUN-95 22:56

IHM for being a lunatic megalomaniac and squandering my own and other's lives.

404:1252) SuZin　　　　　　　　　　**05-JUN-95 22:56**

I hate ragged paul for squandering my life.

404:1269) neandergal　　　　　　　　**06-JUN-95 16:35**

IHM for not knowing how to French braid my hair.

IHM because I have no playground mommy friends because I am a social misfit and reject and as a result I am an angry bitch and they can see it in my face and they hate me and Max will have no friends and I have ruined his life.

404:1313) piercing boy (stahl)　　　　**09-JUN-95 0:31**

I hate myself for skipping everyone else's reasons for self hatred just so I could post my own.

404:1456) MP　　　　　　　　　　　**24-JUN-95 11:38**

I hate myself for walking past someone I know and like on the street and pretending I didn't see her 'cause I didn't feel like talking.

I hate myself for thinking I heard her say "hey, I know him" and still walking on.

404:1550) neandergal　　　　　　　　**30-JUN-95 15:03**

Oh and I hate myself because this nice Mommy in the playground said, "well we have to go now. Ben needs to take a nap and I need to start dinner."

When, in fact, I NEVER think more than 15 minutes ahead, ever in my life, and Max falls asleep whenever he collapses in his stroller and I never cook a decent dinner, and I'm just, like, not doing this June Cleaver thing correctly at all, ugh.

404:1553) Lisa J. Cooley   **30-JUN-95 15:22**

Fuck, fuck fuck fuckfuckfuck

fuck

fuck

that's all.

Fuck.

And, oh, yeah:

I hate myself.

ECHO POLL

Source: From an online survey of 224 members of Echo, March 1996.

Margin of Error: Sure. Like they're all going to tell me?

Do you ever repeat what you have read in a private conference outside the conference?

27% said yes.

39% of the women said yes.

20% of the men said yes.

09% said they didn't belong to any private conferences.

Face-2-Face   And Now?   Mystery Button

IN CYBER-
SPACE, WE
ARE NOT WHAT
WE THINK
ABOUT!

AND WHO
INVITED
YOU?

When was the last time you
thought, while planning a party, "I think I'll invite . . . *everyone.*" I'll
just open my door here and whoever wanders in, I'll talk to them,
tell them personal things, listen to whatever they have to say—I'll
be the same way with them as I am with my friends. I mean, why
should I talk to a stranger any differently than I do with someone
I've gotten to know? I don't care who walks in the door, or if we
get along. Hell, I could hate them. Come on in.

That's how some people envision cyberspace. I keep hearing the
voice of Zelda Rubenstein from the movie *Poltergeist:* "*All are welcome, all are welcome.*" Again, it's the virtual utopia. And to some that
means instant friendship, automatic intimacy with all—you can go
anywhere you like and all doors will open to you and everyone
there will accept you and we'll all get along with everyone else. Tra-
la-la-la.

No, no, no, no, no, PLEASE GOD NO. Like we're all some

mutant strain of Miss America contestants? All are welcome. But that doesn't mean that we're going to make friends with everyone who walks through the door. I don't want to talk to everyone. I don't want to share the intimate details of my life with everyone. You like some people, you dislike others. And people naturally form groups. They gravitate toward some people and away from others. When someone logs in and assumes that everyone is their friend, I can guarantee you that this is the person everyone is going to hate inside of a week. If you walk in as if we're all already close instead of going through the actual process of becoming close, people will distance themselves from you. They feel manipulated. Unless you are terribly charming. Some people are so adept and so intuitive, they can walk into a room full of strangers and instantly make friends with everyone there. For the rest of us, however, establishing friendships takes time. There are no shortcuts.

People form cliques. You can't stop them. Cyberspace is lousy with cliques; cliques here, cliques there, we've got cliques within cliques within cliques. On Echo, sometimes newcomers object. What do they expect? When a group of people get together they form affinities with some and not all. Should I step in and say, "Okay you guys over there, break it up"? As a matter of fact, I encourage them.

Private spaces exist everywhere. Sometimes I want to talk to my girlfriends, I have friends I go to the movies with, friends I go dancing with. I go to all my high school reunions. I share something different with each group. Eliminating similar private spaces on Echo would be that enforced niceness, the utopia I never wanted. I can't tell people whom to talk to, or whom to like. It is up to you to make friends. The cliques aren't a barrier to friendship. *Cliques are what happen as people make friends.* If they weren't open to new people, we wouldn't be growing. It can be daunting though, if you're new. We do what we can to smooth the way. That's the hosts' main job. The rest is up to you.

We learned our very first year that opening something up to everyone on Echo isn't always such a great idea. Echo has a lot of musicians. A number of them got together and organized a jam session. They searched everywhere and found a space that they could afford if they all split the cost. Then they made a public announcement and invited anyone who wanted to sing or play to join them. They weren't expecting the ton of people who came who couldn't play or sing a note. These people went to the studio and sat and chatted like they were at a cocktail party. The musicians complained. "We can't play music like this. Stay home," they begged. We went back and forth. "Well, are only professional musicians allowed, or can anybody who had piano lessons come?" Nobody could agree about who could come and who couldn't, and the jam sessions stopped.

Some people will always feel, or genuinely are, excluded. Whose fault is that? The first person I can remember complaining about cliques was The Red Queen. She kept insisting there was an in-group. I didn't know how to respond at the time. I was not prepared for the reaction that we got (and continue to get) about cliques. What did she think? That Echo management had formed an official group, voting about who gets in and who doesn't?

I asked her and others who were complaining to tell me who the in-group was exactly. The answers were amazing. I was, of course, queen of the in-crowd, most believed. Never mind that for the first few years of Echo I was working practically twenty-four hours a day and had no social life whatsoever beyond calling my friend Joe to cry, "I don't know what I'm doing. Please shoot me." Then they named Echoids who barely spoke to each other. They assumed friendships between people who were either indifferent or who actively disliked each other. "Well we all know so and so and this guy are Stacy's good friends" and people would be named who most certainly were not. Everyone had a different idea of who was in and who was friends with whom. Their guesses were revealing.

And most were, almost without exception, entirely wrong. We're all in the dark in the beginning. In time, if you're paying attention, it's obvious who is friends with whom. And who is dating whom. Relationships on Echo are public. For some, the darkness of cyberspace is a clean black slate onto which they project their fears. People choose their own friends. And in The Red Queen's case, because she complained about so many of us so relentlessly, she didn't have a lot to choose from. She was friends with the people she made an effort to be friends with. Her place within the society of Echo was entirely her own doing.

Most people get past the feeling of being excluded however, because in time, they find their place. Friendships are not instant or automatic. It takes time to carve out a place for yourself when you're someplace new. When you don't know anybody. Meanwhile, I responded to the growing need for private space. People couldn't, and shouldn't, have to conduct all of their Echo social life on center stage, for all to see. They need places to go to be alone. Private spaces give Echo depth. This is how people take evolving friendships and connections deeper. In private.

The first private conferences were MOE and WIT, the ones for men only and women only. We made the Sex Conference private and invited people over twenty-one to join (we later changed that to over eighteen). This wasn't to protect children. It was to protect the adults. We wanted to be able to talk about sex without having to worry about a child wandering into the room and hearing about Mom having sex on a desktop. We had a feminist conference for a while called WON (Women's Online Network) that evolved into the *Ms.* Conference. Later we added a 12-Step Conference for people in various twelve-step programs, Alcoholics Anonymous and the like.

Not many people had a problem with these particular private spaces. A few grumblings, nothing major. Now, usually I can tell beforehand if something I do is going to cause the Next Big Thing. Change of any sort, I learned, even something positive, always stirs up a few voices of complaint. People hate change. I hate change. I was completely blindsided by the intensity of the response to Under 30, however.

The majority of people on Echo are in their thirties and forties. Big surprise. I'm thirty-nine as I type this; I was thirty-three when we opened. Susan Campbell, aka SuZin, approached me a few years ago with a new idea. SuZin, a young Echoid, whose contributions to *I Hate Myself* are among my favorites, and whom I've watched grow from college student who always did her homework and her laundry at the last minute to married lady with a dream job writing about television, wanted to start a conference for gen-Xers. Yes! We give book lovers a place to find each other in the Books Conference, the movie lovers head to the Movies and TV Conference; well, sometimes you want to hang with people your own age. You have shared history, shared culture. You watched the same cartoons as kids, listened to the same music. In person, you can find people your own age easily. Online, what were you going to do? Walk in and say, "Okay, everyone in their twenties, please raise their hands"? Yup. It was a great idea. Even better—let's make it private. Only people under thirty can get in. It will truly be their own spot. Susan got it ready and in a month we announced a new private conference called Under 30. Email SuZin to get in.

The Echoids went ballistic. The Echoids over thirty, I should say. No one under thirty objected. I was caught completely off guard. So what if they want to talk among themselves? If they want to have a private conversation, shouldn't they be able to? A number of people couldn't stand the idea of being excluded from conversations simply because of their age. Steve Barber explained:

> "Personally, the not-so-subtle ageism that an 'under 30' conference represents violates the whole notion of what online communication and Echo in particular has been about, at least for me."

We have thoughts on the same issues, others added. We should be able to express them. John Neilson, aka jneil, disagreed:

> "If Echo is to have an Under 30 Conference it should reflect the thoughts and feelings of people under 30. And like it or not, the thoughts and feelings of the (sizable) group of folks who used to be under 30 is not the same thing."

As long as we stay on the topic, that is, issues of being under thirty, what difference does it make how old the person is? still others asked. We should be transcending the age differences, they argued. We're interested in these issues, too. Well, based on that logic we should open up the conference for women only to men. They are interested in many of the same issues and there are plenty of Echoids who believe we should be transcending our gender differences as well. But sometimes members of a particular group want to talk exclusively among themselves. What effect would allowing anyone in have on the conversations that were taking place there? Also, it wasn't like the under-thirty crowd was going to stop participating everywhere else.

SuZin asked:

> "Is it really so wrong to have a space where people of a certain age and experience level can talk about their feelings and experiences, without having the voices of their Olders and Wisers pipe in?"

Kevin joked about a conference for toddlers and posted a sample of what they might talk about.

> 1 Gerber strained squash, don't ya just hate it?
> 2 Playpens, set my people free!
> 3 Your favorite potty tricks

4 Pampers vs. Kimbies, the debate rages on!

5 GET OUTTA MY FACE MOM/DAD! (Goo-Goo this sucka!)

6 What I wanna be when I'm 2

7 Mr. Rodgers, the man, the myth, the party animal.

8 Baths, who needs em¿

9 Teeth, more trouble than they're worth¿

10 Hair, Yipes!

11 Blankie love

A number of Echoids made snide comments about the new Kiddy Conference. Some called it the Nursery. One Echoid claimed the whole conference itself was illegal. They were just hurt. I tried to think of a way to please everyone. I know: we'll let people over thirty in, but they can't post. That would address the problem raised by the under-thirty crowd who didn't want to deal with the "when I was your age," attitude. A compromise.

What was I thinking¿ It's a horrible idea. It would be like having your parents lurking in the corner at a party, listening to your every word. I scratched that idea quick.

Ms. Thang added:

"If Echo was an old fashioned drug store we would probably group according to certain ages and talk things over. But Echo removes all of our outer characteristics and opens up to us different booths to sit in according to what is being talked about and occasionally, who is sitting there.

"I would like to meet people my own age on Echo. I would like to be able to get into a dialog with them without being in a fishbowl for others to watch. I think of the Under 30 Conference as the back booth at the soda shop, where it's probably smokey and the music is very loud. I'd like to be able to sit in that booth with people my age."

Some argued that the great thing about the online world is that it breaks down these barriers to communication, and here we are, replacing them. Jaze didn't think so.

"Y'know, I really think that a strong effort should be made to resist the homogenizing influence of some phony concept of cyberspace as a democratic medium. It's not."

How do we know people are under thirty anyhow? We take their word for it. SuZin asks them if they are under thirty and she lets them in if they say yes. As far as we can tell, no one has ever lied.

The controversy was dividing Echo. Bad feelings were everywhere. Virtual communities are new, none of this stuff had been worked out on Echo or other online services. The proper etiquette had not been established—we're still making this stuff up as we go along. I was *that close* to either shutting it down or opening it up to everyone when a few members of the Under 30 Conference sent me mail. Like I said, I'm on the tail end of the baby boomers and Echo was crawling with late-boomers. These people said it was hard to speak up sometimes in the rest of Echo, they felt so outnumbered, but after a month of being able to talk all the time in Under 30 they were posting more outside of it as a result. I checked and it was true. Then I remembered how the women of Echo lurked until they developed their online chops in WIT.

Under 30 stays as is, for people under thirty only, I announced. Although many threatened to, no one huffed. People got used to the idea. The Under 30 Conference has an item called *Logan's Run,* where people say good-bye to the members turning thirty before they are kicked out. And, we've opened another private conference called Over 40. I'll be a member of that by the time you read this. (No 30–39 Conference. There's no demand.)

One of the ongoing and trickier problems with private conferences is, ironically, protecting the privacy of the people and the conversations within. Some of the thornier issues that can come up include, what about when people talk about Echoids who are not members of the conference? Those people can't respond to what is being said. You're talking behind their back. And what about the people who tell their friends what is being said about them in the private conference? If they don't respect the privacy of the conference should they be allowed to stay? Also, what if someone makes a personal attack in a private conference? Is it okay because it was said in private? Since a select group of people can see, it is really private? As The WELL developed similar private spaces on their system, they struggled with the same issues. I would read in private conferences on Echo about someone huffing a private conference on The WELL because someone else was talking about what was being said there.

There used to be an item in WIT called *Is Someone Bothering You on Echo?* I opened it our first year because I heard that a woman was getting bombarded with YOs and, rather than complain to me, she was putting up with it. This was not good. I didn't know how widespread this particular problem was. How many other women were dealing with this or other problems? The item was a godsend in the beginning. Cyberspace was all new territory for many of the women on Echo and the item helped them negotiate it. Echo was also all new territory for the men who came here from other online services. The culture of Echo is very different than that of the Internet and it takes time for some people to realize they are in someplace new. While it might be okay on other online services to ask a woman about her breast size, here it's considered rude and tasteless. (Unless it's between friends who are in a rude and tasteless mood.) If a guy said something questionable, a woman brought it up in WIT, and sometimes another woman would speak up and say, Oh yeah, I know that guy, he's okay, just tell him to lay off, he will. Or they'd say, He's a friend of mine, I'll talk to him. But every once in a while, someone creepier would come along and we would discover through that item that we were all experiencing the same thing. In 1990 this was very important. It gave us the relief of, "Oh good, then it's not just me." We'd work out an appropriate response together, and either they were "cleared" or they were told to stop.

Here's the first problem with this. Since there is no such thing as a secret, sometimes someone would hear that he was being talked about and he would be, understandably, indignant. There was something unfair about it all. It was like not being able to participate in your own trial. But I refused to remove the item. No one was getting slandered there. We were all very careful about that. I was sympathetic to the men's discomfort, but the item was serving a real and important need. Again, this was all so new to us and we had to work this out. Besides, as unfair as it may be, people talk about other people all the time. I may talk about Fred with Ethel, and I don't feel Fred is entitled to listen in on my private conversation and respond. We made sure that the topic stuck to things that someone actually did and didn't drift into name calling or conjecture.

The second problem. Sometimes a woman reads one of these discussions and goes back and tells the guy everything because he's a good friend. The women find out and they're furious. If you can't respect the privacy of this space you shouldn't be in it, they fume. The woman is frequently torn between loyalty to her friend and loyalty to the members of the conference. The others want her kicked out. This scenario is repeated in every private conference on Echo.

Some breaches of conference privacy go too far. We had a New York University student print out a conversation from MOE (the conference for men only) and circulate it back at school. I believe the person's intentions were good, but it was a horrible mess. A woman on Echo had refused the advances of one of the men on

Echo and he and others had ripped her to shreds in MOE for it. It was ugly. And the guy who started it was a friend of mine. I could have killed him. When the members of MOE found out their conversation was making the rounds at NYU, all Hell broke loose. They were mad for two reasons, the violation of their privacy and the fact that the entire story wasn't being told. When my friend made these comments, the men in MOE called him on it, and he had apologized to them and the woman, but that information wasn't also making the rounds. The student who distributed their words was unmoved by the apologies. In his heart he was defending his friend and all women. Others were unconvinced. Bob Knuts posted:

> "The real world contains a lot of personal remarks about people that are privately made outside of someone's presence. Such remarks only become tangibly 'hurtful' when someone else with an ax to grind decides to disclose the remarks to the subject. The discloser breaches a confidence by making the disclosure. And since the comments would never have existed but for the assurance of privacy, there's a sadistic element in the intentional disclosure of private conversation."

I knew the student and although I was as disappointed in his response as I was with my friend who made the original comments, I knew, like my friend, he was not a monster. But they both fucked up big time. My friend went way overboard in his comments, but the guy who distributed them? Like you've never said bad things about anyone before? No one was right, but like every situation that rocks the community, everyone had a point.

People should have a right to say whatever they want in private. But how private is it if a select group of people can see? And, unlike a regular conversation, our words are saved. They are always there. It's as private as a bathroom wall in the men's room. In this case, the woman was being skewered and everyone was reading it but her and the other women on Echo. Until the NYU student hit the photocopy machine. Who was more right? Who was more wrong?

Neither.

In the end I decided this: We are not going to tell you what to say in private, but personal attacks are still frowned on. So say what you like, but we will not protect personal attacks made in private conferences. If your words get out, it is up to you to answer for them. We're not going to try to legislate around the fact that no one can keep a secret. You know that. Take responsibility for it. If you don't want it to get back to the person, don't write it. That said, we're not thrilled with tattletales either, or the harm that can be caused by the self-righteous with an agenda, so while we will not kick out of Echo someone who repeats what is said in a private conference, we will kick them out of that private conference.

This position was going to be seriously tested by the most notorious conference on Echo: X. If people didn't like arbitrary criteria like age, they hated how we handled memberships to X even more. The only way to get in is by invitation. X was not announced. It doesn't appear on the list of conferences, there is no host to email to get in. You're either invited or not. It was some Echoids' worst fear. If you aren't friends with any of the members, or if your posting style does not match the tone, you are never going to see the inside of X. If you lurk you can just forget it because someone who remains a stranger will never get into X.

It all started with one of my worst screw-ups. For a while Miss Outer Boro was cohosting the Culture Conference with someone I will call Drama Man (he is an active theater goer). He was well liked on Echo but never an effective host in Culture. He wasn't strong on the topics that took place there and he could be a difficult cohost. Culture is the most popular conference on Echo, but this was not, unfortunately, due to him. The usage reports showed that posting went way down whenever Miss Outer Boro wasn't around. The Computer Conference was without a host at the time, Drama Man was a computer consultant, it seemed like a good fit. I made Drama Man the host of the Computer Conference and Topper the new cohost of Culture. Drama Man was devastated, he didn't want anything to do with the Computer Conference and the Echoids were outraged. (Drama Man had a lot of friends on Echo. How could they not like the guy? He once got stabbed in the subway protecting an older woman from a mugger.) Drama Man called me in tears. Then he got mean. Everyone went back and forth in the Feedback Conference about what to do for weeks.

Was there a way out? I could see he was terribly hurt; what would fix this? I got it. I told him he could dream up any conference he liked, and as long as it wasn't a duplication of the Culture Conference, he could do whatever he wanted and he could host it all by himself. The Echoids who were upset were happy with the solution. No response from Drama Man at first. Then he told me privately that it was too much to ask him to create a new conference out of thin air. (Someone else had created the Culture Conference, Drama Man was not the original host.) I got on the phone with Miss Outer Boro, Topper, and Jaze and we brainstormed for him. We came up with the idea of a theater conference. Drama Man didn't like this suggestion. It would be too small, he said. Then he announced publicly that he had proposed a Drama Conference to me and that I had turned the idea down. Huh? Things had begun to settle down so it was not the time to call him a liar. I said no, I loved the idea, go for it, and he got to work on a conference he called Stages. He also posted an open letter to me about the whole affair in our Feedback Conference that was seething. The pressure must have been enormous. He said many times that he was a fabulous host, that he should never have been removed from Culture—now all eyes were on him. I wish I had been better, but after months of nastiness from him I was without sympathy. The conference failed. He sent me email full of bile and huffed. I felt awful. Sometimes I hate this job. Managing people in cyberspace isn't any easier than it is at the office.

Stages was abandoned. Like squatters in an abandoned building, people move into deserted conferences and take over. We call them graffiti conferences because people go in with virtual spray cans and mark up the place, opening topics that have nothing to do with anything and generally having a fine old time. We figure whoever gets in there first has squatters' rights and we leave them alone. Knock yourself out. This time was different. Someone, I have no idea who, but it had to be someone who works for Echo, gave Berg access to the host commands in Stages. He went to town. He changed the names of all the discussions, it was like rearranging the furniture, and then he played around with the banner that greets you every time you visit. Meanwhile, Phil, (27% of the Echoids polled felt Phil was the worst thing to ever happen to Echo) was at his height of creepiness. He was active in Plain Wrapper and his participation was ruining it. Once Berg got Stages the way he wanted it, he led the people of Plain Wrapper away to Stages (or Stooges, as some people briefly called it), and then he made the conference private. John Gabriel joined him as cohost. They decided who got in and who didn't. Since these graffiti conferences were not official, I thought of them as throwaways, or light entertainment, I didn't care what people did with them. A few users complained when they couldn't get into Stages all of a sudden. That conference is gone, I told them, and I asked the spray painters to change the name. They christened it Xenophobia, but it came to be known affectionately as X. Then we loaded a new version of the software we use to run Echo which allowed more than one person to have access to the host commands. Flying Fish suggested making everyone a host in X. Gabriel and Berg loved the idea. Total anarchy. Since the hosts maintain the list of users who can or cannot get into a private conference, once everyone was a host, anyone could kick anyone else out. Even better and more subversive, anyone could use the edit commands available to the hosts to change what anyone else said. It did come to be known for a while as the Anarchy Conference. I was thrilled. I was sick of rules and I loved the idea of a space on Echo where even I had no say. The timing couldn't have been more perfect. I was still reeling from the whole Drama Man affair and feeling like the manager from Hell. I was glad to have a place where I had no official responsibility. It was a relief. I took a peek. Nothing in there that interested me, but it wasn't my conference. I hadn't looked closely.

Around this time, John Seabrook was writing a Talk of the Town piece about Echo for *The New Yorker*. He chose to write about X. He was brand-new to the medium so he didn't have an understanding of private dialogue in cyberspace, but the article wasn't half bad even if he didn't get it. He thought of X as some hip, downtown NYC club with a velvet rope and bouncers. (A revealing projection, I think.) He wanted to take a look, but I couldn't change the rules just because of an article, even though I was tempted to (and I was). When I think of how the Echoids would have responded if I let a journalist who was writing an article about us into X—it would not have been pretty. Besides, I also thought at the time that the best stuff on Echo was elsewhere. I was wrong.

As far as I can tell, one of the main things driving early X was the joy of having a place where Phil wasn't. It gave them a space to vent their considerable frustration. Because of our personal attack rule, no one could come right out and say how they felt about him. Well, they let it out in X. As I said earlier, they had an item for it. And they called it, simply: *Fuck Phil*. Oh yeah, there was a lot of nastiness in X. When I saw *Fuck Phil* I felt I had to tell them they had gone too far, but to be honest, I essentially looked the other way. Sure, I told them they had stepped over the line, but then I left them alone. I didn't shut the thing down as I could have. Until I got a note from an old friend telling me that he and his wife were going to sue me and Echo because of things that had been said about her in X, I didn't do a thing. I wanted a place where I didn't have to do a thing. I went back. Sure enough, they were going at her. A tad eccentric, and very sensitive, she had some difficulty getting along with some people, and there it was, being played out yet again, in cyberspace. She had a good heart and I knew these comments must have hurt her deeply.

That was it. I had to put an end to them. Attack each other all you like, you can kill yourselves for all I care, but you may not attack people who are not also members of X. Then I looked closely for the first time. Some of the best stuff I have ever read on Echo was right there next to some of the worst. They had built up a level of trust and opened up to each other like nowhere else on Echo. There was a sense of camaraderie there that was stronger than what could be found in the public spaces.

It all makes perfect sense once you stop to look at it and don't try to separate cyberspace from life. It's all very well and good to be nice to everyone and try to make friends with everyone, but it's not going to work. Friendship takes time and history and something that can't be described. Chemistry. The people in X are friends. Of course they would go farther and deeper in here, alone, among friends. Duh. This was a good thing. Something I wanted to support. It has its sick moments. From Oedipa: "Disembowel me and find a PRIZE!" But I like sick.

Word of X got out of course. What did I say about secrets? And I suppose an article in the *The New Yorker* about the conference must have been a big tip-off. We want to see! Well, you can't. You have to be invited. Who decides? The people already in there. That's not fair! You have to make friends with them to get in. Oh, we're not cool enough? The projections of the uninvited. It's just like high school. That's not it. How can you expect to be invited to a private party if the hosts don't know you? People wanted in, instant acceptance and intimacy without the work. It's not that they don't like you, you haven't made friends. Are all the people out there who aren't your friends people you dislike?

I wanted more Xs. There are times when I want to call in an air strike and obliterate the place. When people think no one is looking they can get mean. But it's amazing, ultimately, how civilized anarchy is. I let people do whatever they wanted and they acted out for a while but in the end, they were terribly polite. Once a year someone removes all the items in X. Because everyone is a host in there, everyone has the power to do this. You would think it would happen more often, but people cherish that space. When it happens everyone grumbles about it for a while and then they go back and rebuild it. They use X to pour their hearts out mostly, and joke around. The people in X were definitely onto something.

A few months later Tank, aka Jennifer Tanaka, and NYD (Not Your Daughter) opened a couple of items in WIT that were unlike anything else that came before. (NYD is not this woman's real pseudonym. NYD was concerned about her mother's reaction to what is about to follow, so I have named her Not *Your* Daughter in order to strike fear in the hearts of paranoid New York mothers everywhere, and that would be, essentially *all* New York mothers, wouldn't it?) The topics they started were *Five Guys Named MOE: Who would you do on Echo?* (it was a place to name the guys on Echo you'd like to fuck), and *Ask NYD and Tank*, a Dear Abby style advice topic with attitude. WIT has a very supportive atmosphere, but it can be too damned nice sometimes. These items were a breath of fresh air. When someone asked for advice NYD might come back and say, "Oh go hide in a cave. You are so lame, girl." And people were saying whom they'd like to go to bed with and naming names? Was this okay? We were always so careful about talking about other people in WIT.

"If only we had a whole conference like that," I said to Jennifer. Wait a minute. I'm the boss. We can do whatever we like! NYD (that's right, she's your neighbor's daughter) and Tank created

BITCH. It was WIT in black leather jackets <tm MOB>. And it was made to order. To preserve the tone we made it invitation only. Girls with attitude only, please. BITCH was the place for your inner wicked witch, dark but with a sense of humor. The women who complained "that's not very nice" in the items in WIT were not invited. Another X.

It was time. Miss Outer Boro had been holding informal gatherings from time to time that she referred to as the House of Outer Boro.

> "It wasn't a 'place' on Echo. There might be mentions of it here and there, but it was mostly a thing of YOs and email and f2f's. A bunch of us; me, Neander, SuZin, Cham, can't think of who else right now—detested the syrupy nicey-nicey B.S. of WIT and got together at this sleazy dark dive in the very lower very east side—NOT a hipster place but a genuine dive—to get wasted on Scotch before watching jneil's band play."

Bonds had been formed. They needed a place.

Invitation-only places were new in cyberspace. The whole dos and don'ts of how to invite some people and not others still had to be worked out. Again: etiquette had to be established. My first mistake: I announced the place publicly. If it wasn't open to everybody, was this wise? The second mistake was made when Ms. 50 Smartest People in New York was invited. (Not her real pseudonym. *New York Magazine* had listed the 50 Smartest People in New York that summer and she was one of them.) Smart woman. Absolutely no sense of humor. Instead of playing, she stayed on the sidelines, commenting on everyone else's game. "Oh, that's not so funny," or "you people this," or "you people that." What a wet blanket. She didn't get it. NYD (or is she?) and Tank put her on read-only first. They should have just kicked her out. Better yet, we decided we had to be much more careful about who we invited in the first place. It's kinder to tell someone no and never let them in than to push them out the door after they've joined the party.

BITCH was the Next Big Thing for a while; some people were hurt. Again, cyberspace was supposed to be better than this, they thought. We're all one big happy family here. And again, here was this supposedly awful thing producing some of the best discussions on Echo. One of my favorite items in BITCH is an exchange we have going between the women in BITCH and the men of MOE. Each week a different man and a different woman is chosen as BoTW (Bitch of The Week) and MoTW (Moe of the Week) and they agree to answer whatever questions are thrown at them. (The men question the woman and the women question the man.)

A few examples follow. For a while we found a rare middle ground where we could try to explain and understand the differences between the sexes without anger or defensiveness. The fact that it happened in a private conference between people who had already gotten to know each other is important, and the fact that it occurred online. A little distance, even between friends, produces interesting results. The questions are the same questions we've been asking each other, or have always wanted to ask each other, for forever.

Dear BotW,
Is it all about clitoral stimulation or penetration?
Asking for a pal,
Joey X

Dear Joey X,
GOOD QUESTION. Glad you asked!
Of course I must start by saying that everyone is different, and likes different things, blah blah blah. But I can tell you that the lit-

tle man in the boat down there is ALWAYS happy to get attention, no doubt about it.

BUT—NEVER underestimate the power of having Little Willie go home (if you know what I mean). You can always get a nice warm fuzzy feeling with the little man in the boat, but once that feeling travels inside, you just HAVE to have Willie in there. That's the type of thing that sends you over the edge.

At least, that is what I hear. How would I know? I'm frigid.

See you at 8—My house.

Love,

NYD (Not Your Daughter)

Dear BotW,

Why don't more of you swallow? Does it taste that bad?

Love and syphillis,

Berg

Dear Berg,

Have YOU ever swallowed? Think about this for a second. Imagine, if you will, the thought of swallowing some goo that just squirted out of something that expels human waste. Add to it the fear of AIDS, STDS and all those fun lil bacteria, and you aren't exactly talking creme caramel.

Given that, however, it is NOT that bad. Personally, I think the longer you are in a monogamous relationship (I can see all the MOEs cringing at this), and the more you trust your partner, the easier and more fun it becomes to gulp the goo. Dare I even say enjoyable?

Not that I know. I just heard it from a friend.

Squirting at ya —

Love,

NYD (Not Your Daughter)

Dear BotW,

What's the deal with shoes? Why do women need so many of them?

The Strange Apparatus

Dearest Jack,

Let me express this in terms you can understand.

Why must you possess every Hawaiian War Chant ever recorded? NOW do you understand?

Here's to Les Elgart —

Love,

NYD (Not Your Daughter)

Dear NYD (Not Your Daughter),

I've got a really small dick. Does dick-size matter?

I've been told it doesn't, but I find that really hard to believe when I'm thrusting away at full steam and my bitch du jour says: "Is it in yet?"

Also, where is the clit? What are the best ways to give a woman head?

Love, Shivers & Spurts

Dear Shivers & Spurts,

OH BOY! I was WAITING for this one! YAY!

Actually, this is a topic currently under discussion in Bitch (what a surprise!)

First, I will say that women are like men in one respect: They superficially lust over "bigness". Guys always ogle women with big breasts, and we always talk about wanting men with huge penises.

Well, what is the reality? You MOES don't always get the 44D, and we Bitches don't always get the third leg.

Now some women swear by huge schlongs, and you can be sure that there are women who are disappointed when they finally see a guy naked and their ain't much there.

BUT, you know what? There are some REALLY valid reasons why average penises are much more desirable (according to ME).

1. Bladder infections. Bigger penises cause bladder infections in some women. Ever have one? IT REALLY SUCKS. IT REALLY SUCKS.

2. Pain. Bigger penises HURT. Especially for those of us with petite frames. Now, sometimes it can "hurt so good" but not MOST of the time. That is NOT fun sex. Unless the woman is used to a bigger penis, they can bring fear and terror.

3. Blow Jobs (now I know you are listening). They are easier and more fun on smaller penises. Bigger ones cause the gag and choke reflex. They are just too difficult to handle. (heh).

Of course, if you are truly hung like a pimple <tm Howard Stern> then you gotta make up for the lack of friction. If you can't do that, then, ummmmm . . . . GOOD LUCK!

But if you are just average, then stand tall and be proud!

Now, for your other question.

Weren't you paying attention to my response to Joey?

Remember The Little Man In The Boat?

And just think of licking an ice cream cone. Or something.

Phew. I'm exhausted—

See you in the 6X section!

Love,

NYD (Not Your Daughter)

It isn't just about the answers. It was also about the spirit in which the questions were asked and the answers given. There was a generosity here, and such a level of unabashed honesty. It was fun. People were dying to be the Bitch or MOE of the week. Some people lobbied for the position. They couldn't wait to answer questions that would normally make them roll their eyes, groan or run screaming in horror.

Janet,

Why are so many women petrified? Are there SO many psycho-fuckup-pricks out there that a gal must be e x t r e m e l y careful that she not saddle herself with an unreliable maniac?

Is New York a minefield, when it comes to dating?

Simon

Dear Simon,

Women are petrified for a variety of reasons, only one of which is that the world (and especially New York) is filled with psycho-fuckup-pricks.

But that's a pretty good reason to be terrified.

Other reasons have to do with:

Early traumatic relationships with psycho-fuckup-pricks who called themselves fathers who grew out of the 50's in such a scary way.

Early traumatic relationships with psycho-fuckup-pricks who called themselves teachers during our childhood and adolescence.

Early traumatic relationships with psycho-fuckup-bitches who called themselves our mothers.

Later traumatic relationships with our adjustments to a changing society that gave us the mixed message that we should have a successful career AND a successful relationship AND a successful family and on and on and on when no one gal in her sane mind can Do It All.

All of these reasons can leave the average New York gal's head spinning, wondering where to place her trust and deepest affections.

But you know, we gals, we're brave. We keep on trying. Or at least, I do.

So take heart.

Cuz there's one gal in NYC who signs herself

Looking for the reliable maniac,
Janet

Dear Tingey-one,

Do women bitch about all the "cute and intelligent" men being taken as much as men do about all the "cute and intelligent" women being taken?

If so, shouldn't there be an obvious remedy to this problem?

Jelly-one

Dear Jelly-one,

From time to time I may be found on a Sunday evening, in a depressed huddle, whining pitifully to my cat that "all the good ones are taken" (tho I would never go so far as to limit "good ones" to just the "cute and intelligent" ones).

Since my cat is an unsympathetic listener, I am left to talk myself out of my depression, which I do by reminding myself that while it's sort of fun to imagine that evil, mysterious forces in the universe are whisking the "good ones" away before I can get at them, it's really not very productive.

It is much more productive to remind myself, (quoting from my best friend's grandmother) that men are just like city busses, and there'll be another one along sometime soon.

Then I'll go read a good book, or watch an interesting movie, or call a friend, or do SOMETHING that makes me feel like I'm living my life, not being controlled by forces beyond my will.

Which is very helpful, because if I live my life, I'm bound to have something interesting to say the next time I happen to stumble across a "good one" who hasn't been taken away.

One of the "good ones" who isn't taken,
Janet

Dear Topmost:

Whom would you rather do, Barry White or Lou Reed?
Chanson son goute,
Ro@

Dear American Song Lover:

Hmm . . . When I was younger I dug the BoHo Rebel . . . but why do I suspect that Lou is just a bit too distant for me because of it? HEY! It's BARRY WHITE all the way because of That Voice. A sexy voice can Do A Lot for me! In the words of Salt n' P:

Now tell me baby how many hits must I make before you get the picture / that I like it when you talk to me /
You say it aloud what you say don't shy away, say it to my face
Talk sweet to me
Go up and down and around and do all that
But don't forget I'm a sister with a thing for the sound
So make a sexy noise when you're on the way down
Yeah, all the way down.

Signed,
B Sharp, not B Flat

Dear Topper,

What do women care about?

Why can't they care and talk about the same shit as guys? Wait, scratch that. I can't talk to guys either.
Sincerely,
Too luststruck to speak.

My reply:

One Dozen Popular Female Discussion Topics (in order): 1. Feelings; 2. Relationship with current beau; 3. My Job From Hell; 4. Relationship with mother; 5. I need to lose 10 pounds by next week; 6. Feelings; 7. Politics; 8. Where Did You Get That New Lipstick?; 9. Feelings; 10. Relationship with Sister; 11. He's Hung Like A What??; 12. Feelings.

Sorry. My first reaction to these questions is to be entirely flippant. Do you want to know what women care about so you can talk TO/WITH them or do you just want to talk them into something (you signed your letter "luststruck")? You'll have success with the latter if you concentrate on the former.

Topper

For a while people were able to say fuck it and tell the truth. With humor. And everyone could accept the answers. Not one "men suck" or the single expletive, "women!" out of anyone. From Rilke's letters about his Sonnets to Orpheus: " . . . there is neither a here nor a beyond, but only the greater unity, in which the 'Angels,' those beings that surpass us, are at home." An angst-free truce in the battle of the sexes had commenced, and the Echoids were finding the sublime in a discussion about blow-jobs.

Dear jneil:

Why is it that a blow job doesn't seem to count unless one swallows the hallowed fluid?

Or is this a line guys use to get us to gulp?

Signed,
It Ain't No Chocolate Milkshake

Dear Milkshaker,

I know some guys take it as some sort of primal affirmation if you swallow—and get weirded out if you spit—but personally, once I'm done with the stuff I don't care where it ends up.

If swallowing is abhorrent—for whatever reason—at least be considerate in what you do with it. Drooling it out sluttishly and rubbing it around on your partner and yourself can be a turn-on for both of you. Making gagging sounds and mumbling "you bathtard" as you run for the Listerine bottle, on the other hand, can bring festivities to a quick halt.

Signed,
Just Say 'Ah'

Dear jneil,

Do guys hate fat guts on women, even if they themselves have fat guts?

Signed,
Asking for a Friend

Dear Asking,

I wish I could say "Of course not, how shallow do you think we are?!" But that would be a fib.

You see, we really are shallow. You may be a Rhodes scholar with your own business who does volunteer work on the side, but our first impression is some variation on what we are always on the lookout for, i.e.:

```
( ) ( )
 )   (
(     )
 \   /
```

In the meantime, regardless of what kind of lard we're packin', we barely notice it. In our minds we're the same 14- or 20-year-old who first ogled the women in *Playboy, National Geographic*, and the underwear section of the Penney's catalog. The fact that we can no longer see our belt buckles is lost on us.

So what should you do if you have developed—how shall I put this—a tummy? Distract the hell out of us. Dress smart. Make a lot of eye contact. Be funny. Give us reason to believe that if we play our cards right you'll make us forget all those waifs with chest implants ever existed.

Before long you'll have us rationalizing to ourselves that, hey, you're not perfect, but you're not bad . . .

Signed,
Eating Famous Amos Cookies Even As I Type This

Dear Jneil,

Do you ever have male bondage <tm> with other musical MOEs like Joey and White Courtesy Telephone and stuff? Do you ever get together and talk about music and beer and touch each other's monkeys? If you do, would you ever write a song about it?

Signed,
Groupie Girl

Dear Groupie,

Sure, we do that all the time. Drink beer. Talk about music. Play music. Talk about beer. We don't touch each other's monkeys, though. Heck, if I were to accidently bump into Joey X at work we would have to punch each other in the shoulder and pretend to wrestle so people don't think we're homos or nothing.

Seriously, we'll hang out if there aren't any gals to hang out with. Soon as someone gets a girlfriend it's Yoko Oh No all over again.

And we certainly wouldn't write songs about hanging out and talking about music and drinking beer. That would be sad and pathetic.

Signed,
Trying Not To Be Sad And Pathetic

Dear Jneil:

Boxers or tightie whities?
Love,
NYD (Not Your Daughter)

Dear NYD (Not Your Daughter),

That's a dilemma. Briefs basically make everyone look like an overgrown little boy, which may work for some, but not when you're as overgrown as me. And the tightness and whiteness last for about one wash, after which they're saggy and grey and depressing. And I've got enough sagginess and greyness and depression without that.

Boxers on the other hand tend to make everyone look like their dad. And they seem to have some hellish ability to ride up into one's nether parts on hot days, which can lead to unsightly tugging and squirming.

Which is why I'll often as not choose None Of The Above. It's cooler, more comfortable, and I get to walk around with that li'l "I'm not wearing anything underneath my clothes" look on my face.

Signed,
Do I Or Don't I?

Dear jneil:

What REALLY goes on in the Men's Room?
Signed,
A Bitch With a Lurid Imagination

Dear Perpetual Tonight,

If there's no one else in there we go in, check our hair, make a few muscle poses in the mirror, see if we can write our names on the little scent cake in the urinal with our piss, dribble a few drops on the floor to mark our territory, tug it once or twice for kicks, and leave without washing our hands.

If someone else does happen to be in there we either stand around pretending to wash our hands until they leave or go in the stall and leave the seat up when we're done.

Signed,
Barely Housebroken

The uproar over BITCH and conferences like it died eventually, and now we have even more invitation-only spaces on Echo. The whole concept was so controversial at the time they were talking about it on The WELL. A few months after X opened, I logged into The WELL and found a topic about it that was started by their conference manager: *Echo, the xenophobia story and other evidence of community!* The WELL later went through their own Next Big Things over private spaces. The one I followed mirrored the Echo experience exactly—the same angst over who's getting into which conferences. I find it comforting that no matter where you go, we're all fucked-up in much the same ways.

Outside cyberspace, you can choose where you go and whom you go with. Sometimes you go to a big party, sometimes you just want to hang out with one friend, no one complains. Now we have these choices online. Private spaces make cyberspace richer, and more real. They give it a variety in intensity as well as subject. You'll say things in the private conferences that you won't say in front of everyone. The thing is, private conferences are still group conversations. What if two people want to talk alone, just the two of them? On Echo we have email and YOs.

Because email is even more select, you'll say things in email that you wouldn't reveal in a private conference. Someone might say something publicly, and another person reading it may want to respond to it without the whole world listening. Email is where two people go when they want to continue a conversation in private.

Then there are the things that people say to each other in YOs. Running all through Echo and all that is happening there is the subculture of YOs. YO is a feature that people use to say something to the other people online right then and there. If I YO you, only you can see it. YOs are the undercurrent of Echo, the subtext. People comment on the public and private life of Echo via YOs. It is the *Mystery Science Theater* of Echo. Whenever there is a controversy on

Echo, there's a corresponding powerspike in the exchange of YOs. "Can you believe what she just said⸮⸮" During a recent uproar on Echo, I watched the YOs fly by, fast and furious. (I couldn't read them of course, I could only see that people were using the command.) Not surprisingly, much of the gossip of Echo is exchanged via YOs. "Guess who got fired yesterday!" YOs have a different flavor than email and that's because they are not permanent. They glide across your screen and off. They aren't saved anywhere. They're off the cuff. You might be sitting at your computer, reading about opera when your screen freezes, beeps three times, and a message appears on your screen:

[. . . YO!!!!!!! This message comes from joe (Joseph Hobaica) @ 10:00 . . .
I want to be in you like a train.
Right now.
]

To be followed a few seconds later with some more beeps and:

[. . . YO!!!!!!! This message comes from joe (Joseph Hobaica) @ 10:00 . . .
Actually, make that a golf cart.
The three wheeled, electric kind that tips over easy.
]

That YO was sent by Joey X. Using cut and paste, a computer trick that allows you to take words on the screen and copy them elsewhere, the Echoids regularly share their favorite YOs in an item in X called *Pathetic YOs of Love*. Here is another he sent to Cathy Young (aka cafephreak). I have no idea what inspired this particular outburst.

[. . . YO!!!!!!! This message comes from joe (Joseph Hobaica) @ 10:00 . . .

Okay, Cathy. You fucking ROCK MY MOTHER FUCKING WORLD.

I am going to name my first son after you.

Mr. Cathy Hobaica.

He will get beaten up, but it is worth it!

]

Relationships grow through YOs. Joe Rosen, aka Joro, posted something that concerned me, so I asked him what was up. His response:

[. . . YO!!!!!!! This message comes from joro (Joe Rosen) @ 14:03 . . .

Depressed . . . ask again later <tm the angst ridden Eight-Ball.>

]

People will YO each other to support something someone has just written in a public conference. "Great post. Keep it up." Or they can be critical.

[. . . YO!!!!!!! This message comes from visigoth (Doug Cooper) @ 18:21 . . .

Yeah. Real sensitive. Kick em while they're down why don't you. Don't you have a Meen Pierced Person on Ludes' Anonymous meeting to go to?

]

They are frequently playful.

[. . . YO!!!!!!! This **message comes from
lorenzbc (Lorenz Wyss) @ 03:10 . . .**

Well, in the movie, the vampires seduce all these women,
and it was very sexy with those period dresses and stuff and
then . . . they like . . . killed them and drank their blood.

Yuck! Where's the fun in that?
]

To Marian from fellow Echoid Luce.

[. . . YO!!!!!!! This **message comes from
lwollin (Lucy A. Wollin) @ 01:49 . . .**

Why am I here?
]

Marian's response: "Existential crisis strikes late nite echoid."
This one was sent to visigoth, who is six feet tall and shaves his
head:

[. . . YO!!!!!!! This **message comes from
dreaming (Julie Alix Robichaux) @ 23:50 . . .**

Do you ever stand in front of the mirror and smile at yourself, arms folded, and assure yourself in a deep voice that your
floors will sparkle like never before?

If I were a six-foot bald guy, I wouldn't be able to get
enough of that.
]

Visigoth's response: "We like her."

Playful or serious, YOs are usually exchanged by people who
have gotten to know each other, or, by people who are interested in
getting to know each other. And because they're fast, it's so easy—

they pop up on your screen and seconds later they are gone—
Echoids take their chances with YOs and the subtext of these YOs
is frequently flirtation.

> **[. . . YO!!!!!!! This message comes from joe
> (Joseph Hobaica) @ 02:01 . . .**
> Penn Station, Wednesday, 1 AM. Last stall on the left.
> You make the choice, men's room or women's room.
> **]**

> **[. . . YO!!!!!!! This message comes from
> dada (Pavia Rosati) @ 20:33 . . .**
> I'm in love with you.
> I fucked myself this afternoon, inspired by the Hasidim in
> the park, and screamed Holy Hosannas in your name.
> **]**

> **[. . . YO!!!!!!! This message comes from
> jet66 (Jack Taylor) @ 00:15 . . .**
> Can I wear the Hello Kitty mask?
> **]**

From Theresa to Molly:

> **[. . . YO!!!!!!! This message comes from
> janedoe (Theresa M. Senft) @ 23:43 . . .**
> I love you so much.
> **]**

Molly's response:

> **[. . . YO!!!!!!! This message comes from
> molsk (Molly E. Ker) @ 23:44 . . .**

Then MARRY ME!

We will register at Tiffany's and both wear nice white dresses!

]

One of my favorite exchanges took place between Alice Bradley, who calls herself Alice, Part of a Complete Breakfast, and Doug Cooper, aka Visigoth. I've included the YOs that were copied into the *Pathetic YOs of Love* item, and because it demonstrates how a community can get swept up in a public flirtation, I've also included everyone's reactions.

To visigoth:

[. . . YO!!!!!!! This message comes from abradley (Alice Bradley) @ 12:41 . . .

I have many tiny and ugly friends.

Me? I'm 5'7", brown hair, blue eyes, pale and wearing a lot of black, 36-20-30, and I like sensitive men and long walks in the park.

]

Pavia's response:

"Doug [visigoth's real name] yer search is ovah."

New York Jew's response:

"Birddog ya beddah geddah Chicken Little of yer own . . . Evvahboddy knows that she fuckin' me."

visigoth's response:

"She's mine. All mine! (Nyah ha ha) Anyone touches her, I send em: The Cake of Death.

"Actually, she's here in my apartment RIGHT NOW! (ahem: Alice, care to say a few words to the rabble?)

'I'm here with Doug. I love him. He loves me. We're very much in love. Now leave us in peace, as we quietly (or not so quietly) celebrate our newfound love together.'

"I rest my case."

ragged paul's response:

"So that was your right hand, huh, Doug."

My response:

"PLEASE PLEASE tell me you made that up and I will worship you."

visigoth's response:

"Actually, Stacy, I'm afraid I did not make that up. And NOW: I'm logging in from Alice's apartment.

"(Uh, Alice? Care to say a few words to the rabble?)

"'No. Could you please leave now?'

"I, uh, rest my case."

SuZin's response:

"I went to camp with Alice. Really."

ragged paul's response:

"So dish!"

SuZin's response:

"She's very bright and very funny and cute, too. I know this 'cause I saw her on a train two years ago after not having seen her since she was 14."

ragged paul's response:

"That's not dish, that's just annoying."

SuZin's response:

"Like me!"

Alice's response:

"It's true—I'm so fucking cute that total strangers run up to me and grab my cheeks and squeal, 'Aw, izza witta cute-ums! Yezzzshe is! Yezz!'

"(Thank you for not telling them what an adolescent FREAK I was, Suzin. I love you.)

"And I don't know what the hell Visigoth is talking about. I've never met the man. I swear."

visigoth's response:

"Izza witta cute-ums."

Alice's response:

"Cut that out! And get OFF of me, would you?"

visigoth's response:

"<climbing carefully off of Alice>"

Alice's response:

"It's about time, too."

Berg Man of Alcatraz's response:

"GET A ROOM!"

To Alice:

[. . . YO!!!!!!! This message comes from visigoth (Doug Cooper) @ 14:02 . . .
Now everyone assumes you're having my baby <tm Paul Anka>
]

To visigoth:

[. . . YO!!!!!!! This message comes from abradley (Alice Bradley) @ 14:03 . . .
The DNA test will reveal just whose it is . . .
]

To Alice:

[. . . YO!!!!!!! This message comes from
visigoth (Doug Cooper) @ 14:10 . . .
you mean: satan's¿
      (ulp)
]

To visigoth:

[. . . YO!!!!!!! This message comes from
abradley (Alice Bradley) @ 14:06 . . .
I mean . . .
            Jew's.
He's here right now. (ahem: Peter, care to say a few words¿)
"Yeah, it's me. I'm old and fat, but I'm fuckin' her. So fuck
you."   SEE¿ Don't you just LOVE him¿
      ]

Berg Man of Alcatraz's response:

"GET A FUCKIN' ROOM ALREADY!
"JESUS H. CHRIST ON A POGO STICK."

Jim Baumbach's response:

"If the child is born bald, it's Visigoth's."

To Alice:

[. . . YO!!!!!!! This message comes from
visigoth (Doug Cooper) @ 14:40 . . .

Did you know that a whip made of stretched bull penis can put a hole in a brick wall?
]

To visigoth:

[. . . **YO!!!!!!! This message comes from abradley (Alice Bradley) @ 14:39 . . .**
KNOW it? I've LIVED it.
]

Jane Doe's response:

These are the only PYOL's that have made me laugh in some time.
Fuck Herb; carry on!

Berg Man of Alcatraz's response:

"Yes.
"Fuck me and carry on."

visigoth's response:

"<fucking Herb, and carrying on>"

Public and private interactions mix nicely in this example from the conference called X. And while people who are not members of X may feel left out, that exchange never would have occurred if everyone on Echo was in X. It happened because of the chemistry between a particular group of people who hit it off and got to know each other a little better privately.

*　　*　　*

Imagine you have just moved into a new town. Now look at that person across the street. He is showing movies at his house tonight and you are not invited. He doesn't know you, he didn't invite you. Is this wrong? If he can't invite everyone, should his friends not get together at all? Invitations come once you start making friends. The same thing happens online. Unless you are that rare soul who is loved by all, you will never be invited to everything anyway. There's always going to be some party you're not invited to. And it's true, there are people who are rarely or never invited anywhere. Again: whose fault is that? Should cyberspace be expected to artificially correct this sad reality?

When people get to know each other and establish affinities, they break off into separate groups. As cyberspace grows, it will only become more and more like the rest of the world. Not an even bigger global village, but a bigger *collection* of villages. And it is these combinations of ways of interacting—conferences, email, YOs and places to speak, both private and public, and others that will develop, that give cyberspace the same complexity of human interaction that is found outside. There's more than one place to talk to someone here, and there's more than one way. Online services that offer only chat, or only conferences and have no private spaces, tend to be flat and lifeless.

Without all these tools, there cannot be as great an outpouring of self. And community. (This is why the World Wide Web is so flat and lifeless to me. And it is also why you won't find people returning again and again with such passion to a home page. They are too solitary. You can't feel the presence of people.) What would life be like if there was only one room to go to, and only one way to talk in that room; no telephones, no letters or faxes and everything you said was listened to by everyone else? And open to comment by everyone else? If we didn't have anywhere to go to be alone, you'd have to watch what you say—what if the boss was listening? Or your children? Total strangers? Without privacy and variety there'd be no depth, no poetry, little emotion—you can't open up in front of someone you think is creepy, you can't make love in front of your mother. And even those who long for utopia, a place where everyone gets along and no one is excluded, would come to hate the unrelieved sameness that would invariably evolve in a place where you could never choose whom to talk to, and you could never go off and be alone with your friends.

I HATE MYSELF CONTINUED...

404:1562) SuZin 30-JUN-95 19:53

I hate myself because I am going to the shore this weekend with women who worry about their manicures and bikini lines and by golly, I'm finding myself worrying about mine.

404:1572) Jackie Blue 01-JUL-95 21:43

IHM for renting 3 movies at Blockbuster instead of 2 just so I can get my Congo <tm> box of free goodies.

404:1711) Clem . . . again 10-JUL-95 9:54

IHM for not changing the station when KCR started playing selections from every recorded version of *Showboat*, and liking it (particularly the 1936).

What a freak, am I.

404:1755) Amy R. 12-JUL-95 0:11

IHM for recognizing just about every ABBA song, even though the part of my brain storing that info would be best used for True Knowledge.

271

404:1806) Bottomer Forever   13-JUL-95 21:52

I hate myself for thinking that pride is a deadly sin, even though I'm saying basically the same thing as the Pope.

404:1815) Amy R.   14-JUL-95 2:46

I hate myself.

In particular, I hate my head, throat, stomach, body temperature, and subconscious.

404:1818) Yooey's Plushy Militia   14-JUL-95 22:22

I'm better today.

404:1828) Miss "Outer" Boro 1991   15-JUL-95 16:38

I JUST HATE MYSELF, OK?!?!?

404:1829) Rob Tannenbaum   15-JUL-95 16:39

But I love you, Maud.

404:1830) Miss "Outer" Boro 1991   15-JUL-95 16:43

Please come here and prove it.

404:1831) Rob Tannenbaum   15-JUL-95 16:49

Ah, an offer . . . with no address.

404:1833) Miss "Outer" Boro 1991   15-JUL-95 16:52

I'm in midtown, darling.

404:1834) Rob Tannenbaum   15-JUL-95 16:53

Oh, MIDTOWN, why didn't you say so?
I'll be right there.
'Cab driver, take me to MIDTOWN.'

404:1835) Miss "Outer" Boro 1991   15-JUL-95 16:55

I'll be waaaiii-ting!

404:1837) Ah. . .Bottomer   15-JUL-95 17:11
Greybar Building.

404:1838) Rob Tannenbaum   15-JUL-95 17:14
Great, by midnight maybe I'll even have a floor number.

404:1839) The Lonesome Drifter   15-JUL-95 17:19
I could give it to you, but you'll have to blow me.

404:1840) Rob Tannenbaum   15-JUL-95 17:25
How do I know you REALLY have the floor number?

404:1841) ragged paul   15-JUL-95 17:29
If it's wrong, you don't have to swallow.

404:2067) Amy R.   30-JUL-95 1:13
I don't hate myself, honest. I'm a kinda ok person with a cynical streak to keep things interesting. The messy crapola I've dealt with lately are just the remainder of one of those "Smart Women, Stupid Choices" incidents.

404:2078) KZ   31-JUL-95 13:28
Hurricane warnings have been issued and everyone is stocking up on water, batteries and other necessities. So what do I do? Run down to Dolly Duz's fabulous shoe sale to stock up on expensive shoes at cheap prices.
IHM.

404:2079) Amy R.   31-JUL-95 13:29
It is very important to be well-dressed during crisis. You may get on tv!

404:2110) The Strange Apparatus 01-AUG-95 21:54

I hate myself for feeling badly that my new favorite movie is no longer BUFFY THE VAMPIRE SLAYER, nor KILLDOZER, but:
CLUELESS.

404:2126) Mary Beth 02-AUG-95 11:07

IHM because I went to see Paul Rudnick read last night and he said, "There are two kinds of people in this world—people who go see Kids and people who go to see Clueless" and I knew which one I was.

404:2127) tiger lily molsk 02-AUG-95 11:08

Okay, fine, now IHM for going to see 'Clueless' and loving it. Happy now?

404:2222) Miss Outer Boro 1991 05-AUG-95 2:51

IHM for so many reasons I don't have room to post them.

404:2223) Charles 05-AUG-95 2:55

Go ahead. We'll post fewer of our own to make room for yours.

ECHO POLL

Source: From an online survey of 308 members of Echo, October, 1995.

Margin of Error: They liked this question.

Have you ever had a crush on an Echoid? Have you ever fallen in love with an Echoid?

52% have had a crush on an Echoid.

24% have fallen in love with an Echoid.

6% said not yet.

THIS IS THE CHAPTER ABOUT SEX

I started Echo to meet guys.

It's at the bottom of everything I do. That and this obsession with death I may have mentioned once or twice. The promise of sex. Whether I'm reading, writing, watching TV, at the movies, or dancing, it all has a sensual element, and if it doesn't, on to the next thing. Without it, what's the point? Boys, boys, boys. I haven't changed a bit since I was sixteen. Of course everything is sensual, especially at a certain point every month when I want to walk out my door, point to the first guy I see, and say, "You! Yes, you. Come upstairs please." The men on Echo have left me breathless—something they said, it made me laugh, made me think, made me mad. Nowhere else am I so surrounded by the words of men. Having them isn't always the point, most of them I just like to have around, they raise the air of possibility and keep it there always, up, up, and every day I log on and think, Well, you never know. It's irresistible, I tell you. And it isn't just me. If Echo didn't offer and ful-fill this promise, the Echoids would be someplace else. What is work, art, career, or anything without sex? And it isn't just Echo. Cyberspace is a most erotic medium. Expectation. It's thrilling. Keeps you alive.

I'm going to tell the story of four couples who met in cyber-space: me and Max (not his real name), we're the normal, straight, heterosexual couple; Jack and Vivian (also not their real names); Lisa and Jonathan, the not-so-normal, not-at-all-straight, hetero-sexual couple; and Mocha and Donna, a normal, pretty straight I'd say, lesbian couple. The circumstances of how we met is different but the results haven't changed for a katrillion years. No! In cyber-space we've figured it all out. We've finally got this love thing down. Yup. Sure we have.

I usually work the weekends straight through. Two days of uninterrupted time. I might go to a movie in the middle of the day during the week, an exquisite feeling, but rarely on a Saturday or a Sunday. On the weekends I can work in peace. Except on one par-ticular summer Friday night when I got sucked into a heartbreak-ingly dark book about one family's history. I couldn't put it down. I can order food in all weekend, I thought, I don't have to pick up the phone unless it's a friend and they sound desperate, and only if they sound really desperate, otherwise I can call them next week. Oh God, I hope Echo doesn't crash or something. Monday morning I told Sue Grady that I was going to marry the author, whom I am calling Max. First I called all my friends to see who might know him. I found two. "Introduce me to him," I begged them. Then I went to the public library on St. Lukes Place, one of the loveliest streets in Manhattan. There's a ballpark on St. Lukes Place. Books and baseball. What more could you ask of a block? I was looking for an article about the author which also had a pic-ture. Okay, I'm shallow. I found it. Yeah! He's handsome! Then I wrote a letter praising his book and just before I mailed it I discovered he had an account on Echo. Is life great or what? I emailed the letter instead.

Jack is alive. These words make my friend Vivian stop breathing. She lives for them. She's a television producer, a writer, has fabulous friends, she's dated the rich and famous, but when these words flash up on her computer screen, there is no other world but the world online. When Vivian gets to the *And Now?* prompt she can type a command that tells her if the love of her life, who lives in Holland, is online right now. If he is, the computer tells her he is alive. Some programmer decided that. It could have said *Jack is online* or *Jack is logged in*. Nope. Some programmer decided it would say *Jack is alive*. Some poet.

If Jack is alive she can type a command, a demand, that he talk to her. If he types the same command back, whatever is on their screens disappears at once and suddenly they are in the same place. He can see what she is typing and she can see what he is typing, nothing else, right then and there. It's their mating ritual, their dance. Only he hasn't left his dark studio in Holland and Vivian is still in bed on the Upper East Side of Manhattan.

But when his words appear—"I need you, I need you! Come to me now!"—she is nowhere near that bed, she is in there with him, hearts racing, excited, alarmed and falling. But where is she? What is she thinking?

Flirting online is intoxicating. On other systems, where people are anonymous, it's more like a game, but on Echo everyone uses their real name. It's real. They know who you are. They know who's saying this to them. It's a much bigger risk than what passes for flirting on systems like AOL, where you don't know whom you're talking to. It makes your heart beat harder. Can you fall in love without meeting them first? Would you have sex with that person without ever having laid eyes on them? Lisa met Jonathan on Echo and several months later she put on a blindfold and made love to him before actually meeting him. She hadn't looked him in the eye until the blindfold was ripped off at a moment when she couldn't resist, she had been on the edge for month after month, ready to fall and she fell, they both fell when they saw each other for the first time, the faces of the hearts they had already come to know and neither was disappointed. Lisa Palac lives in San Francisco. She was new to Echo, but not to the online world. She was the editor of *Future Sex Magazine,* producer of an audio CD called *Cyborgasm,* she was young, beautiful, and when it came to technology and sex she was absolutely fearless. Jaze spotted her the very first night she logged in.

"Hey! I'm Jonathan Hayes. We have some friends in common and I know your work. Welcome to Echo," he YOed her. Things moved quickly through YOs and phone calls and email. By the time they actually met, they had already had sex countless times and, though neither was prepared to admit it, they had fallen in love.

Donna was terrifying online. Everyone thought so. She was confident about what she knew, she got straight to the point, and you had better be very sure of what you said if you were going to challenge her. She was formidable. We once talked about throwing Donna and another user together for a public debate online, someone whose ideas we couldn't stomach, just to see what Donna would do to him. She'd go after him like a pitbull, we knew, and wouldn't that be fun to watch?

While we were all enjoying her strength, another Echoid was falling in love, an intern who was working for me at the time, Mocha Jean Herrup. The flirtation began in public, while we all watched.

5:306) Donna Minkowitz   08-MAY-94 22:17

Hi Jane Doe. Would love to hear about the process of your getting willfully misread as a straight girl. It sort of echoes off some ideas I've been thinking about a lot . . .

5:307) mocha jean   09-MAY-94 11:05

Donna, I believe the trendier word choice there would have been "resonates." Tsk, tsk, I think someone needs to brush up on her buzz words. . . .

5:308) Donna Minkowitz   09-MAY-94 16:53

I was a trendy radical when you were in 4th grade, Mocha Jean.

5:309) mocha jean   09-MAY-94 16:56

Yeah, well, I was a conservative republican when you were a Leninist!

5:310) Donna Minkowitz   09-MAY-94 19:18

And you can imagine how exciting I find them.

Max, my new interest, wrote back right away. Nothing flirtatious, perfectly polite. What a disappointment. I wrote what I could to keep up the correspondence. I didn't want to be direct. Something he had said in his book made me think I would scare him off if I got right to the point. I could be a psychotic fan for all he knew. I found out from him a year later that he had seen my picture many times, had already formed a crush himself, and was thrilled to get my email. Not knowing this at the time, I told myself: tread carefully. I was dying to meet him. Then Vivian called to tell me he was going to be in town for a talk show. Max lives on the other coast. Great! I had mentioned that I would love to have lunch with him if he was ever in town. Maybe he'll call. I watched his TV appearance. He was graceful and articulate and I got further hooked. Careful, careful, I told myself. Let him get in touch with you. I called Jaze. He suggested writing Max and saying, "Saw you on TV. You're cute! I'm cute! My address is . . . " I couldn't. He was skittish, I was sure of this. "Do something," I said into the machine of friends who know him, but they were out of town. Perfect timing. I didn't hear a word. Two days later my out of town friends called to tell me that Max left a message on their machine asking how to get in touch with me. Moron, I thought. He couldn't call information? But maybe, I thought hopefully, he was moving equally carefully with me. But what if he had a girlfriend?

When Jack and Vivian started the dance of *talk*, the name of the program they use to communicate across the Atlantic, she barely knew him. She had met him in Holland when she was on a business trip. They knew each other for exactly a week before she returned to New York and they were both sending desperate faxes back and forth, fast and furiously, but not fast enough, and Vivian was telling all the women online every single last detail.

It was like watching some soap opera, only here you could talk back to the characters. Every day she got online and filled us in on the latest. We learned all about him along with Vivian and we advised her daily. People who never met her before were putting in their two cents' worth alongside those of us who knew her for years. On Echo, when someone is in love we all get to watch, their love life is public. To be so close when others are around you, taken away by that bliss, gives the community another level of intimacy, the sharing of that joy. Everyone feels it. The place comes alive when people are in love.

Right now what Vivian needed was our approval, and if she didn't get it, the words stung. A woman halfway across the country could send her into a tailspin if she didn't choose her words carefully. Rosemary, someone Vivian admired and respected, gently reminded Vivian of the book she was supposed to be writing and Vivian was crushed. She knew it was madness, but her mind was made up and it was not the time for gentle reminders. She needed our support.

He's married, has four kids, he's an active alcoholic and he's unemployed but I haven't had sex in five years, I haven't wanted to have sex in five years and I want him, she told us. Of course we all tried to tell her as politely as we could that she was out of her ever-loving mind, but those of us who knew her a little better had also never seen her so interested in anyone before. We knew her unrelenting loneliness, and having been online we knew that the truth of a lot of our stories was just as insane, love is not rational, and besides, there was no stopping this train. I said, "Vivian. Tell him to buy a modem." Vivian lured him online with love and a conference on the Internet (not Echo) called alt.sex.bondage. That's how people on the Internet name things.

If any of us were shocked at the extent to which she was revealing herself we weren't saying so, and this was nothing compared to what Jack was to tell the world about them when he got hooked up himself. Jack had awakened some desires in Vivian that she had long suppressed, and as she was exploring these issues, S&M, Mocha and Donna were flirting with the very same ones and they were all advising each other, publicly, but in WIT, an area that only the women could see. We were on the edges of our seats.

Lisa got on Echo after she and I, and other women, were featured in a *Mademoiselle* article about "cybergoddesses." I offered her a free account and she jumped. She had just broken off an engagement and she was looking for sex, sex, only sex, she wasn't ready for love again so soon. She was on the West Coast, the men of Echo were on the East Coast, she thought she'd be perfectly safe. Big mistake. What have I said over and over? You can't leave yourself behind when you get online. Yes, there's a distance, but it isn't a safe distance. It's the kind of distance that can make you take risks—good ones *and* stupid ones. You are not protected from yourself and your heart here. She had a thing for British men, she told me when I interviewed her, and I smiled, knowing Jaze. She never had a chance. She thought, Oh, here's a good way to meet people and have some erotic adventures. She had tried a few other places, using her own name because it "was mysterious enough not seeing someone's face." However, when she made her feelings known, she was often mistaken for a man. "You're a guy aren't you? No woman would talk like this." It just made her mad. For her it was liberating. Fuck these losers.

When Jonathan YOed Lisa, he mentioned a mutual friend who worked for *Screw,* a porn rag. So! They had something in common. Lisa YOed back. He was funny and charming, but also a bit snotty. Lisa might have logged off, but she was in the mood, she had to have someone *now, now, now,* or hang up and use the vibrator, and then Jonathan mentioned that he was British. "Were you caned in public school?" she asked him. They talked about dominance and submission for an hour and a half, then Lisa asked him, "Do you feel like taking control now?" "Maybe I do," he answered. "Well then, maybe you should give me your phone number."

While Donna and Mocha Jean were openly flirting in the Lambda Conference and in WIT, they were also trying to learn in email if the other was serious. It was all very playful and funny and both were too afraid to admit that they meant every word. It was real, what they were feeling was real, they were dying to meet, but neither wanted to be the one to take the first step out of cyberspace. I saw it all. I knew that agitation well. Vivian knew Donna, so she and I plotted on the phone to get them together. Vivian was having a birthday dinner and Donna was coming. "Invite Mocha Jean along," she told me. Mocha learned that I knew, we all knew, and she started showing me Donna's email. "What does she mean by this?? Is she interested you think?" If you type last, you can see when someone was on . . . last. Mocha typed last constantly. If

Donna logged in and out quickly Mocha would cry, "She's avoiding me!" But she made up her mind, she was going after Donna. Their first meeting was disastrous.

Donna went to an Echo face-to-face in Brooklyn. Mocha didn't live in Brooklyn so Donna never expected her to come. She hadn't been feeling well and didn't pay much attention to how she looked. Who's going to be there anyway? she thought. But Mocha had read that Donna was planning to go and she spent the morning putting together the perfect outfit. Twenty-four years old and the picture of health, Mocha came bouncing in. Donna was only thirty at the time but she felt she was too old. Mocha was sure her youth would be an attraction. Believing Donna to be a super-confident chick, she went right up to Donna and smiled. "Hi! I'm Mocha!" Mocha was thinking, I'm young! I have a charming smile! This is exactly what she wants. Donna, who terrified us all with her intelligence and courage, was intimidated. And shy. I look terrible, she thought. Mocha wondered why Donna kept scowling at her.

Months would go by and Max would be absolutely silent. I would email him from time to time and tell him stories about myself, the stories I thought he might recognize. But I didn't say a lot. I was dating one guy after another, and while none of them had gotten through to my heart, I was concentrating on the men right there in front of me. Slowly though, Max and I got to know one another. Then a friend called to tell me he was going to be in New York to accept an award. Why hadn't Max told me? Moron, I thought again. I knew instinctively that he was interested in me. I couldn't be sure of the nature or extent of his interest, but I knew I had him on some level. Why didn't he tell me he was going to be in town?

When it comes to matters of the heart I try not to wonder about why people do the wacko things they do, who can know? I just went to the NYU building where he was going to appear on a panel before receiving the award that night and worried, Is this the way stalkers behave?

I was early. I found a seat and then went out to bring back a cup of coffee to drink while I waited. When I walked back in the door I looked up and straight into his eyes. Wait a minute. I was going to go up and say hi *afterward*. Totally unprepared I said only, "Max! I'm Stacy!" And I tried my best to smile and be friendly even though I was completely flustered. He didn't say anything immediately, so I took off my sunglasses and said, "Stacy. From Echo." He was friendly but not overly so. Think fast. On my way out for coffee I passed by the most beautiful wooden door, something about it I couldn't resist, and I went in. It was a room like no other I had seen at NYU. I'm an assistant professor there and we don't have rooms like this where I teach. Dark wood, long drapes, thick carpet, and big fat couches and chairs and antiques all over the place and it was so peaceful. "Come see this room I've found," I told him. I'll show it to him like a present, I thought. He followed. We talked until he had to join the panel. I went up to him afterwards to say good-bye and he asked me to dinner the next night.

"If there's a purpose to life it's to love and communicate," Vivian told me. She had always been interested in telecommunications. First writing, then television journalism, and now cyberspace. And when it came to men, after being hurt so often, she was scared. The setting was perfect. She had just the distance she needed to get to know the heart of the man who had made himself unforgettable their very first meeting. Email, faxes, letters, telephone calls, she was in an orgy of communication and they got to know each other deeply. Fast. We were having horrendous problems with the equipment at the time, and Echo was crashing constantly it seemed. When it did, I'd get desperate phone calls from Vivian. Me, Scotty, Kevin, Mark, and Sue would all be on the floor with screwdrivers, cables and keyboards, rolling in cat hair and dust, and Vivian would plead, "You MUST get Echo back up." We worked hard for her. We all have known the agony of love. All the while, the women of WIT continued to follow the *Days of Our Lives* of Vivian and Jack. Most were cautious, but there was one woman who was supportive. This person didn't even like Vivian, but Vivian's predicament made her kind. She had also had an affair with a married man and this married man had left his wife for her. "You never hear those stories," Vivian said. And she was right. You never hear stories about adultery with happy endings. In cyberspace you hear it all, you hear every side of the story eventually. Vivian had just started seeing someone when she went off to Holland and met Jack. Jack was jealous of this man and Vivian was jealous of his wife and all the women on the Internet. Jack's stories in alt.sex.bondage made him a popular man among the S&M girls of the Net. He was a shameless flirt. And, he was an exhibitionist but, like Donna, he could also be very shy in person. Being online was like public speaking, but he had more control. He could choose his words carefully. Unlike being up in front of people when there's no time, he was back in his room, taking all the time he needed to say just what he wanted, creating just the right effect. And he could write. Vivian told me that if those first letters had been poorly written, the relationship would have ended right there.

They had resisted each other when she was in Holland but that was gone now. She was ready. He was ready. They had met in Holland in October. Jack came to America in January. When they finally got together they had the most extreme sex of their lives. They stayed in bed for two weeks and we didn't hear a word. The women were furious! We were used to daily reports, we'd been with her all through this, rooting for her, and now she dropped us cold. What was happening? I called Vivian and she logged in briefly to tell us everything was great. And when they were done, and Jack was back in Holland, he told everyone on the Internet absolutely everything. He was scared and needed their help.

" . . . Over the days, the sex became more and more extreme. We began with some gentle bondage, which rapidly degenerated into strangulation and restrictive breathing. Then we moved into physical violence. It was relatively gentle at first, but we were both unable to stop ourselves from raising the stakes with extreme rapidity.

" . . . At that point, I underwent an emotional collapse. How could I love somebody (and I do love her, more than life itself!), how could I love somebody and bear to hurt them like that? . . . Is it possible to really love somebody and yet wish to hurt them so severely? . . . I need some help in trying to think through these issues—for my own sake as well as Vivian's. I throw myself on your mercy."

Lisa wanted to come to New York, but Jonathan was reluctant. "What? Are you the Elephant Man?" she asked him. No, but he was in the process of getting back into shape and he didn't want her to see him until he was. Later, Lisa went to have a facial. When it was over they dimmed the lights and placed cold packs on her eyes. So relaxed. Just dreaming. Eyes covered, thoughts and pictures drifting. Then, that's it! "I'll wear a blindfold. I'll be able to meet Jonathan and maybe we'll have sex and maybe we won't. But we can be in the same room together and I can hear his voice and feel him hold my hand." In her original plan, the blindfold would never come off. She just wanted to touch him. She just wanted to be in the *same room*. Cyberspace gets you close, so close, but there comes a time when you have to put out your hand and touch. The waiting and the playing, thoughts and hearts from a distance—it makes the touch, when it finally happens, just that much more exquisite. She would come to him blindfolded and then return when Jonathan was ready to have her see him. He agreed. But Jonathan made his own plans. He elaborated on Lisa's fantasy. He had a friend, a dominatrix, waiting in the hall to put the blindfold on.

First she walked Lisa in and gave her a cocktail. Then they both held her and touched her and kissed her for hours. The blindfold made Lisa acutely and deliriously aware of every single thing that went on. When it was removed everything was blazing. "You're my hero! You are a national treasure!" Jonathan told her.

"Oh my God she's seen me and she doesn't like what I look like," Donna moaned. Mocha found her very odd but very endearing. When they got back online Donna sent her a message. "What a strange meeting . . . " she wrote in despair. She hadn't been feeling well. No fair. If only she had had a chance to prepare. "Mocha was so intimidating." And Mocha had worn her best shoes! So the tables were reversed. Online fearless, offline shy for Donna, and just the opposite for Mocha. Donna needn't have worried. Mocha had had a backburner thing for the outspoken Donna Minkowitz for some time it turned out. She read her stuff in the *Village Voice,* had seen her at a meeting a couple of years before, and she was attracted to people who were goofy and smart—nerds. That was Donna. When Donna logged into Echo for the first time, Mocha thought, Well! Echo just got a little more interesting. Then Donna started posting everywhere about sex and Mocha was amazed: "What guts." Most people lurk for a while until they get a feel for the place, but Donna came out blasting. It was one thing for Mocha to flirt with Donna, she knew who Donna was. But for Donna to flirt back! Mocha could have been anyone. "I could have been a man," Mocha said, laughing later. Courageous as she seemed online, Donna felt vulnerable when her physical presence was attached to her words. Mocha didn't know. Donna's style led her to be more flirtatious than she had ever been in her life. She took risks. For Donna.

After meeting, they started talking more frequently in the item Vivian had started about dominance and submission. In it, they formed their very own cyberleather community. They were posting about what was really important to them and loving it. It's a heady experience to let it out. To risk. And their words won them all over. Now the trick was to win over the flesh. Neither Donna nor Mocha had lost interest but both were sure they had lost ground. They knew they had to reconnect with words. They got back online like it was a reconnaissance mission. When Mocha got Donna's message she took the plunge. "I love it when you get didactic. It makes for such sexy writing." Yes! Donna was having a horrible day at work, it was just what she needed. All was not lost. Their false start only brought them closer and they opened up like they never had, both in front of us all and in email.

"There was so much pleasure doing this publicly," Mocha told me. And being caught in the swirl of romance is delicious for anyone who comes close. We were all drawn in. She ran into another user, Diamond, and Diamond asked, "So? Is she taking you to breakfast now?" Donna had just thrown down the gauntlet in Lambda and invited Mocha out to eat. Everyone was talking about them. The editors and I chatted about them during a planning meeting at *Ms.*

The breakfast lasted hours and a week later they were an official item.

Max and I had dinner and talked until two in the morning. He didn't make a move though, and I began to doubt my instincts. I took him home but he sat at my desk the entire time and never joined me on the couch. He left New York and we resumed our correspondence. And, there it was again. The spark of interest. That's it. I wrote him and said, "Max. When it comes to us I want you to think of that Abba song, 'Take a Chance on Me.'" (Yes. I adore Abba. Just be quiet, you.) Finally it came out. He had a major crush, but he was sure I wasn't in the least bit interested. We went at it. We told each other everything. In email and in phone calls, in the program *talk,* and in YOs we said the things we'd been waiting a year to say. He was the one I flirted with on television when we did the interactive TV show with the SciFi Channel. On national TV, in words that scrolled across the bottom of the screen, I joked with him about snow during a heat wave because we both love snow. I couldn't work and I didn't care. At any time, in the middle of whatever I was doing, his words might appear on the screen: *I love you.* Constant anticipation. And that boy certainly had a way with words. It was madness. But we shared a similar darkness and a similar hope.

He came back. The next time he YOed me when he returned to California he could speak with authority: *I was just lying on the couch dreaming of what I will do to you when I see you again. It involves your couch, opening your legs, tongues and blindfolds.* Even though I was on the computer, my body was right there with me, flushed, heart racing. For those of you who think the computer is taking us away from our bodies, I can assure you we take our bodies with us when we go. My heart and mind wouldn't let my flesh miss out on this.

Vivian and Jack were astounded by the response they got to his declaration on the Internet. *Get help. Stop what you are doing.* They had expected support. Here they were, among S&M enthusiasts around the world, and they surpassed them all their very first time at bat. Total newcomers and they had shocked everyone. Well, not everyone. A few women invited Jack to visit them. Vivian was beside herself. Was it betrayal? The women started emailing Jack privately. If nothing ever happens, is it cheating? he asked her. It felt like cheating to Vivian. We talk about this on Echo occasionally. We usually decide that if feelings are involved, it's getting close. Vivian was afraid. Email had brought them together, after all. Sharing their fantasies online for months had allowed them to go as far as they did. It felt safer to confront what terrified and attracted them there first.

They started having cybersex. It's like phone sex only you type in what you want to say. I know people who have never tried it sometimes dismiss it—you type it instead of do it? But it does have its attractions. It's a matter of taste. I tried it once and didn't like it myself. I tried phone sex once, too, and didn't like that either. While it's not a substitute for real sex, it's something to do when you're not in a position to have physical sex with the person you love. It's a form of foreplay. To dismiss it would be like asking why flirt, or rent porn films or look at magazines or read erotic literature, or anything else instead of actually having sex. Why? Because it can be fun. Unlike physical sex, Vivian told me, "You know what's going on in someone's head."

Think about it. When you're making love, you are up and down and in and out and wrapped around someone and while you may or may not know their heart and how they think, you rarely know just what it is that they are thinking at that moment. It is interesting, more than interesting, to think that you can. Not better, just different. "The words go right into your head, like telepathy," Vivian explained. When you're having physical sex with someone, you could be thinking about anything or anyone. When you're having cybersex, you're right there, you can't go into yourself for too long or it won't work. To keep each other aroused, you have to tell each other what you are thinking and feeling. "Half the time you don't want to know . . . " Jack told me. It's scary. It's a responsibility to know. Email and talk with Vivian became Jack's lifeline. He told her things he couldn't tell other people. It took their actual, physical relationship deeper. It's a strange intimacy.

It also makes me understand why Vivian got nervous when women emailed Jack asking him to explore his fantasies with them. "It's like walking into a room and seeing him flirting with someone," Vivian told me. "Women are threatened by emotional infidelity and men are threatened by sexual infidelity." When I asked Jack if it would have been cheating if he had explored these fantasies with other women in email only, he said no. What if Vivian had? "It would be cheating," he answered. Double standards extend into cyberspace.

After they got over the initial shock, their Internet friends were more supportive. A telephone counselor in California was particularly helpful to Jack, and he used him like a therapist. Jack went into a rehab and took his computer with him. While they wouldn't let them talk online, he was able to keep in touch via email. Vivian went to see him when he got out.

Lisa found the one man who was not afraid of her sexuality. In *Future Sex,* she wrote about him as the man "who knew how to finish what was on his plate." They flew back and forth and tried everything. They took mutual pleasure in every erotic toy, adventure, and game. "It was magic," Lisa told me. But they were not to be forever. When they broke up Lisa wrote me to close her account. She couldn't bear to be *that close* to him and not have him. This happens frequently. Again, Echo is like a small town, and everyone knows who's seeing who, and you break up, but there they are, all over the place, every damn day, you can't escape it and whenever a couple stops seeing each other I wonder—which one will be closing their account? Her exile only lasted a few months. They got back in touch and Lisa returned. They are now good friends.

And Max and I learned all the things that you can't learn about someone online, what they feel like, smell like, make love like. Physical chemistry can't be accurately gauged online. What is behind those words? Is he loud or quiet? There's so little sound in cyberspace. In person Max was stern, tentative, and distant. Everything he already was in email, but the message wasn't strong enough without the power of his every move inescapably right there in front of me. Hope makes you miss things, just like anywhere else. We simply didn't get along as well in person as we did online. Online, we left a few things out. We're friends. We still talk and email and YO and we send each other gifts. There is a warmth and generosity there that is also inescapable.

Mocha Jean and Donna didn't last either, but it was to be the longest relationship either of them had ever had. Donna was the one to leave Echo. It seems whoever found Echo first gets to stay. Of the four couples I have written about, only one is still together, Vivian and Jack.

I wonder how the odds in cyberspace stack up against any other situation. You win some, you lose some, nothing new in cyberspace here. But there are a few problems, that while not unique, are exacerbated by this environment. In cyberspace you have more control over how someone sees you. Everything begins with words. You are who you say you are. And you can make yourself sound really good. Then, when someone meets you in person, they may be disappointed by the complicated reality of you. No one's *that* good. But cyberspace plays with our hopes. People who are prone to project pull out all the stops in cyberspace. We aren't so much who we say we are to some, we are who they hope (or fear) we are. Longing and distance create the most perfect (or nightmarish) pictures. Finally, cyberspace invites risk from the inexperienced. Years of romantic wisdom go right out the window and some people act like teenagers again. They just don't think.

These patterns are not necessarily bad, in some cases they're good, in moderation—sometimes we think too much and we should act more like teenagers when it comes to matters of the heart. A little. In any case these patterns are all certainly human and familiar. Misrepresentations and overexpectations are troublesome everywhere. It just happens in reverse online. In the physical world, sometimes you get fooled by what someone looks like on the outside. Online, you can get fooled by what they look like on the inside. But these are the risks you take in love. As people become more familiar with cyberspace they regain the sophistication they abandon when they first get online.

How can it happen? people ask. How can you fall in love online? The answer: *The same way you fall in love anywhere else.* And if you've had bad patterns in love elsewhere, then you're going to get to watch in horror as you repeat those patterns online. Pain, heartache, and all the unspeakably nasty things we do to each other in the name of love, they're all here. When Jonathan and Lisa, and me and Max, and Mocha and Donna broke up, I would guess that they all ended much the same way all our relationships ended. The course of any relationship is the same online. Perhaps cyberspace favors people who are comfortable with distance. It must be true, I think. But that doesn't mean that the only people who are falling in love online are the people who are comfortable with distance. When I look at the people whose stories I have just told, it's true for maybe half. The other half are active online because they are very social and expressive people. Painting, writing, words, music, telephones, this is just another medium to them. Does cyberspace prolong relationships that would have ended sooner, like other relationships that have a long distance element? Or does it give people who would not have gotten together otherwise just the distance they needed to see that this person was the one for them?

There have now been more marriages among Echoids than I can keep track of. More babies, endless romances, I swear we are the Peyton Place of the online world. Part of that is probably due to the fact that we have more women, there's more opportunity. And again, the fact that it's not anonymous. It's the perfect combination of distance and intimacy. These ready-made boundaries make it easy to play. You can tell your sexual secrets.

This is what's so great about romance online: it brings back the extended courtship and that's exciting. Becoming emotionally and intellectually intimate before you have sex makes the sex more thrilling. You have all these simultaneous dialogues going on when you're at the point where you just can't get enough, when drowning feels so, so good. And, unlike life, your words linger here. The conversations don't disappear. You can go back to them again and

again. Sometimes I look at the drives that store everything that is
said on Echo and see cardboard boxes of love letters that the
Echoids save. With electricity wrapping their words like red rib-
bons, I think—sex, love, that's what wires Echo.

I HATE MYSELF...
THE FINAL INSTALLMENT

404:2376) Everyone Likes Josh Karpf   16-AUG-95 7:29

I hate myself for making the only woman I've ever proposed to late for her plane in my dream, when it was really nice of her to show UP in my dream; I hadn't thought about her in years, and had forgotten her face.

404:2427) tiger lily molsk   17-AUG-95 23:34

Okay, IHM for trying to clean Joey Cat's infected paw and accidentally getting hydrogen peroxide in his eye, and now it's all red and awful-looking, and IHM for freaking out about it and being useless, and IHM for being a bad cat-owner and feeling inadequate and crying and shit.

404:2453) Amy R.   20-AUG-95 2:17

IHM for my paranoia and low self-esteem. However, I do have most excellent fingers.

404:2485) tiger lily molsk   23-AUG-95 13:11

IHM for having cramps and eating cake for lunch and calling it 'therapy.'

404:2551) brindle coyote   25-AUG-95 17:56

IHM for thinking that asshole fifi dog owners should all be shot.

**404:2558) It's not the Hebe,
           it's the Jewmidity**   25-AUG-95 22:53

IHM for owning a fifidog <tm>.

404:2601) Neandergal   31-AUG-95 22:13

IHM for getting Nebraska confused with North Dakota.

404:2602) The Once and Future Rotator   31-AUG-95 22:22

That's okay, I can't keep Idaho and Iowa straight.

404:2603) Charles   31-AUG-95 22:42

But do you hate yourself?

404:2604) The Once and Future Rotator   31-AUG-95 22:45

Well, sure, that's a given.

404:2621) The Reverend Bottomer, Deathist.   01-SEP-95 19:56

IHM because I control the entire universe and, lets face it, it sucks sometimes, doesn't it?

404:2666) Mary Beth   14-SEP-95 14:01

IHM for having a damn good sex dream about Chandler from *Friends*. IHM for feeling like my subconscious is laughing at me.

404:2718) ragged paul   16-SEP-95 17:14

IHM for trying to be a social butterfly when I am really a beetle.

404:2786) Charles   23-SEP-95 4:55

IHM for going to bed at 7:30 pm Friday evening and waking up at

4:30 a.m. Saturday morning—WIDE awake.
And wanting: donuts.

404:3014) Extra T. (formerly almost known as ET)   04-NOV-95 8:39
I hate myself for being taken out to a fancy restaurant and making poor ordering choices due to lack of focus.

404:3016) Extra T. (formerly almost known as ET)   04-NOV-95 8:42
I hate myself for using all passive verbs in the post above.

404:3036) NYC shrink   06-NOV-95 22:53
IHM because I'm really good at it and everyone has to have a strength.

404:3038) Topper   06-NOV-95 23:41
I hate myself for not becoming the Fabulous Girl I was meant to be.

404:3089) Amy R.   13-NOV-95 9:28
IHM for being up yet again for the dumb abominable snowman owning family show at 4:30 on this bout of insomnia. However, the former-Oscar nominated actor dude probably hates himself more for being in it.

404:3090) Shallow Bottomer   13-NOV-95 10:06
I hate myself for knowing this is Alf.

404:3091) Glen Rogers   13-NOV-95 10:07
No, it isn't. It's HARRY & THE HENDERSONS.

404:3092) Shallow Bottomer   13-NOV-95 10:08
Isn't that a movie? Or was that made into a TV show? Now I don't hate myself!

404:3093) Crooked Clem   **13-NOV-95 10:12**

I think it IS Alf.

404:3094) Shallow Bottomer   **13-NOV-95 10:22**

IHM.

404:3095) Crooked Clem   **13-NOV-95 10:25**

IH us both.

404:4179) Skyvue   **30-JUN-96 2:26**

IHM for being the only person on Echo who isn't a Metrobeat contributor.

404:4180) oedipa   **30-JUN-96 8:38**

IHM for telling Skyvue that I have never been a contributor to MetroBeat, iGuide, or WORD.

404:4181) Jaguar   **30-JUN-96 8:44**

So just what the hell are you doing with your life, pal?

404:4182) oedipa   **30-JUN-96 8:45**

I try to Hate Myself here and there. It passes the time.

A CHRISTMAS MOMENT . . .

A Christmas moment from our Central Conference. This is Echo to a tee. It's hard for me to imagine anything like this springing up in any other online community, it so perfectly reflects the style and personality that is Echo.

196:76) Joey Davis, Jr.　　　　　　　**16-DEC-95 12:37**
Bring me some figgy pudding!!!!
Molly, bring me some fucking figgy pudding!!!!

196:77) molsk in boots　　　　　　　**16-DEC-95 13:04**
Yes, dear.

196:79) Avenging Disco Godfather　　　**16-DEC-95 14:40**
Tiny Angry Tim <tm>

196:81) goat noise　　　　　　　　　　**16-DEC-95 21:07**
Bring Us Some Goddamn Fucking Figgy Pudding in Seven Parts

Part 1
bring us some goddamn fucking figgy pudding
bring us some goddamn fucking figgy pudding

Part 2

whats the wait

whats the fucking delay

were hungry

were out here in the cold and youre in that big house of yours
    that sits there grinning idiotically on its cool green lawn

your whole damn familys pigging out on turkey and tater tots and
    figgy fucking pudding

youve got barrels of the stuff

youve got crates of the shit stashed in your basement

you export your leftover figgy pudding to your grandmother in
    Montana and you wont give us any

you goddamn little Republican prick

Part 3

I tell you what

we wont go until we get some

thats the deal

we wont go

until we fucking get some

were hungry were cold and were pissed

well stand out here on your lawn like demented howling lawn
jockeys

as cars go flying by through the ham-stinking night

well stand out here and wail

well set up a sound system on your lawn and blast you with
    Southern Culture on the Skids songs till your ears bleed prick

Part 4

I kid you not

we want some figgy pudding

Part 5
Mr. No Figgy Pudding
Mr. No Figgy Pudding,
feh!

Part 6
no you dumb jerk we dont want chocolate pudding
we dont want goddamn butterscotch pudding
we dont want banana frigging pudding-and-pie-filling
and we sure as hell dont want no goddamn figgy custard
I said figgy pudding   I meant figgy pudding

Part 7
and now well say it one last time
well say it one last time before we lose it asshole
before we lose all semblance of self-control
before we rise up bigtime and spray your house with the automatic weapon fire of our souls
and burn it with the napalm of our wanting hearts
and piss our pain on your stupid petty stingy-ass ashes
were cold
were hungry
and were not all that pleased with your attitude
NOW BRING US SOME GODDAMN FUCKING FIGGY PUDDING!

Face-2-Face And Now? Mystery Button

ECHO POLL

Source: From an online survey of 321 members of Echo, November 1995.

Margin of Error: I don't know, do you think they're just trying to be nice? Frauds.

Why do you stay on Echo?

35% said because the people are: rude, fascinating, bright, opinionated, caring, smart, superior, the best minds on the Net, strange, clever, frightening, interesting, cultured.

27% said because Echo is: rude, friendly, homey, scandalous, unique, personal, loud, scintillating, creative, cool, a nice place to come home to.

14% had no idea why they stick around.

5% stay purely out of habit.

2 people said, "Good question," and immediately closed their accounts.

THAT'S LIFE IN THE INFERNO OF POST MODERNITY

Before I wrap this up I want to include an item from Culture. It's a special item because reading it is like flipping through a photo album of the very heart of cyberspace. It demonstrates what is most unique about this medium. Although we are talking about O.J. Simpson, this chapter is not about O.J. Simpson. It is about a group of people talking about O.J. Simpson. It's a community talking about a community event.

Jacked into the home version of the multimedia game, with their TVs on and their computers hooked up to Echo, people reacted, debated, deconstructed, and ultimately shared an intimate moment over the electronic back fence through what had to be one of the most surreal media events of 1994: following that white Bronco.

When it was just the TV, we had the bond or connection that we get from watching televised history together. Remember watch-

307

ing Bobby Kennedy's death train? Armstrong walking on the moon? The *Challenger* explosion? With cyberspace, now we watch and we talk about it as we are watching. We're not just a silent group of witnesses anymore. We're sharing our responses and we're sharing them in realtime, as history unfolds. Think what it would have been like if you could have talked to the rest of America while you watched the young JFK, Jr. salute his father's coffin. Cyberspace takes the connection we had before and revs it up until we know like we didn't know before, that none of us was alone when these things happened.

Our reactions, the collision and integration of online and offline life, are all now part of the history. The participants in this particular discussion include the director of an art museum in New York City, the editor of a newspaper in Los Angeles, a medical professional, a graduate student, a professor, a performance artist, an editor at *Ms. Magazine,* musicians, lawyers—in twenty-four hours they said enough to fill over ninety pages.

I've edited their discussion mercilessly. They may seem heartless because I have taken out pages of analysis and sympathy for every character, every element of the whole tragic affair. Even with my cutthroat editing, personalities emerge from this singular commentary on media, culture, O.J. Simpson, and the New York Knicks.

Item 550 17-JUN-94 22:31 Jonathan Hayes
That's Life in the Inferno of Postmodernity!

On my TV right now, OJ Simpson is driving down a highway 3,000 miles from me, holding a gun to his head. I am watching it live on TV.
What's going on?

550:1) Jonathan Hayes   **17-JUN-94 22:32**
This is incredible.

550:2) Ann   17-JUN-94 22:33

It's very sad.

550:3) doktor dorje   17-JUN-94 22:33

They are reading his letter, psychoanalyzing him, and following him in a copter on 1010 WINS.

550:4) Ann   17-JUN-94 22:34

Don't you think they'll run out of gas soon?
I didn't even know who he was before yesterday.

550:7) Jonathan Hayes   17-JUN-94 22:36

I think it's fascinating that this banal image, a white car moving down an empty road, should be so rivetting.

550:8) Twang   17-JUN-94 22:36

You're right Jaze—this is the Inferno of Post Modernity at its most bizarre and fascinating. This hero is self-destructing live on CNN.
I keep thinking of Lee Harvey Oswald getting shot on Sunday morning TV.

550:9) Jonathan Hayes   17-JUN-94 22:36

It's like foreplay.

550:10) Twang   17-JUN-94 22:37

Great shot right now on CNN—you can almost see into the car.
Just heard they have a hostage negotiator standing by.

550:12) Jonathan Hayes   17-JUN-94 22:38

The radio is now nothing but a series of highway numbers and offramps and intersections.

550:13) Twang   **17-JUN-94 22:38**

Interesting tidbit: they traced him via a call he made on the car phone.

550:15) Ann   **17-JUN-94 22:40**

I think he's sort of heroic now, in a sad way. I mean most people watching will be so pleased if he gets to his mothers house and it will seem a heroic act. I haven't expressed myself right. This is so bizarre.

I wish he had email in the car.

550:17) Jonathan Hayes   **17-JUN-94 22:41**

No, Ann, most people are wanting him to:

A) Shoot himself

B) Die in a fiery crash like in a movie

C) Be shot by the Police

If he's shot by the Police, THEN he'll be a hero.

550:19) doktor dorje   **17-JUN-94 22:42**

Email in the Van—that is the next step.

This is just so fuckin crazy! The TV movie is happening NOW!

550:26) Snoop Trouty Trout   **17-JUN-94 22:43**

This needs music—something dramatic and tragic.

550:27) Jonathan Hayes   **17-JUN-94 22:43**

I'm waiting for a helicopter crash. The sky must be packed with them.

Ah. Brentwood. Mom's place. THE DENOUEMENT.

550:28) Twang   **17-JUN-94 22:43**

If it goes to trial he could get the death penalty. What is it in CA? Chair? Lethal injection? Gas chamber?

550:30) Ann   17-JUN-94 22:44

They used gas last year in SF for the first time in years.

550:31) Jonathan Hayes   17-JUN-94 22:44

They usually use acid in SF.

550:35) Snoop Trouty Trout`   17-JUN-94 22:46

You think he would call first?
Hello Ma?

550:36) Ann   17-JUN-94 22:46

He's not even been found guilty yet.
He may not have done it.

550:41) Jonathan Hayes   17-JUN-94 22:47

Oh, DO get a grip, Ann! It isn't that he's guilty or innocent, it's that
he's RUNNING!

550:45) Jonathan Hayes   17-JUN-94 22:47

I hope that OJ makes a detour from Brentwood and nails this hor-
rid radio psychiatrist.
I wonder what they're listening to in the Suicide Bronco.
Thank God he did this while it was still light.

550:60) Ann   17-JUN-94 22:51

He may not have done it, and it was an act of passion, something
that has been excluded from the death penalty in many countries
that do use it.

550:66) Twang   17-JUN-94 22:53

They found a bloody glove at his house afterwards—suggesting it
may have been planned.

Also, he flew off to Chicago right afterwards, tried to establish an alibi there—really sounds premeditated.

OOH OOH! They're exiting the freeway now!

550:67) GreenPig   17-JUN-94 22:53
This thing—I mean us—reminds me of Tertullian, who said that the greatest joy in heaven would be watching the torments of the damned below.

550:69) viadyer   17-JUN-94 22:53
He should take his own life, or spend the rest of his life in jail. He should pay the government's cost of this spectacle.

550:71) Jonathan Hayes   17-JUN-94 22:54
Great! More directions! I feel like I could drive from Orange County to Brentwood in my sleep.

550:72) Ann   17-JUN-94 22:54
I don't think he should pay for it. This is what we pay taxes for.

550:75) Jonathan Hayes   17-JUN-94 22:55
AH! SO THIS IS WHY WE PAY TAXES!

550:76) Twang   17-JUN-94 22:55
THEY BROUGHT IN A SWAT TEAM!

550:78) Jonathan Hayes   17-JUN-94 22:55
A SWAT Team? Now THAT's what we pay our taxes for!

550:79) doktor dorje   17-JUN-94 22:56
The radio guy started blabbing the SWAT tactics on air—mentioning the camoflauged snipers and right after saying he didn't wanna compromise security. The announcer interrupted him to go to the exit ramp.

550:80) Ann   17-JUN-94 22:56

I don't understand why he hasn't run out of gas yet. That car looks like a gas guzzler.

550:84) Jonathan Hayes   17-JUN-94 22:57

Well, that's where you're wrong, Ann! The Bronco gets a very reasonable 23mpg city and 30 mpg highway.

550:85) Snoop Trouty Trout   17-JUN-94 22:57

MOM!

I'm hoooome!

550:87) doktor dorje   17-JUN-94 22:57

HE'S THERE!!!!

HE'S THERE!!!!

550:89) Jonathan Hayes   17-JUN-94 22:57

I wonder what the camouflaged snipers wear in Brentwood.

550:95) Twang   17-JUN-94 22:58

Ford's getting some great publicity here.

550:96) Ann   17-JUN-94 22:58

If they don't let him see his mother I'm going to cry.

550:98) Twang   17-JUN-94 22:59

Ann, you are CNN's ideal audience member.

550:107) Twang   17-JUN-94 23:00

THE FUGITIVE is on pay-per-view tonight, by coincidence.

550:108) Snoop Trouty Trout   17-JUN-94 23:00

Ch 2 has a ground shot.

550:117) Snoop Trouty Trout   **17-JUN-94 23:02**
Give him a mic and let HIM do the play by play.

[An announcer uses the term 'lookie-loo.']

550:120) doktor dorje   **17-JUN-94 23:02**
A "lookie-loo"?

550:123) Jonathan Hayes   **17-JUN-94 23:03**
THAT "lookie-loo", my friend, is why we live in New York City, rather than in fucking California.

550:126) Twang   **17-JUN-94 23:03**
Boy, was Kurt Cobain a boring suicide.

550:130) doktor dorje   **17-JUN-94 23:04**
He's outta the car!

550:139) ur-Josh Karpf   **17-JUN-94 23:06**
EVERY BROADCAST CHANNEL BUT 13 IS CARRYING THIS LIVE. I've never seen anything like this. I used to advocate broadcasting executions to educate people about the horror of capital punishment but not any more; this is gratuitous entertainment for the giggling, squirming masses.
The choppers are being ordered to pull away from the car now—the sheer number of aircraft over the car are fucking up c-phone communication with the negotiators. I'm waiting for a newshound to stick a microphone in the driver's window: "What are your feelings now, Mr. O.J.?"

550:141) Twang   **17-JUN-94 23:06**
Look! His dog has come out into the driveway.
What's on Channel 13?

550:148) Jonathan Hayes   **17-JUN-94 23:07**
Still no groundshot on Fox.

550:168) David Yamada   **17-JUN-94 23:13**
Wow.
Stunning and bizarre.
I hope he doesn't die here.

550:175) Ann   **17-JUN-94 23:14**
I hope he doesn't die at all. I hope he didn't even do it. I hope
something miraculous happens soon.

550:179) Twang   **17-JUN-94 23:14**
Deus ex machina, Ann? Worked for Medea!

550:181) Snoop Trouty Trout   **17-JUN-94 23:14**
Is this a great country or what?

550:187) Vantage, jAe   **17-JUN-94 23:15**
He's coming out.

550:191) Jonathan Hayes   **17-JUN-94 23:16**
If he blows himself away, do you think he will get out of the car and
do it for the cameras?

550:196) Snoop Trouty Trout   **17-JUN-94 23:17**
In Hawaii, they have a place that you can run to to be absolved.
But I don't think you can get there in a Bronco.

550:200) ur-Josh Karpf   **17-JUN-94 23:17**
Peter Jennings is pontificating now, representing sad America's
conscience.
I'll let him do it only because he shut up Baba Wawa.

550:203) Jonathan Hayes   **17-JUN-94 23:18**

Has this pre-empted the Knicks game?

550:212) Twang   **17-JUN-94 23:19**

No, the Knicks game is on, or rather was a while ago. Ch 4's gone to a commercial now.

550:215) ur-Josh Karpf   **17-JUN-94 23:21**

Cops are trying to patch a phone call to mom. Place your bets as to whether it goes on the air.

550:220) Snoop Trouty Trout   **17-JUN-94 23:21**

If it's a cellular phone call they could capture it and broadcast it.

550:234) Jonathan Hayes   **17-JUN-94 23:25**

THERE IT IS AGAIN! A "lookie-loo"!

That expression makes me want to off an Angeleno.

550:236) Ann   **17-JUN-94 23:25**

How old are the children?

550:238) Twang   **17-JUN-94 23:25**

Kids are under 10.

550:243) Vantage, jAe   **17-JUN-94 23:26**

Ah well, the lights are going.

550:248) Twang   **17-JUN-94 23:27**

Like I said, good thing the car's white.

550:261) Jonathan Hayes   **17-JUN-94 23:29**

What's the score in the Knicks game?

550:273) Twang 17-JUN-94 23:31

OJ's trying to phone the house, but the battery on his cellular phone is dying!

550:276) Josh Save the Juice Karpf 17-JUN-94 23:32

Now he's writing a message on the window with a Twinkie.

550:284) gail j 17-JUN-94 23:33

Houston up by 1 point, 3 minutes remaining.

550:285) Jonathan Hayes 17-JUN-94 23:33

Well, I tell you one thing: when I take it on the lam after my murder spree, I shall be taking two dixie cups and a length of twine.

550:286) Jonathan Hayes 17-JUN-94 23:34

Which game in the series is this?

550:292) Vantage, jAe 17-JUN-94 23:34

Game 5 Jaze.

550:297) Josh Save the Juice Karpf 17-JUN-94 23:35

He's on the phone!

550:307) doktor dorje 17-JUN-94 23:37

"I'm sorry but your call cannot be connected at this time . . . "

550:312) Ann 17-JUN-94 23:37

Oh my God . . . they are implying that he has AIDS I think.

550:314) Jonathan Hayes 17-JUN-94 23:38

Ann! Cut down on your meds!

550:315) viadyer   **17-JUN-94 23:38**
Knicks game is back on, 1:50 to go.

550:317) Twang   **17-JUN-94 23:38**
This is indeed Hollywood Babylon.

550:319) Vantage, jAe   **17-JUN-94 23:38**
Knicks up by 5, 1:25 left, 4th quat.

550:321) Twang   **17-JUN-94 23:38**
CNN announcer is commenting on the "party-like atmosphere" of
the crowd.

550:335) Twang   **17-JUN-94 23:40**
OJ says he'll consider coming out after talking to his mother.
This is gonna be a long night.
What if he has to pee?

550:344) viadyer   **17-JUN-94 23:41**
1:08 left, Rockets on the line.

550:349) Josh Save the Juice Karpf   **17-JUN-94 23:42**
He should have went before, Twang.

550:350) viadyer   **17-JUN-94 23:42**
Knicks lead 85-81.

550:370) Twang   **17-JUN-94 23:45**
Almost totally dark now.

550:371) Ann   **17-JUN-94 23:45**
The police look really scary. I bet he's really scared. I am scared.

550:372) viadyer   17-JUN-94 23:46

Starks is on the knicks. Knicks at the line.

550:376) Twang   17-JUN-94 23:46

Lawyer Schapiro has arrived.

550:377) Jonathan Hayes   17-JUN-94 23:46

Ann! Increase your medication immediately!
What's the betting Shapiro's still charging his hourly rate?
And what's a "lookie-loo", you SF types?

550:394) molerat   17-JUN-94 23:50

Is anyone else struck by how much the TV commentary sounds
like golf coverage?

550:396) viadyer   17-JUN-94 23:50

Rockets score 3, 88-83. Knicks up!

550:403) Twang   17-JUN-94 23:51

I am SO glad I stayed in tonight.

550:409) Ann   17-JUN-94 23:52

I may be sick soon.

550:410) viadyer   17-JUN-94 23:52

22 seconds . . .

550:418) sarah m   17-JUN-94 23:52

They say they're arresting him now.

550:421) Jonathan Hayes   17-JUN-94 23:53

Radio is behind. They don't have the arrest news yet.

550:424) viadyer   **17-JUN-94 23:53**
Knicks wasted ball. Knicks get it back and are fouled.
Mason at the line 19 seconds left.

550:426) Jonathan Hayes   **17-JUN-94 23:54**
OJ is in custody.

550:428) Vantage, jAe   **17-JUN-94 23:54**
Just said lookie-loos on TV. Must be the rubberneckers.

550:430) Ann   **17-JUN-94 23:54**
He was framed.

550:431) Jonathan Hayes   **17-JUN-94 23:54**
Hands up who's happy it ended peacefully?

550:433) viadyer   **17-JUN-94 23:54**
Mason gets first foul shot.
Miss the second.
Knicks by 6 4 seconds left.

550:436) Josh Save the Juice Karpf   **17-JUN-94 23:55**
No stun or flash grenades were needed. No more hurt people. Just
the formalities in further destroying a shattering life.

550:444) viadyer   **17-JUN-94 23:56**
Knicks Win!

550:445) Snoop Trouty Trout   **17-JUN-94 23:56**
Knicks Win!

550:448) Jonathan Hayes   **17-JUN-94 23:57**
KNICKS WIN!!!!!

550:476) Snoop Trouty Trout   18-JUN-94 0:00
Let's see it again!

Just before midnight, as if both events were choreographed by
some bizarro God with one wack sense of humor, the two dramas
ended within minutes of each other. The Echoids were left asking
themselves: "What just happened?" Why was everyone glued to
their computers and their television sets? "Let's face it, it was a
pretty banal story, considering the intensity of the media scrutiny
it produced. The coverage was more about the medium than the
event," Jonathan Hayes commented. Yeah, it was about that. But
the television wasn't the only compelling element of all that took
place that night. Seconds later Josh Karpf posted: "Night, all. The
dishes are calling. *Thanks for sharing this.*" That's it. It wasn't just
the event that riveted them. They were watching it and they were
watching it together. And once the event was over, it wasn't what
kept them there, still talking, late into the night. The audience for
the real life drama had a right then and there direct connection
into the thoughts and feelings of their fellow spectators and
together, in the aftermath, the Echoids examined the complexity
of their feelings. From Skubik: "This circus is disgusting. Why am
I so engrossed? This is a low point for American culture."
Jonathan, the realist, and Ann, the humanist, kept going back and
forth and the conversation continually turned. There was so much
they had to say—610 responses in two and a half hours. The topics jumped from domestic abuse to race and the Echoids started
throwing in what they know, what they've read, and what
they've experienced. One talked of Oedipus, another of Tertullian,
and one Echoid pinned us to the spot with a glimpse of a tragical-
ly similar event, the murder of her father. Through it all a group
picture or documentary of the whole cast of characters emerged—
what happened and who are we anyway? Everywhere you go,
cyberspace is developing into one great big home movie of human-

ity. The Echoids took note. And not everyone felt the same about the virtual response.

550:600) Twang   18-JUN-94 0:53

What made this event exciting, for me anyway, was the fact that there were so many of us experiencing it at the same time, and feeding on each other's excitement. Isn't that the definition of media—group experiences, more or less simultaneous?

550:607) doktor dorje   18-JUN-94 1:05

I was much more excited by the fact that we were in this multimedia experience than I'd ever be unless I was actually on his front porch with some sampsonite filled with sammiches and ammo for his prolonged showdown.

550:610) Cloud in Levis   18-JUN-94 1:09

I was watching the Knicks game when they broke away to show the white van driving through LA. After watching for 15 minutes or so, I got bored and came to Echo. I don't find the story compelling, and I found the media feeding frenzy disgusting. So I was doing my Echo thing when I came to this item, and found it much more interesting than the television coverage. I understand the fascination, revulsion, compassion, and, with all of that going on, people still wanting to know the score of the Knicks game. But I am slightly disgusted with the blood lust, both here and on television. The actual murders were horrible, but the fascination with them, and the aftermath, is revolting.

550:645) Twang   18-JUN-94 14:44

I'm interested to know, for those of you who didn't watch the live coverage—if you read this item and our as-it-happens commentary, to what extent do you feel like you "experienced" the event? What was it like to read what we were typing in the midst of the frenzy? How well does this medium (Echo) communicate experience?

Obviously (to those of us posting last night) the medium does well with immediacy—though I'd like to hear some more comments on that, too.

550:646) TomF   18-JUN-94 15:30

The first 250 responses in this item are like Mystery Science Theater 3000, where the commentary is much more entertaining than the media material. Maybe that's what Echo does well.

550:648) GreenPig   18-JUN-94 15:34

I watched the event entirely through postings last night. I don't have a TV and the radio was just too repulsive. I think I preferred to have it filtered through Echo precisely because it didn't make me feel like I was "experiencing" the event, just reading about it, albeit with lag approaching zero. The event itself was just a blank slate: none of us knows O.J., none of us knows if he's guilty or not, none of us finds the picture of a car moving down a highway all that inherently interesting. So there didn't seem much point in watching it. But to see all of us trying to come to terms with it, now that actually had content. And I felt less like a jackal, awaiting my turn to dig in.

550:657) Tally ho, Telos!   18-JUN-94 18:32

Twang: I have no TV or radio (My motto: No television No Microwave No Therapist). I caught it but only in background. It didn't register with me that something culturally significant was going on till I read this item.

I found it wonderfully evocative and it made me feel like I was "there."

I do feel this was a special event in our cyber history, and frankly I'm a little jealous that I missed it real-time.

550:668) Driftwood   18-JUN-94 21:03
It has yet to be mentioned, so I will.
Another level of postmodernity is added in all the posts talking
about the posts talking about witnessing the tragedy.
And we spiral ever upward.

One Echoid was taken aback by the tone of the group. She wasn't
online when it happened and all she saw was coldness where the
participants felt electrifyingly, can't sleep, can't log off, connected.
She missed the subtext. This wasn't just about O.J.

550:670) xue   18-JUN-94 21:55
It was bizarre for me to read this entire item. I didn't come on last
night because I was riveted to the drama, the near-Othello drama.
The ultimate Crime of Passion. Medea. I was really surprised at
how cynical New Yorkers seemed to be. Some New Yorkers, that
is. And maybe it isn't just New Yorkers, but it seemed so cold. Was
it cold? Or is my impression wrong? Is it wrong because I don't
know you? Or is it wrong because the cold things you said were a
way of letting off natural human tension in the face of tragedy.
Are you that cynical when you read *Othello* or *Medea*? Do you
say, essentially, that you're glad to see Othello die in the end?
Isn't his tragedy (Othello's) as profoundly sad as the death of his
love?

550:678) Jonathan Hayes   18-JUN-94 22:23
Some years ago I watched (in a professional capacity) the video-
tape of the death of Larry "Bud" Dwyer, a Pennsylvania politician
who had been accused of financial improprieties. Dwyer held a
press conference, and, clearly suffering, spoke a few words against
the charges and apologized to everyone for all of the trouble. He
then pulled out a gun, and, amidst screams and shouts of "Larry,
NO!", stuck it in his mouth and pulled the trigger, blowing a hole in

the back of his head. He collapsed back against a wall, and slid to the floor, the blood gushing from his nose and mouth, the cameraman zooming tight, the screaming in the background.

I found this emotionally devastating. I had watched the entire tape, maybe 7 minutes of him coming into the press room, speaking, handing out envelopes to his staff. I had some sense of the man, of what he was feeling, of what he was thinking. And then, when he finally killed himself, it was really really horrifying. This was the death of another person, a real person, a person like me.

But with OJ, it was different. There was no preamble, we just cut away from whatever program was on to some bizarre shot of a white car driving along the highway, pumped by the bloodlust of the reporters and the choppers and the psychoanalysts. NO ONE SET UP THE CLIP. There was nothing human there to which I could attach myself, no narrative space in which to install pity, or compassion. This was an historic event, a sequence from a movie where I had missed the first hour.

Xue was right in one sense. The interactions in and between the two mediums, television and cyberspace, are complex. There are varying levels of distortion. Sometimes they make an event devastatingly real—at others, like a cartoon. And if you're not a part of it all, it's hard to tell what people are feeling. Going back to my earlier example of a virtual community where the membership was almost entirely black—I had logged into this place a few months after a jogger in Central Park was brutally attacked by a group of teenagers. It was everywhere in the news all the time, you couldn't escape it. "Wilding in Central Park," the headlines bellowed. Like xue, I was struck by the lack of empathy I thought I found on this service. But it wasn't that the people there didn't have any heart, they were every bit as full of heart and empathy as anyone anywhere else—it was me. I was visiting an unfamiliar culture and I was lost. It was there, I was missing it. They were more sensitive to the race issues involved, for one. And, like the Echoids and O.J., they were more real to each other than the Central Park Jogger.

550:692) doktor dorje　　　　　　　　　19-JUN-94 1:13

Sorry—the thought of OJ fuckin Simpson with a gun to his head in a high-speed chase in a Bronco is far too absurd for me to take seriously.
Like Brecht directing THE LAST BOY SCOUT.
Shakespeare gets to me much more.

550:693) jneil　　　　　　　　　　　　19-JUN-94 1:25

It's even more absurd in a low-speed chase.

550:877) Tangerine Telos　　　　　　　01-JUL-94 9:20

Check this out: Last night I went to Equinox for my third session in three days with my new personal trainer (ouch!). As I enter, I notice there are these TV cameras, cables, reporters, etc milling around. Nothing too unusual about that—I thought, well, maybe they're here to shoot something on aerobics, or the new workout routines of Echoids, or whatever.
So I'm sitting on this bench next to the lifecycle/stairmaster area, that has a bank of TVs above it. Suddenly it dawns on me, and I say to these two people next to me: They're probably filming for a story about people following the OJ case [on the TV monitors], so this way people can watch TV of people watching TV.
One of the two was with the station (Fox Live at Five) and confirmed my guess. At which point I cried: "Do I have my hand on the pulse of post-modernity, OR WHAT?" They looked at me like I was nuts.

What happens is important. What is equally important, and certainly more far reaching, is our experience of events and our response to them over time. How we incorporate them, how they emerge as stories, and then how those stories are used to instruct and to connect. Robert Coles, quoting an old teacher of his, Dr. Alfred O. Ludwig, said: "The people who come to see us bring us their stories. They hope they tell them well enough so that we understand the truth of their lives."

This is what we are doing online. We are finding the truth of our lives. That conversation continued for years, as the drama itself continued, and as we added more facts, lies, and mostly, our take of the whole ongoing spectacle. We construct a collective truth—truth by consensus—like the truth that emerged in Faulkner's *As I Lay Dying*. History doesn't come down through the top of established hierarchy. It emerges through the shared wisdom of everyone who has their tiny piece of it.

Cyberspace makes historians of us all.

LOG OFF, BYE, QUIT

"Echo is dying." The first couple of years we were in business I'd call my friend Joe Rosen at least once a month and cry this into the phone. Echo is dying, Echo is dying. I was sure that at any moment it would collapse. Nice try, girl. Now get a real job. I haven't said this in a long time. It's not that I don't think it still might die. It probably will or has to. It's just that in spite of my fears and inexperience we kept growing and, slowly, I came to concentrate on growth instead of the prevention of death. I felt a lot better when we finally moved Echo out of my apartment. I was ambivalent at first. It felt like the soul had been ripped right out of my living room. I missed the electrical hum. It was quiet, but a loud quiet. Like the sound of hundreds of people raising their hands at the same time. Now I relish it. I have a home again. Echo is a place I go to, just like any other Echoid.

Seven years ago (only seven years ago!) I couldn't convince anyone that the Internet was worth investing in. Everyone just looked at me with smug expressions on their faces. "Stacy," you poor deluded innocent, their eyes said, "it's never going to take off. And," they told me, "smart people will never want to talk to each other over a computer." Ha, ha, ha. LOSERS.

Not that I'm some hotshot visionary. I wish. I disappointed a large group of people the other night when they came to NYU to hear me talk about success. I told them that I was nothing more than a hard-working opportunist, who wasn't the smartest person around either, come to think of it, and who, quite simply, got lucky. Go to school or not, wear the right clothes or not, the best advice I can give you is pay very close attention and pounce. It's your only advantage because so few people do. And then, be prepared to make an idiot of yourself. Figure for every ten things you do, nine of them will be idiotic. They were furious. I'd thought they'd be relieved to know that someone without vision or money and just a few months out of rehab could pull something like this off.

Where is cyberspace going? Fuck if I know. Anything I write will be out of date in six months and that's about as far as my vision extends. Okay, maybe a year because, as I said, so few people pounce. I was watching Bill Gates on TV last night and I thought, "Now there's someone who knows how to pounce." But wait. He's a multibillionaire and I'm a not-very-many-at-all-come-to-think-of-it-thousandaire. Hmmm. Who am I to be talking about success anyway? I'm an idiot! (And I hate myself.) And any idiot can tell you that in the future we'll have what we have now only more MORE MORE. A big mother of a broadcast and interaction on demand hybrid of everything they can stuff on whatever bandwidth we have at the time. A lot more talk radio or talk TV-types of things than traditional magazines or one-way broadcast-type television shows. What is important and new about the Internet is connecting your viewers (or your customers) to each other—not you. This is how you create community. Everything we put on it will look a little different, but what's underneath it will be the same.

The Internet is a recreation of what we already have and who we already are. I was asked recently if the Net is going to bring us together or distance us. That depends on us. Does New York City bring people together? Does any place bring us together? It's like Maya Angelou says, it's not that you can't go home again, you can never leave. There's nothing like cyberspace for slowing things down just enough for you to see how true this is. There should be a war sometime down the road as a result of some misunderstanding or power struggle online. For all the talk about how freeing cyberspace is, I've found you can't pry people's personalities from their furiously typing fingers. The same goes for how wonderfully vast it all is—you can go all over the world! It's been my experience that people want what is familiar. They want borders. They may go 'out there' for a visit but they hang out in the place that they call home. What are we doing trying to predict the future anyway? We don't know what we have now. We should look at one day in the life of any virtual community and then figure out just what happened. That should keep us occupied for a while, except we won't do it. No. We want to see the future.

Cyberspace. In the end, it's just a place like any other place. As we realize this, as we become more sophisticated users, it won't be such a big deal anymore. People born in the eighties are probably reading this book and saying: duh. As more and more people get online it becomes more and more like us. DUH. That said, it will be interesting to see the effect that participation in such a nonlinear medium will have on our culture after another ten or twenty years or so of this. What will the artists do? How will books and movies reflect this experience? I believe the concept of maneuvering in a space of no beginning, middle, or end is starting to feel more natural. When we let go of the linear we open up to new connections; most are unimaginable to me now.

I've had a number of companies approach me about buying Echo, but I pursued only one—The WELL, of all places. I decided not to sell because Bruce Katz, the owner, had a different vision at the time for The WELL and Echo, and that included turning them into America Online. Shortly after I told Bruce, "Sorry, I don't think so," he announced that he was creating a "New York WELL." "Let's crush Echo," he cried at their business meetings I was told. Uh-huh. Not that I didn't think he could. Quite the opposite. The guy had millions to spend and years of successful business experience and I had what? Zip money, no business experience whatsoever—I got ready for a good fight. Then I heard his plan. They would create a few New York conferences on The WELL and when they got big enough, like Rhoda from *Mary Tyler Moore,* they would spin them off into a separate New York WELL. I started to relax. I knew they wouldn't become "New York" conferences. They would become conferences about New York on The WELL. They would quite naturally be incorporated into The WELL culture and assume The WELL style, with all their traditions, language, and so forth. Then he talked about sending children door to door in New York City to sell WELL accounts like girl scouts selling cookies. I stopped worrying about Bruce.

I thought I would open other regional systems myself at one point. Based on the response to Echo that I've gotten over the years from around the country, I picked cities I thought would be able to support virtual community. I also chose cities I'd like to spend time in: Boston, Los Angeles, New Orleans, to name a few. Okay, New Orleans is a long shot, but I so long to live there (in the winter at least). I put the idea aside, however, because I knew it would take as much work as Echo did. I'd have to find people locally to host, build relationships with local organizations and businesses—it's an incredibly delicate and gut-wrenching process—I simply couldn't go through it again and again unless some big huge company paid me a lot of money to oversee the local people they would also pay a lot of money to do the actual work of building a local virtual community from within a physical one.

So I'm going to movies more and dancing less these days. That's because I'm turning forty this summer and I'm getting fucking lazy. Uh-oh. I just hung up the phone. I signed up for drumming lessons. It's something I've always wanted to do.

We're having a party for our sixth anniversary and I was trying to decide between two dresses. "This one is sophisticated and this one is sexy," the saleslady told me. I bought them both, but I'm going to wear the sophisticated one to the party. "Mistake," Lisa Cooley warned. Oh dear. I don't wear high heels anymore either, which is too bad. They look so good. Unfortunately, it's been so long, I think I passed the high-heel-wearing tolerance threshold years ago. If I put them on today I'd walk funny. It'd be like going back to my teen years and starting over. Doesn't *that* sound like fun?

Whenever someone closes their account I send them a letter and a poem to say good-bye. I hate ugly breakups, don't you? Things *can* end gracefully. I'm still friends with most of my former boyfriends. My ex-husband is on Echo! It was between a Frank O'Hara poem and one by Robert Penn Warren. I went with the Warren poem, but I may change it to O'Hara later because that's the kind of girly-girl without heels I am.

Dear So and So,

What? No! WAIT! You're not really leaving us are you?? Sorry, I just wanted to say that it was great to have you. Good luck with what ever you do, wherever you go. From Have You Ever Eaten Stars? by Robert Penn Warren:

Question: What can you do with stars, or glory?
             I'll tell you, I'll tell you—thereof
             Eat. Swallow. Absorb. Let bone

Be sustained thereof, let gristle
Toughen, flesh be more preciously
Gratified, muscle yearn in
Its strength. Let brain glow
In its own midnight of darkness,
Under its own inverted, bowl-shaped
Sky, skull-sky, let the heart
Rejoice.
    What other need now
Is possible to you but that
Of seeing life as glory?

Regards,
Stacy Horn

INDEX OF THE ECHOIDS MENTIONED IN THIS BOOK

Mark Abene (aka Phiber Optik). Former Echo system administrator, hacker, programmer, and ex-con.

Steve Barber. Software consultant, recovering attorney, cyberspace activist and occasional writer, host of the Matrix Conference.

James Barnett (aka Spingo). Web Guru, cohost of the Web Conference.

Jim Baumbach (aka Bottomer). Unemployed polymath and Internet pioneer.

Bucky Berg (aka Bucky Dave). Cohost of the Hightimes Conference, plays guitar for White Courtesy Telephone.

Stephen Berg (aka Berg Man of Alcatraz aka Herb). Editor, writer, cohost of the Books Conference.

Stephen Biegner (aka Stahl). Web designer/production drudge. Both shameless and painfully shy.

Bradley Bloch (aka telos). Bradley first learned the Hollerith Code in the seventh grade, in 1974. He wishes he had stuck with it.

Mark Bloch (aka Panman). Multimedia artist since 1976. Publisher of the zine *Panmag* since 1980. Host of Panscan.

Marisa Bowe (aka Miss Outer Boro 1991). Former conference manager, editor-in-chief of *WORD*.

Abby Bowen (aka Crunch Monkey). Former Echo employee, web producer living in London.

335

Alice Bradley (aka Alice, Part of a Complete Breakfast). Managing editor of *STIM,* a webzine.

Rosemary Bray. Author.

Jacqueline Broner (aka Jackie Blue). Graphic/Web designer, host of the Shopping and Handmade Conferences.

Susan Brownmiller (aka susanb). Author.

Alan Cabal (aka Garbled Uplink). Circus roadie, member of the band White Courtesy Telephone.

Mike Caffrey (Maggot Boy). Guitarist for White Courtesy Telephone, founder of Monster Island Records.

Susan Campbell (aka SuZin). Editor at TV Guide Online, original host of Under 30.

Leila Change (aka Kiwi). Producer of video at CD-ROM games at Disney Interactive.

Josh Chu (aka Slacker). Echo employee, producer of the film series Alt.Film, founder of NonProphet Organization.

Scott Connor (aka Scottso). Cohost of Plain Wrapper, street artist. Liberal to a degree and thinks everyone should be free.

Lisa J. Cooley (aka coollit). Playwright and new media slacker.

Douglas Cooper (aka Visigoth). Novelist.

Liza Cowan (aka Diamond). Anthropologist and lesbian mom.

Alec Cumming (aka Bite the Wax Godhead). Bassist, new dad and writer/producer for the USA Network and the SciFi Channel.

Patricia Decker (aka Ms. P.). Tarot reading systems consultant, earth mother whose idea of tech support is to ask you how you feel.

Neil deMause (Null Dogmas). Freelance journalist and coeditor of the zine *Brooklyn Metro Times.* Cohost of the Zines Conference.

Wendi Denman (aka Shrink). Psychotherapist specializing in trauma, sexual abuse, and eating disorders.

Daniel Drennan (aka Xixax). Editor of the zine *Inquisitor.* Host of the Media Conference.

Holly Duthie (aka binki). Echo button and T-shirt designer.

Peter Dworkin (New York Jew). Art and antique dealer, and personal property appraiser.

Simon Egleton. Shoe-gazing guitar thrasher, New Yorker.

Matthew Ehrlich (aka Oedipa). Matt Ehrlich (oedipa) is a writer and editor. He still hasn't finished his Ph.D. He works for MTV Networks, but doesn't get to play that Portishead video whenever he wants. He is host of Echo's Art and Lambda conferences.

Carmela Federico. Computer activist and teacher.

Eric Fixler. Multimedia programmer and designer living in San Francisco.

Jake Fogelnest (aka Squirt). Creator of *Squirt TV.*

John Gabriel (aka Gabriel). Computer consultant, currently in the process of getting a life. Hobbies include: finding new hobbies.

Debbie Geller (aka nottinghill). Producer for British television.

Mike Godwin (aka Avant Garde A Clue). Lawyer for the Electronic Frontier Foundation, writer.

Ann Goodstein (aka Grace). Direct marketing consultant, lapsed art historian, Web producer, new mother.

Harriet Goren (alto artist). Design director at a World Wide Web studio and an a cappella singer.

Sue Grady. Former general manager of Echo, now works at American Express.

Andrew Grant. Lives in NYC, loves his wife, hates his job, and still hasn't written that first novel.

David Green. Host of the Jewish Conference.

Jason Guy (aka Jae Cen). Internet technologist. Macintosh evangelist.

Hugh Haggerty (aka MCHuge). Bass player for White Courtesy Telephone, original host of the High Times Conference, multitalented freelancer.

Jonathan Hayes (aka Jaze). Dilettante writer, cohost of the Movies and TV Conference.

Andrew Hearst (aka Asterix). Writer and editor, Andrew has both the optimism of a midwesterner and the cynicism of a New Yorker.

Mocha Jean Herrup. Writer, media producer, information activist; doctoral student in the department of radio-TV-film at the University of Texas at Austin.

Joe Hobaica (aka Joey X). Freelance music writer and owner of Stickboy Records. Cohost of the Music Conference.

Eric Hochman. Cohost of the Central Conference.

Douglas Horn. My brother! A financial guy who works for Merrill Lynch, father, and a golf pro in a Richard Linklater-type alternative reality.

Edward Hutchinson (aka The Lonesome Drifter). E.H. recently quit his job as a book editor and currently seeks an employer who will pay him handsomely just for being generally quizzical and acerbic. Cohost of MOE, the men's conference on Echo.

Gail Jaitin. A born and bred New Yorker who will be spending the next two years in Ohio, pursuing a master's degree and hating herself.

Phil James (Goat Noise). Author and musician.

Jeff Joseph (aka Kilgore Trout). President of Joseph Audio, a high-end speaker manufacturer.

Arthur Johnson (aka artj). Hermit, thinker, computer scientist, and ex-online junkie.

Toni Kamins (aka tonik). Writer.

Lisa Kamm (aka Camel). Lawyer/Web designer/geek currently working for the ACLU.

Josh Karpf. Editor.

Molly Ker (aka Molsk). Former general manager of Echo, currently a communications producer at Time Inc. New Media, ever snippy.

Mary Kessler (aka Maz). Everyone's favorite YORB caller.

James Kim. Currently selling vanity email addresses on kim.com to the millions of Kims in the world.

Daniela Kirshenbaum (aka Danski 181). Lives in San Francisco, met her husband through Echo, and works with inner-city teens.

Terry Knickerbocker (Flying Fish). Adjunct Professor of Acting at NYU, freelance theater director, cohost of the Performance Conference.

Robert Knuts. Attorney for the SEC.

Dean Koga (Cloud in Levi's). "I look younger than I feel, but I extend the life of buildings as a restoration architect."

Vera Kraus (aka Mouse). Double threat: Wellesley girl/Hunter girl. Teacher, editor, linguist, occasional pedant.

Leslie Kriesel (aka girl next door). Editor, brought to Echo by her good friend Josh Karpf.

Kevin Krooss. Host of Feedback and Computers.

Sue Laris-Eastin (aka xue). Editor.

Brett Leveridge. Freelance writer and publisher of the zine *BRETTnews.*

Jaime Levy (aka Kurt's Brains). Creates electronic magazines and virtual environments for the politically incorrect out of her East Village loft.

Mia Lipner (aka Chameleon). Cyberspace researcher/writer/artist, with a low tolerance for the over-hyped and/or stupid. Former cohost of the Internet and Elsewhere Conferences, lives in Seattle.

Liz Logan (aka Liz L.). Writer and editor.

Alice Lord. Writer, editor, HTML designer, aka Dearest on AOL.

MG Lord. Author, cohost of the Books Conference.

Carol Lowbeer (aka Carolinda). Writer, cartoonist, photographer.

Henry Lowengard (aka Nemo). Electronic artist, animator, musician, and programmer. Cohost of Comix and Writing; married to Nancy Graham (ngraham) the other host of Writing.

Angus MacDonald (aka Fourway Flytrap). Itinerant knowledge worker, currently rearranging chairs at Prodigy. The bad lieutenant of Echo.

Liz Margoshes (aka Neandergal). Psychologist, crepuscular endomorph, host of the Psych Conference, and Dr. Lovelady on WORD.

Sarah Maupin Wenk (aka Sarah M/). New media producer, host of the Parenting Conference.

Amy McCutchin (aka Mame). Manages Internet and online development at BMG, host of Sonic Cynic.

Peter McDermott. Writer, researcher.

Peter Merholz (aka Driftwood). Know-it-all twentynothing, Web designer who fled New York for the calmer climes of San Francisco.

Donna Minkowitz. Writer for *The Village Voice, Ms.* and *The Advocate.*

Kristen Mirenda (aka Twang). New media producer and cohost of the New York Conference.

Isaac Nahem (aka Ike). Amtrak locomotive engineer, New York Jew, and unrepentant Marxist.

Ivan Nahem (aka Jaguar). Poet, novelist, and cohost of MOE, the men's conference on Echo.

John Neilson (aka jneil). Musician, web developer, freelance writer and cohost of the Music Conference.

Morgan Noel (aka Mono). Web designer and writer who has learned to ignore all the dogs on the NYC street that tell him to "kill the pigs (and cats)."

Cleo Odzer (aka Cleo the Goa Freak). Anthropologist and author.

Mary O'Shaughnessy (aka Oshma). Trainer and consoler of frightened computer users.

Lisa Palac. Writer and producer of Cyborgasm, a CD series.

Bill Paulauskias. Dadaist, lion and gorilla tamer, magician and poet.

Michael Peck (aka MP). Editor at *TV Guide* Online, afraid of babies.

Marianne Petit (aka MR Petit). Multimedia artist and educator.

Sukey Pett (aka Chow Bella). Host of the Food Conference, writes about food.

Reuben Radding (aka Ah Clem). Writer, musician, world traveler, Satanist.

Magdalen Radovitch. Teacher, writer, mother, vampire.

Erik Rieselbach (aka Greenpig). Editor, book designer, and typesetter.

Julie Alix Robichaux (aka a little black cloud in a dress). Manager of online services at *The Village Voice.*

Nick Rosato. Self-employed and "more interested in writing, sailing, coaching sports, whatever, than my business."

Pavia Rosati. New and old media writer/editor, email addict. Flirt.

Karen Rose (aka KZ). Artist, realtor, and host of the Sex Conference, cohost of Handmade.

Joe Rosen (aka Joro). Multimedia artist, programmer.

David Ross. The Alice Pratt Brown Director of the Whitney Museum of American Art.

Amy Roth (aka Amy R.) Cohost of BITCH.

Susan Sabatino (aka Lana Tuna). High school teacher, host of the Love Conference.

Michael Sansonia (aka Singer). Musician, conductor (*Little Shop of Horrors*), arranger/producer (CNN), composer (Showtime).

Bruce Schechter. Writer.

Nicholas Scheer. Manager of electronic imaging at a historical photo agency.

Vanessa Schnatmeier (aka Dali Good Jello Biafra). Ex-computer journalist who chucked it all for art, ramping up in the Web world, back in school for her master's.

Margaret Segall. Host of the Politics Conference.

Theresa Senft (aka Jane Doe). Doctoral candidate in the Department of Performance Studies at New York University, cohost of the Lambda Conference.

NancyKay Shapiro (aka Perpetual Dawn). Author of 2½ as-yet-undiscovered novels, who lives, works, and walks her dog south of Twenty-third Street.

Susanne Skubik. Student.

Charles Smith (aka OpPhantom). A lifelong devotee of New York City and its people, who lives and works in Connecticut.

Lianne Smith (aka Topper). Refugee from the Lone Prairie. Can be found singing in various NYC clubs. Echo's conference manager.

Stuart Statman (aka Gurustu). "Raconteur without peer."

Robert Sterbal (aka viadyer). Computer sales person, got married on October 1, 1996, moving to Pittsburgh.

Leslie Sternbergh (aka Mrs. Hippie Queen). Comic artist, host of the Comics Conference.

Eric Swenson (aka Mr. Happy). Principal of Necro Enema Amalgamated, publisher of the BLAM! CD-ROM series, *Momu's Stop Must This!,* and Hans Neleman. www.interport.net/~swenson

Daniel Swerdlow. Telecommunications engineer, cohost of Parents, founding host of Science and MOE.

Jennifer Tanaka (aka Tank). Writer, editor.

Rob Tannenbaum (aka Ro*). Contributing editor at *Details Magazine,* and colead singer of White Courtesy Telephone.

Ellen Tarlow (aka Extra T.). Teacher, writer, and editor.

Michael Taustine (aka Senor Voce). Assistant Treasurer at the Music Box Theatre.

Hadley Taylor (aka coyote). Echo system administrator, theatrical sound engineer, cohost of the Web Conference.

Jack Taylor (aka The Strange Apparatus). Graphic designer/artist with a rich fantasy life involving dairies. Cohost of the Culture Conference.

Janet Tingey. Designer, art director, who does not read posts longer than ten lines. Cohost of the Digital Arts Conference.

Astrida Valigorsky (aka Aeonflux). Artist and Web maven who spends her time divining the true ingredients of Twinkies, cohost of the Art Conference.

Paul Wallich (aka Ragged Paul). Writer, troublemaker, renovation survivor. Host of the Science Conference.

Chris Weller (aka Dorje). Host of Into the Mystic, rumored to appear on Echo on or around the full moon.

Nick West. Producer of YORB, an interactive TV show on public access in Manhattan.

Mary Elizabeth Williams (aka Mary beth). Freelance writer and host of *Salon Magazine*'s Table Talk (www.salon1999.com).

Luce Wollin. Retired NYC school librarian, researcher for writers, and host of the Over 40 Conference.

Lorenz Wyss. Electronics technologist. Aspires to be a real human.

Cathy Young (aka Cafephreak). Web designer and owner of the Grouchy Cafe, a special spot on the Web devoted to the celebration of angst.